The Culture of Recovery

Elayne Rapping

The Culture of Recovery

Making Sense
of the Self-Help Movement
in Women's Lives

Beacon Press · Boston

Beacon Press
25 Beacon Street
Boston, Massachusetts 02108-2892

Beacon Press books
are published under the auspices of
the Unitarian Universalist Association of Congregations.

99 98 97 96 95   8 7 6 5 4 3 2 1

Text design by Wesley B. Tanner/Passim Editions
Composition by Wilsted & Taylor

Library of Congress Cataloging-in-Publication Data

Rapping, Elayne
The culture of recovery : making sense of the self-help movement in
women's lives / Elayne Rapping.
p.   cm.
Includes bibliographical references (p.   ) and index.
ISBN 0-8070-2716-2
1. Recovering addicts.   2. Feminism.   3. Women—Mental health.
4. Self-esteem in women.   5. Twelve-step programs—Political
aspects.   I. Title.
RC533.R365   1995
305.42—dc20   95–14095
CIP

For the Women of the Second Wave
Who Did, Indeed, Make a Revolution

&

For Marion
Who not only Survives, but Thrives

Contents

Acknowledgments

Many people have of course helped me by commenting upon the ideas in this book, as it evolved from its earliest phases to its current form. I wish first to thank Elsa Dixler of *The Nation* for commissioning the 1991 review article—a critique of several self-help books about, and for, women—which became the germ, or core, of the book. It was Lauren Bryant, then of Beacon Press, who first approached me, shortly after the article appeared, about expanding it into a book. It took a good two years of gentle but persistent—and increasingly compelling—prodding from Lauren to convince me that she was right in her instinct about the larger importance of the ideas first sketched in that article. In the two years in which I continued to play with and discuss the idea with her, her acumen became apparent. In those years, I saw the movement's impact grow and spread, in the press, in casual social conversations, and most dramatically—and this was what convinced me, a media theorist first and foremost, to get started—in bookstores and on television, where recovery-talk and its genres now take up so much time and space. It is to Lauren, and her successor as my editor at Beacon, Marya Van't Hul, that I owe the most gratitude. They are the editors every writer dreams of working with, smart, thorough, committed, and involved. Both have the great ability to be at once firm and tough, and warm and supportive. Marya, who inherited the project in midstream, went through the entire first draft with a finetooth comb, I'm certain, and offered countless large and small suggestions—from chapter reorganization to word choice—which have found their way into these pages, to its great advantage.

Many others have listened to and read many of the ideas in the book and encouraged me to undertake, pursue, and often rethink the project. Versions of some of the ideas have appeared in *The Progressive, On the Issues: The Progressive Women's Quarterly,* and *The Guardian,* all of which have elicited a variety of helpful comments and responses from readers. Early on, friends and colleagues, especially Pat Mann, Diane Neumaier, Susan Weisser, Janice Wetzel, and Peter Costello, talked to me about the project and offered much encouragement and many suggestions about approaches, authors, and texts which proved invaluable in helping me sort through the many angles and issues raised by the recovery movement and its phenomenal success. Ethan Nadelmann and Stanton Peele were extremely helpful in leading me to ideas and sources in my struggle to come to grips with the aspects of U.S. drug and treatment policy and philosophy—a new field to me—which I needed to understand to write chapter 3. The members of the Adelphi Humanities Institute heard and commented upon a version of chapter 4, and offered several useful suggestions; and the participants of the 4th Annual Console-ing Passions: Television, Video, and Feminism Conference who attended the panel at which I presented a version of chapter 1 were similarly helpful. I am also indebted to the writing of many feminist therapists, especially Harriet Goldhor Lerner, who was among the first to critique the movement from a feminist perspective and from whose writings on women and psychology I have learned much over the years.

As ever, my students and my children have been my most constant source of feedback, interest, and support. My daughter, Alison, and son, Jonathan, have by now become experts in the subjects of addiction, recovery, self-help, and drug policy, and have offered me endless bits of insight and personal anecdote from their own experiences and readings, as the book progressed.

And then there is Marion, to whom the book is dedicated for reasons she alone understands and appreciates. Thank you all.

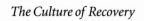

The Culture of Recovery

Small art or love or beauty, their starving spirits knew,
Oh yes it's bread we fight for, but we fight for roses too.

"Bread and Roses,"
Working Women's Anthem

'Twas in another lifetime, one of toil and blood,
When blackness was a virtue, the road was full of mud,
I came in from the wilderness, a creature void of form,
"Come in," she said, "I'll give you
Shelter from the storm."

Bob Dylan

Introduction

One day a few years ago, I found myself sitting in a "Beginners" meeting of Overeaters Anonymous (OA). I was there with an old friend whose therapist had urged her to attend, and who was, as she put it, "weirded out" by the idea of going alone. The room, in the basement of an old church, was furnished with wooden straight-back chairs arranged in a circle. The group members who straggled in were all women, few of them noticeably obese.

The group leader for the day, a veteran of one year, passed around Xeroxed copies of the official OA literature—essentially the classic 12 Steps and 12 Traditions of the "parent" organization, Alcoholics Anonymous (AA), revised to fit the "addiction" of overeating. Then came her own "Qualification" story of compulsive overeating, binging, purging, and endless battles with the scale. She told of teenage humiliation at having to shop in the "Chubby" sections of department stores and facing ridicule and rejection from her father and then from boys. She told of taunts and stares from men on the street, as she compulsively gobbled bags of candy and cookies, and grew larger and unhappier by the year. And then a saleswoman, in a shop for "the larger woman," recognized her desperation and told her about OA. There she found support and was able to conquer her addiction and regain her self-esteem (if not her preadolescent slimness; she was still noticeably overweight).

Other women, at first fearful and hesitant to speak, gradually began to "share" with the group their experiences with food and weight, the misery and confusion that had brought them—having tried therapy, crash diets, even suicide—to this last resort. Virtually every story I heard that day involved men in some way—abuse and humiliation by fathers, husbands, boyfriends, and bosses, or the need to live up to their standards of beauty. One woman had just been laid off, replaced by a younger woman. Another had been shamed into anorexia by her father's constant sexual attentions. A third, a full-time housewife, worried about her husband leaving her for "someone smarter and more interesting." And still a fourth, attractive and stylish, was convinced that if she could only achieve a "perfect body" her husband would stop cheating on her.

The group leader assured us that she had heard virtually every story before and that she too had tried every possible cure–including "feminist therapy"–to no avail. But when she found OA, and realized that she was uselessly "trying to control" her problem when what she needed to do–and here she quoted the first Step of the 12 Step program–was to "admit I was powerless over my addiction" and hand my life over to "my Higher Power," things fell into place for her.

I was moved by this meeting. The stories and the pain were all too real and recognizable. I had been hearing them all my life. Indeed, in one way or another, they were the very stuff of women's conversations everywhere.

But what was most intriguing to me about this particular gathering were the strange echoes I heard of an earlier time in my life. As I watched and listened to these hurting women–sitting fearfully but hopefully in circles, sharing stories of self-hatred at less-than-perfect faces and bodies, of shame and humiliation at the hands of fathers, husbands, boyfriends, bosses, teachers–I was eerily reminded of my days of feminist consciousness-raising, in the 1960s, at the height of what's called the "second wave" of American feminism.

This feeling of déjà vu, as if my experience as a feminist in the 1960s was being relived in some odd way, returned to me soon after the OA meeting in another experience with a friend involved in what I soon recognized as a broad social movement and learned to call "the recovery movement." This friend ("What is going on with my friends?" was my private, increasingly bewildered question) began attending a Women Who Love Too Much (WWLTM) group, based on the theories set forth by Robin Norwood, in her best-selling self-help book of the same name, in order to deal with the breakup of a destructive marriage. Again, I found myself steeped in familiar stories of men and women and humiliation, fear of loneliness, loss of self-esteem. Only this time they came from the Norwood book which my friend insisted upon lending me. "Read it," she urged. "This woman really is onto something about men and relationships. They're addictive! That's why we still fall into the same dumb traps even though we're supposed to be 'feminists.'"

As soon as I began reading this book, I saw what she meant and why she was so taken with Norwood's theories. The cases Norwood cited–all based on the lives of her own therapy clients–were, like the OA stories, all too common and familiar. Right on page 3 I found the story of "Jill" and "Randy," for example, one I had certainly heard many times, from friends as well as strangers, in airports and hospital waiting rooms. At first, said Jill, Randy was a dream, romantic and attentive. She "loved to cook for him" and "he loved being looked after." She "pressed his shirts" and he "seemed to like" listening to her talk, which was a new experience. But just when she was sure this was "it," he drew back, stopped calling, didn't show up when he was supposed to. Confronted by Jill, Randy was cold. "He told me not to pressure him or he would just disappear. I got so scared. I was supposed to love him and leave him alone at the same time. But I couldn't do it. . . . The more I panicked, the more I chased him." Norwood's book is filled with such cases, and her analysis and cure, like those of the leader of the OA meeting, are set forth in terms of a model of "addiction"–this time to rotten men–as a "disease" from which one must "recover." (The book is actually dedicated "to the Anonymous programs in gratitude for the miracle of recovery that they offer.")

My friend was right about the book's appeal. Women do indeed find themselves in these "chaser/distancer" relationships with men who avoid commitment and intimacy. And here was a book that said "Hey, you're not alone or weird or a failure. You're sick. You've got a disease called addiction. You got it from your diseased parents and your boyfriends got it from theirs. You don't need to feel angry or stupid. You need to accept your condition and join a program."

Again, I had the strange feeling of déjà vu. The bad relationships with rotten men; the difficulty of breaking out of them, despite our sense that they are bad for us; the need for support and reassurance in our efforts to change; all this–surprisingly yet unmistakably–recalled to me certain elements of my feminist consciousness-raising experiences.

The more I heard and saw of recovery–and I seemed to be seeing and hearing quite a lot suddenly–the more I found myself reliving that earlier period in my life, when I was introduced to feminism. In fact, I now remembered, that period too began with a book urged upon me by a woman friend. In 1962, when I was a young newlywed, a friend slipped me a copy of Doris Lessing's *The Golden Notebook* and, in a hushed, nervous voice, asked me to read it and tell her what I thought. I was puzzled, by her tone and by the book, whose heroine, Anna Wulf, seemed to me incomprehensibly angry and unhappy. I was confused by the graphic descriptions of sex as experienced by a woman, mystified by the insertion of long, boring sections about leftwing politics – but I couldn't put it down. I read it once and began again, inexplicably keeping it hidden in my laundry basket, lest my husband discover it.

My friend and I did discuss the book, endlessly and compulsively, and we found ourselves transfixed by the same seemingly inconsequential scenes and passages. In the one I remember most vividly, Anna's lover insists on having sex in the morning. Anna, preoccupied with her many morning responsibilities – dressing and feeding her daughter, making breakfast, tidying the flat, getting ready for work – grudgingly and joylessly complies.

Reading that passage, and discussing it later with my friend, I understood, for the first time, what the phrase "the scales fell from my eyes" meant. Doris Lessing had dared to give voice and image to a set of female feelings and experiences never before spoken of or acknowledged. And in doing so she had, somehow, made these feelings – previously experienced as crazy or wrong and so suppressed – suddenly seem legitimate. To share this epiphany, first with Lessing and then with other women, was, as we would come to say, "liberating."

Until then, all the books we read, all the movies we saw, all the rules and schedules we followed, assumed a male view of reality. Our mothers, our teachers, our big sisters, and even our Freudian therapists all assured us that we *should* be happy in our feminine roles, and offered all sorts of "cures" for our "depression" or "confusion" or "frigidity" or whatever. But it wasn't until we read Lessing, or Betty Friedan, or Simone de Beauvoir that we found an explanation for our unhappiness that made sense; one that provided a way of seeing and feeling our situations that offered hope. We weren't weird or bad after all. We were living in situations built upon male needs and values, and it was these situations, not us, that were wrong. For everywhere we looked and walked – in school, in the movies, in Washington and on Wall Street, in our families – we were confronted by conventions and beliefs that insisted that women were inferior to men; that women "belonged" in subservient roles and places. Gradually, as we talked and shared and generalized about our lives, we came to see our common problems as socially determined, and to organize ourselves into political groupings to demand changes in the institutions responsible: marriage, the family, the media, the school system, the courts, Congress, the military, the corporate world.

Recalling all this, I saw more and more clearly why the stories of the OA members and the tales of Norwood's therapy clients seemed so poignantly familiar. Here too, I saw and heard of women experiencing that moment of epiphany when "the scales fall from the eyes" and one understands the larger patterns that explain and determine one's experiences and actions. The important difference was that where we feminists in the 1960s had learned to see our problems as socially determined and to focus blame away from our own failings and onto those of society, these women in recovery were learning—yet again—that their problems were grounded in their own internal weaknesses and that the way out was to alter their own behaviors. They were listening to new leaders, reading new women authors, who were telling them—it seemed—that "second wave" feminism had never had any impact on women's lives at all. In fact, they seemed to be saying, all these problems between women and men, between women and their bodies, were really problems of *addiction* to begin with, and we were foolish to think that mere ideas and organizations would change behavior rooted in an inherited "disease." It was all very confusing and troubling. Where had we gone wrong?

Except, I gradually concluded, we hadn't gone wrong at all. For it was not feminism that was being proven false here. On the contrary, I couldn't help but feel that the only thing about these meetings that was *right* was the kernel of feminism that I sensed at their core. For it *was* after all the feminism of the 1960s that had enabled us to understand the situations of these women and their awful men as problematic. Previous generations of women had in large simply accepted these situations and adapted, with more or less "success." Men have always, after all, treated women as though they were inferior. Women have always, surely, feared abandonment by the men they were socialized to become emotionally dependent upon. And women have always suffered through unpleasant, unfulfilling sexual experiences worrying that *they* were somehow "abnormal." But it was feminism (as my memories of *The Golden Notebook* reminded me)—not an epidemic of progressive emotional "addictions"—that had made the acceptance of such pain and humiliation suddenly seem intolerable. Just as it was feminism, I had to admit, that had in many cases exacerbated the common tensions in traditional sexist relationships by making it possible for women to gain a good deal more independence and mobility than our mothers had, through newly acceptable career and lifestyle choices.

The women in the OA meeting, after all, were talking about problems with men and family life which were at once ancient and also very new. Their feelings of inadequacy, fear, and inferiority were familiar and ancient, but their situations were different and new in at least one important way. *Feminism* had, at least partly, changed these women's lives and expectations so as to make previously acceptable gender relationships suddenly seem inappropriate.

One of the many stories about eating disorders that I heard or read while researching this book, for example, was about a woman who had begun to earn more money than her husband, at which point he began tormenting her about her appearance and age, a sure trigger for her to binge and purge. Another was of a young woman who feared she was a lesbian and who ate to the point of passing out, so that she could make herself tolerate sex with her boyfriend. And still another involved a woman whose husband would not allow her to work because he "needed" her full-time care, but who insisted upon humiliating her with stories about his female law partner, young and "brilliant," a "real knock-out."

All these stories struck me as at once familiar and new, new because of the realization, on the part of the speakers, that these situations were somehow not right, not acceptable, not what one should tolerate. And this sense of "not-rightness," I believe, is a direct result of feminism's influence on the way women have come to think about their lives and relationships. Most women in the past did not have exactly these kinds of experiences and problems. Or if they did, they did not see them as problematic, but rather, accepted them as their lot in life.

Feminism has created these experiences and possibilities for us: the experience of earning more money or achieving more status than one's husband and so facing the possibility or reality of resentment; the anxiety-provoking option of acting upon a preference for women lovers; the feeling of being seriously limited by a traditional "housewife" role. And if these experiences have led to ever more troubled and troubling personal relationships with men, and with ourselves, that is not entirely a bad thing.

In fact, I came to see, more and more clearly, that the entire recovery movement—an ever-expanding offshoot of traditional AA, which was originally only for men who were chronic drinkers—is oddly connected to the gains (if at the moment they sometimes seemed stalled) of feminism. The women I heard and read of were in pain—as women have always been in sexist societies. And they were trying to mask that pain in various traditionally "feminine" ways—overeating, shopping, trying to control others. But they were now aware that the pain, and the ways of coping, are in fact "dysfunctional," and what is more crucial, that the pain is important enough to name and resist.

But if the problems of women in recovery are the same as those of pre-feminist women, or else created by the new lives feminism has made possible, the solutions being offered are so radically different from those of 1960s feminism that it is hard to see, at first glance, that there is a connection at all.

And that is because the most important thing of all is missing in these new meetings: the social context in which our suffering is born and grows. For the recovery rhetoric works to defuse the political tensions which fuel so much of what is now called "addiction," by focusing only on the *effects* of our confusion and pain, not the causes.

Do you hate your body or your husband, and yet can't seem to stop eating or putting up with him? Well, never mind the causes of these feelings, or whether they are justified or not. "Here is a set of rules for managing them," say the experts of recovery. "Keep your mind on these rules every day for the rest of your life and don't let anyone or anything distract you from them, because they are all that matters and they are the key to your very survival." And it is this message which makes the movement not *apolitical* as it seems, but highly political, in a most reactionary and repressive way.

When I began to understand how this message works, my first response was a knee-jerk rejection of the whole *gestalt* of the recovery movement. I wanted to tell everyone I met who was involved in recovery that they were being duped by a reactionary, apolitical dogma which blamed *us* as victims and addicts, and preached spiritual solutions to problems which were in fact caused by sexism and other social forces.

But I gradually realized that this line—true as it clearly is on one level—is not adequate to explain the whole recovery phenomenon. For one thing, the pain my friends and all the other women—on buses, on *Oprah*, on Valium, on therapists' couches—are feeling, not only in relationships but in many areas of their lives, is all too real. And the sense that feminism, as we of the "second wave" invented and practiced it, has not (yet? adequately?) "solved" those problems is a valid one. The changes wrought by feminism have indeed been dramatic and transformative, but there is still so much more to do. And any new effort to expand on feminist gains will run up against the backlash, the stress of the Super Woman complex, and the resistance and laggardness of men.

At such a moment in time, in the history of women and feminism, the appeal of the recovery movement, and, especially, its unmistakable links to— borrowings from?—feminism, cannot be so easily or glibly dismissed or even condemned. For the movement, growing by leaps and bounds, is obviously answering a call similar to the call once felt for feminism itself. It is filling a felt need in intriguing and important ways which are related to feminism's past and present, and which feminists need to understand, in order to build for the future.

Indeed, I have come to see the recovery movement as one of the most important and telling phenomena of our day. It is a microcosm, in many ways, of the contradictions and problems that face us, in a postmodern, postfeminist world—a world where we are all tied to obsolete attitudes and beliefs and are struggling in confusion to form and adapt to newer, more appropriate ones. The recovery movement, in adopting so many feminist ideas, only to twist them into the service of so many deeply reactionary ends, is a fascinating and compelling sign of our times.

I had no idea when I set out to write this book how far and deep and wide into American social and cultural life the project would ultimately take me. For in trying to flesh out my insight about the feminist roots of recovery thought, in following the leads and conversations and footnotes and advertisements I stumbled upon at every turn, I found myself moving farther and farther away from the support meetings and self-help books where I had begun. I moved from professional therapeutic and management conferences to inner-city clinics and spa-like treatment centers. I found myself studying mass-market magazines and professional journals, TV infomercials, and mail-order catalogs offering tapes, books, posters, kitchenware, jewelry, stuffed animals, and more. I looked at TV talk shows and docudramas and movies, law enforcement programs, health care and insurance policy meetings, and more. And while to the casual observer, the new recovery jargon, the sudden emergence of shelves full of recovery books at local bookstores, the Bradshaw seminars on PBS, and inside jokes about AA meetings and inner children, all might seem a passing, minor fad, I began to realize that it was anything but inconsequential. For in immersing myself in the world of recovery, I suddenly saw that it was, in one form or another, everywhere, in our popular culture, our workplaces, our schools, our hospitals. What did it all mean? And what, if anything, did all these other aspects of the recovery movement have to do with feminism? I was absorbed and compelled by these questions, by the need to fit it all together and analyze its importance.

And so, I decided to write this book as a cultural and social history and analysis of the recovery movement. I studied its ideas and structures with an eye toward analyzing its roots in feminist history, culture, and theory. My aim was to uncover the ways in which those roots can be seen to intertwine, in often twisted and contradictory ways, with a changing social and cultural world in the nearly three decades since 1968, and to lay bare the deeply reactionary agenda the movement supports. My purpose in writing the book was not to trash the recovery movement, however. Many books and articles in recent years have ridiculed or dismissed or exposed its claims.[1] I am more concerned with understanding and respecting the movement and figuring out how to deal with it. For I believe it has much to teach us about what is wrong not only with American society but also with traditional liberal and progressive ways of addressing our problems–approaches which do not (as indeed the Right very seriously does) take seriously the crucial importance of sexual and emotional issues to the broad welfare and functioning of society.

There are no simple explanations for the evolution of the feminist ideas of the activist sixties to the conservative, antipolitical teachings and practices of the recovery gurus. It is far too easy to say that women in the nineties, recognizing their powerlessness over political life, have turned to personal, spiritual forces. It is not enough to say that the newly embraced rhetoric of helplessness and humility is fitting in a world in which feminism is on the defensive and losing ground to the forces of reaction and backlash generally. And while it is true that women are feeling the power of these forces and buckling under in ways which are humbling, despairing, and politically depressing, it is not satisfactory to delineate the struggle as a simple dichotomy.

That is the model–in many ways true and useful of course–upon which much feminist analysis of what's happened to women and feminism in the late twentieth century is based. It is a model which stresses retreat and loss rather than triumph and victory. It is not, however, the model I am going to use in this book. For one thing, I believe this model seriously underestimates the enormous triumphs of early feminism and the great changes, still firmly in place, which it engendered. But even more important to consider is its misleading view of how social change occurs, which makes it inadequate to explain the very complicated interrelations between feminism and recovery which I want to tease out here.

One of the ways in which the recovery movement has been most destructive to women, and to progressive politics, is in its insistence on a single, very simplistic narrative pattern to explain our lives. This (as I'll explain further) is one of the ways in which the movement resembles a cult, and it is one of its most powerful and frightening features. One is born, or becomes, an addict, so the story goes. One hits bottom; one sees the light; one works one's program, every day for the rest of one's life, and is, from then on, in "recovery."

In the early women's movement we had a similar, cheerier "master narrative," so to speak. In our version, one is born and socialized female. One wallows in oppression blindly. One sees the light of feminism, joins the movement, changes one's life–and one's society–and becomes free. Only, as times changed and things didn't go so quickly or easily that way, we changed the story line. Now, there was a new chapter, a "backlash" chapter, in which male power fought back and won; in which, once more, we found ourselves held back and put upon.

If we come to the story of the rise of the recovery movement from this angle, we will fast find ourselves reaching for the Prozac. (So far there's no Prozac Anonymous, so we are safe to suggest it as a remedy.) But while there is no doubt that the backlash against feminism has been powerful, it is misleading to focus only on this part of the picture. Yes, the euphoria of feminism was gradually undermined by hard times and hard social and personal realities. And yes, many women turned away from activism either in despair and disillusionment or for lack of time and energy and once the responsibilities and problems of marriage, parenthood, careers, took over. And yes, yes, yes, as this book will document in depressing detail, these same women, for understandable reasons found themselves behaving compulsively in relation to substances or relationships.

But what the 12 Step programs and the other recovery philosophies offered could not have taken hold of these women's imaginations and lives, could not have felt so right and true and comfortable, if it had not offered many things—good, true, and positive things—that came straight from feminism. To call this cooptation is, if not to miss the point, exactly, at least to obscure what is truly interesting and encouraging about this phenomenon: that the recovery movement could not have succeeded without feminism is a great tribute to the power of feminist thought and the changes it has wrought in our lives and thoughts and social environments.

And so, while my primary take on the movement is critical, I do not wish to dismiss everything about it, by any means. In fact, to the extent that it does incorporate feminist ideas, it is a positive process, and, for women in pain, far superior to the classic, masculinist versions of AA. I want to stress this point before turning to my story proper, because I think it is often too easy, in looking at the alarming rise in right-wing, reactionary forces in America today—many of which have developed (as "backlash" theorists rightly note) in hostile response to the gains of feminism—to credit these forces with more power than they actually have, and to read their victories as having more long-term significance than they deserve.

It is as though we viewed history as moving either backwards or forwards, along a path marked, at each step of the way, with a clear "win or lose" score for all participants. "Us, zero; them, sum," we seem to say to ourselves with each depressing headline or personal horror story, as though the Reagan/Bush years and all the reactionary forces they brought into play somehow signaled "the end" of our progressive move forward. As though, as feminists and progressive people, we have been pushed back to square one and forced to begin the whole struggle again, from scratch.

The truth, however, is both more complicated and more encouraging. Indeed, it is self-defeating, I believe, to see the current spiritual and psychological crisis of so many women as conclusions to a story. Rather, we need to view them as stages, or segments of stages, of much longer, more complicated narratives. History isn't over yet and the feminist project is not a zero/sum game which we have lost. Indeed, the recovery movement, I would argue, even at its most regressive and apolitical, is more wisely reckoned as a complex development in which the positive, progressive forces of feminism are alive and well, if momentarily hard to recognize. For many of the roots of this movement are planted deep in the history of feminism itself. And these roots, I intend to demonstrate, are its main sources of power, the main reason why women are drawn to it and why, in dark times, they stay.

In writing this book, I want, in fact, not to mourn but to recover, reclaim, and redirect the feminist impulses that do indeed drive the recovery movement, if too often in the wrong direction. The recovery movement is dramatic testimony, it seems clear to me, that the postfeminist world in which we find ourselves is a world which has been radically and permanently transformed by feminism in ways which make it impossible for any mass movement or widespread, influential social or cultural discourse not to acknowledge and so pay deference to the second wave. The "Yes, I'm in favor of gender equality, but . . . ," the "No, I'm not a feminist, but . . . " are tributes to the power of feminism to change the way we are now forced to see and discuss gender, and to alter the ways in which we, and our daughters, understand and negotiate our lives.

The recovery movement, in taking feminism more seriously than the current Left, offers women something which we cannot so easily dismiss because we have nothing, at the moment, to replace it. We cannot say to the many women, especially those who *are* feminists, that they should simply toughen themselves and wait for the revolution. That is absurd. People do have "addictive" troubles in this world. They do indeed engage in self-destructive habits and escapes while trying to find their footing on the rough ground that lies in the outer reaches of social and sexual political struggle. And if the recovery movement has attracted so many converts to its apolitical view of these problems, we need, I think, to listen to what they are saying and watch what they are doing. The ultimate goals of the movement's leaders are dangerously misleading in many ways, it's true. But they are onto something those with more politicized agendas need to consider. And if what they are onto is largely taken from feminism, then perhaps we need to rethink many of our ideas about what *that* movement actually is and was, and give ourselves a bit more credit for our (strangely contradictory) achievements.

This book grew out of my own changing and expanding understanding of what the recovery movement actually is—what it includes and encompasses—and what its primary role has been in American life. The book covers a wide range of arenas in which recovery thought and method are constructed and empowered, and I have tried to give the reader a sense of how these different arenas fit together. Much of the support and admiration that the movement receives is based on a very limited sense of what it actually is and does. And it is my intention to pull the more invisible strands of the movement out into the open. Once exposed they alter the image of the recovery movement as it is popularly seen—and misunderstood.

I begin with television, specifically daytime talk shows and prime-time docudramas, because they are the most common and prominent avenues by which most of us—those who are not personally involved or concerned with matters of addiction and recovery—ingest, almost by osmosis, the movement's messages and theories and terminology. These pop culture forms are often and easily dismissed and trivialized, but I would argue that they operate as powerful forums through which ideas, attitudes, and values are circulated and gain currency and authority. It is here, in the bits and snatches of conversation and drama we unconsciously catch as we move through our evenings, and casually hear about as we move through our days, that the recovery movement has its greatest influence, even—perhaps especially—on those who are least conscious of its very existence.

Chapter 2 briefly presents some historical background on second wave feminism, revealing the way in which it developed and how, over time, its ideas and processes came to be reformulated and put to use in so different a context. Chapter 3 gives an overview of the institutional workings—the hospitals, lobbying groups, legislative efforts, marketing campaigns, and professional organizations—of the recovery movement. Seeing this "underworld" of behind-the-scenes wheeling and dealing is both fascinating and crucial to an understanding of the recovery movement in what it reveals of the normally invisible origins of "trends" and ideas in a postindustrial, corporate world.

Having looked at the material structures, I turn in chapter 4 to the social workings of the movement, the network of 12 Step groups that now pepper the nation, leading people in and out of meeting rooms for the most diverse array of problems, and somehow managing to hold the diversity and (often) near-chaos together under a single ideological umbrella. The months I spent attending, almost constantly, the widest array of groups I could locate–crossing from one neighborhood and addiction to another to get a sense of the movement as a whole–were invaluable to me. They allowed me to go beyond popular generalizations and look more closely at the internal differences and contradictions which mark the movement and give it its flexibility and, I believe, its power to attract so many different people in so many different ways.

Next, in chapter 5, I analyze in some depth the cultural phenomenon which today forms the ideological foundation–the set of "master narratives," if you will–upon which the entire recovery movement rests: self-help books. These books, which fill increasingly large sections of neighborhood and shopping mall bookstores, and which number, today, in the thousands of in-print titles, lay out in clear language, supplemented with even clearer rules and guidelines, just what the recovery movement's main ideas and messages are and just how to apply them to one's own life.

Finally in chapter 6 I look briefly at the ways in which the recovery movement has influenced actual political movements, including feminist ones, in ways which subtly turn progressive agendas away from looking at the real social causes of suffering and injustice to dwell, more and more, on how we can change *ourselves*. For this is the ultimate danger the recovery movement represents: in its focus on changing ourselves as a means of defusing our problems, recovery leads us farther and farther away from the social root causes of these problems–as feminists originally understood and addressed them–so far away that we are in danger of lapsing into chronic political myopia and self-absorption.

✦

CHAPTER ONE

Oprah, Geraldo, and the Movie of the Week: Recovery-Talk Takes Over

Let's start—Hollywood-style—with the dramatic end of the story. Then we'll flash back to the beginning and follow the tricky trail that led to the situation in which we now find ourselves, one in which the recovery movement has become a major force in our collective national life. Let's look at television. For it is through the recovery movement's successful invasion of television—primarily through the very popular daytime talk show and prime-time do-cudrama forms—that the movement has most forcefully found its way into our hearts and minds, our daily lives, and the various social and intellectual landscapes upon which we travel as members of a common community. "Recovery-thought" is in the air these days, wherever we go, because it is on television, and television is—literally and figuratively—in the air.

The recovery movement itself, as a form of therapy, a way of solving problems, has many outlets and forms—most obviously meetings, self-help books, and treatment programs and centers. But while these are the most common settings for the recruitment of active, working "members" of the movement, they are not the most important settings. For they do not spread the word to the general public, and it is the general public, not simply the converted practitioners, who must "come to believe" (as they say in the 12 Step rituals) in order for recovery-thought to achieve the kind of wide-spread, perhaps largely unconscious adoption in public thought parlance that it has by now achieved. Meetings are for select groups of people whose social needs, or extreme sufferings, move them to actually leave home, on a regular basis, to meet with others, get and give support, and—sometimes at least–take action to change their lives. Books, while reaching a larger segment of the population, are still limited in their impact to self-identified (actual or potential) "addicts" whose perhaps less critical sufferings lead them to at least buy and read books–usually many books–and take their teachings to heart. But it is TV–audible and visible, and therefore "consumed," in some way, in 98 percent of American households, on more than one set at a time, an average of $7^1/_2$ hours per day–that brings the message of addiction and recovery to virtually every American who is not in a coma, regardless of whether or not she will ever consider herself an addict of any kind.

This power of home-based television to reach out, communicate, and persuade in ways no other medium in the history of the world has even vaguely approached, makes it the most profoundly important link in the chain of institutions–government, the medical establishment, the church, the Anonymous group networks, the publishing industry, and the electronic media–that has so successfully convinced an entire culture that its social problems are "illnesses" and its social health is dependent upon mass adoption of 12 Step teachings.[1] For we live in a world in which, more and more, it is slogans, stories, and shifting feelings and "identities" communicated through mass media forms that provide our common sense of who we are and what we believe far more than active participation in traditional institutions like the church, the political party, or even the family. In such a world, it is the recovery movement's ability to communicate its ideological message, far more than its ability to "cure" or "heal," that gives it its greatest impact. Through its ubiquitous presence on the small screen, the recovery movement has subtly and gradually led an entire nation–not only self-defined "addicts" but all of us–to rethink, reevaluate, and redefine our common understandings and attitudes about social and emotional problems. And so it is to television that we turn first, to get the strongest sense of the recovery movement's impact.

While the core ideas and narratives of the discourse of recovery are common to all TV programming, from the morning news to afternoon soaps to nighttime sitcoms, there are two forms which have been most responsible for TV's great success in convincing us that the recovery message is not only the best, but the *only* credible explanation of, and cure for, our woes: daytime talk shows and primetime docudramas (or TV movies).[2] Enormously popular, especially in the last few years, these programs have put names like Bradshaw, Beattie, Norwood, and Schaef–the gurus of the recovery movement–and words like "inner child," "dysfunctional families," "working your program," "recovering abuser"–the mainstays of its vocabulary–most solidly on everyone's mental map. A mere decade ago, the idea that someone's face might appear on our TV screens over a label bar bearing a phrase like "compulsive self-abuser" or "shopaholic," as anything but a joke, would not have been conceivable. But today, such terms–and far more bizarre ones– appear all day and evening long, on broadcast and cable networks alike. And the great majority of them show up in the titles and texts of TV movies and daytime talk shows (Rapping 1992; Rapping 1994, pp. 192–97)–forms, it should be noted, with special appeal to women.[3] Here, for all the world–literally–to see and hear, are the endlessly repeated stories and terms and expert advice-givers who have done most to place the truths of recovery in our collective hearts and minds and make sure they stay there.

Anyone who doubts the actual impact of these two forms on public thinking need only listen in on the many conversations that occur on buses, at water coolers, in fast food restaurants, in which last night's Movie of the Week–about the abused "codepedent" wife, the alcoholic teen–and yesterday's series of talk shows–about date rape, bigamy, kidnapped children, lesbian wives–regularly provide the context for much of the casual conversation about life and society in which we all engage, especially, perhaps, women.

Nor is it only–common opinion notwithstanding–the less educated and sophisticated among us that watch and are influenced by these TV programs (although they may be the most willing to admit to it). Everyone watches or–at least–hears and reads about TV movies and talk shows every day. Just press the right button, and your conversational companion will tell you about them. They are the common "stuff" of our lives; the mental wallpaper which decorates our days and nights, adding color and texture to our mundane existences.

Their popularity is not accidental either; nor should it seem surprising, when viewed from a social and cultural perspective. Docudramas and talk shows are the two TV forms which most successfully merge entertainment and discourse, packaging the major, serious concerns of the day–as more traditional news programming does not–in dramatic, moving, personalized forms. They are highly watchable and speak to our need to understand our common plight. And almost invariably, what they dramatize is the particular worldview of the recovery movement.

I have been studying and analyzing these two TV forms, especially the docudrama, a form which became popular in the 1970s, for several years now. I've noticed that their subject matter comes up more and more often in casual conversations and classroom discussions. Students and acquaintances alike are prone (often unconsciously) to pepper their arguments and observations about personal and social life with quotes and examples from TV talk and docudrama almost as a matter of course these days.

It's not that such people are stupid, that they don't "know," intellectually, that docudramas distort and talk shows sensationalize and simplify life. Everyone "knows" these things. The role of major television events is not after all, at least primarily, to inform or explain. It is to socialize and unite us as a nation. And in this project, docudramas and talk shows have come to play a major role. They acquire a de facto authority by virtue of their status as the most widely seen or read "official" version of a situation or issue in which we, as a society, have some stake. They are defining and unifying public events, and as such form the basis for our "common knowledge" about a great number of events and issues.

So powerful is the sway of the "knowledge" gleaned from these widely seen, oft-repeated spectacles of narrative and discourse, that I have even, on occasion, been egged on by journalists, in interviews on popular culture matters, to offer printable quotes to bolster analyses *they* have already settled upon, based on *their* TV viewing. "But didn't you see that movie about Karen Carpenter's food addiction?" one reporter asked me as I was writing this chapter (of course I had), as a way of steering me toward a particular explanation for the early 1990s trend toward near-starved looking, waiflike fashion models. Another journalist, around the same time, actually quoted an audience member's testimony about her own sex addiction on a *Geraldo* show (which I had *not* seen) in an effort to steer me toward her favorite theory about the apparent rise in "fatal attraction" murder cases.

These journalists may not be aware of the extent to which their conversation is informed by such "low" TV forms, because, when they quote television shows, they are simply searching for an apt example, to which the other person may reasonably be expected to respond. And they are right to choose TV movies and talk shows, for they are inhaled by everyone as part of our social environment, like second-hand smoke.

Nor are these shows necessarily a bad thing. The movies and talk shows that so regularly plug recovery are often the most useful, sensible, and compassionate projects in the media. They are also two of the three TV forms (the other is soap opera) most likely to implicitly incorporate feminist analyses and attitudes. They target female audiences and serve a certain function within American society, which has been virtually forced to turn to feminist thinking to address its troubles today. For this reason, they are particularly useful in illustrating the perspective of recovery thought.

WARD CLEAVER, WALTER CRONKITE, AND WESTINGHOUSE COME TO DINNER

Television, ever since its establishment in the 1950s, has been a stabilizing force for a nation in the throes of constant economic and social transformation. The invention of television—actually available since the 1930s, but only adopted in the postwar, postindustrial 1950s—appeared as a godsend to those trying valiantly to keep order in the lives of a population whose traditional ways of doing things had—by then—been sorely disrupted by the radical economic and social changes wrought by industrialization and the new corporate order (Williams 1975). As people gradually were forced to leave traditional small town and rural communities and traditional farm and small business lifestyles, and move to urban centers, to find work in the new industrial and corporate work forces—in factories and offices—much that had traditionally given order and meaning to their daily lives dissolved. Families and extended families, used to living, generation after generation, in a common home, attending a common church and schoolhouse, pursuing and passing on common, gender-specific tasks and functions, began to shrink and ultimately disintegrate. Individuals floundered amidst a wealth of new, seemingly "unnatural" daily regimes and responsibilities. As Americans adopted urban, industrial lifestyles, and home-based production gave way to consumerism, and home-based education and socialization gave way to the ever louder and more persistent commands of socialized workplaces, schools, and commercial media, television itself came to play the central socializing and educating role in American family life. Television replaced the "finger knowledge" and land-based routines which had, for so many generations, determined moral values, family and gender roles and authority structures, and concepts of the cycles of life and death.[4]

Women, it is important to note, were always the primary target of television sponsors and executives because women bought the products upon which the new consumer-based economic order depended, and women—the traditional nurturers and socializers of men and children—were called upon to ease the American family into the new ways of thinking about and living their daily lives which industrialism and consumerism required (Spigel 1992; Taylor 1989; Spigel and Mann 1992). As the stresses of industrial life—and then of postindustrial life—have in recent years led to the rise in "addictive" problems, for men and increasingly for women too, the role of television in addressing such problems and in offering ways of coping with and resolving them, has intensified, as has the medium's attention to women as its most important audience, economically and socially.

It is clear even from this brief overview that television has always been more than an entertainment form. The original draw to buy television sets may well have been shows like *The Honeymooners* and *Your Show of Shows*. But it is no accident that these two early shows were quickly replaced by others—*Father Knows Best, Leave it to Beaver, The Donna Reed Show*—which were far more ideologically consistent with the needs of sponsors and government regulators in their pushing of middle-class norms of consumption and family order.

Television, from the start, told us what was happening, what it meant, and what to do about it. Its white, male patriarchal figures—the Murrows, Cleavers, and General Electric hawkers who stood in, now, for the increasingly disempowered heads of our real families—because our mentors and role models, bringing and interpreting news of the brave new world, and acting out, for our edification, the new roles we were supposed to play in it, as men and women, boys and girls.

The very fact that early television programmers felt the need to stress so much the still-central role of fathers and patriarchy was a sign of the already straining internal contradictions and weaknesses of the traditional model of family life, in the new era. The role of early television was, after all, to shore up the old images of family unity and male domination and authority against the growing pressures—built into the new economic order—which were tearing it apart. Women, and young people too for that matter, had far less reason to accept father-based authority in a corporate world of wage earners, in which advertisers spoke far more directly and emphatically to women and, even youth, than to men (Miller 1986).

One of the most obvious of television's contradictions, from the start—and its greatest difference from theatrical films, which generally assumed a male viewer and male worldview—was its emphasis on female viewers. In a medium built for home consumption, and intent on hailing us all as nuclear family members, out there in "television land," it was assumed implicitly that "father" was the head of the household. Nonetheless—and television was built upon *this* idea as much as on the need to preserve the family—the switch to a consumerist economy made *mother*, not *father* the key target of the TV announcer's messages. The job of the full-time housewife was, after all, to shop (which is why shopping is now one of the most common female "addictions"). Thus was born the phony image of the Cleavers and Andersons, in which Dad was the main honcho and yet seemed to do nothing of significance, while the real activity of family life centered on the kitchen.

That television has always assumed a predominantly female audience can be seen most clearly by looking at commercials, arguably the dominant cultural form of our age. Commercials, the driving force of the medium, have always been geared to women in the home, who have always bought and used most consumer goods. The networks heeded the needs and desires of women, and sought to subtly maneuver them toward acceptable solutions to their problems, all the while making sure that those solutions were in keeping with the needs–for profits and socially "appropriate" messages–of the sponsors and executives and government regulators–who were, and still are, the real "fathers" who "know best" (Barnouw 1975, 1978).

The original "cure" for the "feminine mystique"–the one which recovery-thought now supplements–was to sell women on the meaningfulness of housework. The joy on Dad's and the kids' faces when the ring around the collar disappeared, or the towels were "Downy soft," was meant to give new meaning to a job which corporate consumerist America had, in fact, made increasingly hollow (Ewen 1976, pp. 159–76). Norman Lear's hilarious spoof of soap operas, *Mary Hartman, Mary Hartman,* which ran for a season or two in the late seventies–on late night syndication since no network or sponsor would dare place it on prime time–is based entirely on a parody of this media strategy. While the heroine, a midwestern housewife, copes with every social trauma of postmodern life, she is continuously distracted from her actual situation by her constant, nagging anxiety over the "waxy yellow buildup" on her floor.

As time went on, of course, this precarious balance between the patriarchal authority still stressed by television news and entertainment and the actual changes in gender and generational relationships brought on by postindustrialism grew strained. And television–scrambling madly to contain the many contradictions and potential explosions wrought by the social and political upheavals of the sixties–was forced to reconfigure and renegotiate everything it did. While the Waltons and Bradys denied it, and the Bunkers joked us through it, the sixties and seventies were not, in fact, easy to handle for the men who ran the social and culture industries and agencies.

Against their wills, the TV moguls were forced to incorporate the demands of the unprivileged and disenfranchised into the TV picture of private and public life. Suddenly, the faces of black and female authorities were brought onscreen to read and explain world events. The likes of Mary Tyler Moore and eventually Murphy Brown and Roseanne Arnold appeared along with the Cosbys and various other versions of minority and blended families and workplaces. Their progressive inflections–especially a feminist influence–were added to the increasingly complicated and confusing world of postfeminist, post-Vietnam, post–civil rights America. Suddenly men were housekeepers, women were executives, and some of us were even black or gay. But the point was always the same: no matter how things change, we can accommodate ourselves to new situations and demands without really changing the basic structure of things, the basic rules about power and money and decision-making (Rapping 1994, pp. 5–13).

This promise was hard to keep, however, especially in the realm of gender relations and assumptions. For the issues and controversies raised by feminists have gone to the heart of the most basic ways in which we live and think about our lives. The role of television, as gatekeeper, agenda setter, and negotiator of these matters–as the public sphere through which they are introduced, debated, and reconsidered–is crucial, in such troubling times, if we are to maintain any semblance of a politically and socially unified and coherent national entity. Now more than ever, we watch television for far more than mindless entertainment. (In fact the idea of mindless television is misleading if not oxymoronic. There are ideas present in every frame we produce and consume.)[5] We watch, religiously, if you will, in order to figure out what is going on and how we are supposed to manage it. We watch because we are confused and isolated and embarrassed to share with our friends and neighbors–whose lives, we believe, must be more "normal" than ours–the real problems in our lives.

And when we turn to TV for these reasons, we are more and more often watching docudramas and talk shows, where our problems are most likely to be addressed in terms that resonate with our own realities. How do they manage to speak so truly and realistically–even so helpfully in many ways–to our real sufferings, even as they steer us away from our own *true* best interests, and toward deeper and deeper involvements in their own socially approved, commercially viable, solutions? By invoking the language and methodology of addiction and recovery.

Day after day on daytime, week after week on prime-time, two highly popular and influential forms, docudrama and talk, give us tales of addiction–to people, things, places, feelings, almost anything you can think of to worry about–and lessons in recovery, through groups, in books, with experts. All acknowledge just what feminists have long made clear: that the old family and relational norms don't work anymore. And all present the same addiction/dysfunction analysis and prescribe the same cure: buy a book, join a group, work your program, trust your Higher Power. You can listen to Oprah Winfrey or Sally Jessy Raphael interview "love addicts" and "sex addicts" and lead them, by hour's end, to the teachings of 12 Step gurus like Robin Norwood and Ann Wilson Schaef. Or watch TV movies like *Sarah T: Portrait of a Teenage Alcoholic* and *The Life of the Party*, which dramatize the descent into addiction by women of all ages and then lead them, inevitably, to a recovery meeting where their problems are solved. Both the talk shows and the docudramas serve to lead us all to understand women's problems as "addictive" and their cures in terms of a common, 12 Step analysis.

But that language and methodology itself works so well because of its extensive borrowings from, and incorporations of, feminist thought and process. On talk shows and TV movies, as in the self-help books and meetings of the 12 Step–based recovery movement, we get a potent version of addiction/recovery ideology laced with just enough feminist consciousness and challenge to worn out patriarchal norms and values to make the messages of disease and powerlessness palatable. Indeed, in the tracing of the history of the women's docudrama, joined midway in its development by the phenomenon of the talk show, we can see the final emphatic merging of feminism and 12 Step–ism into a powerful social ideology–at once heartening and frightening, therapeutic and oppressive–for our confusing times.

THE SOCIAL ISSUE FILM
GOES FROM BIG SCREEN TO SMALL

It is not surprising that docudramas and talk shows have been the primary forms through which the new, feminist-informed versions of recovery-thought have been circulated on television. No two forms take women's issues more seriously. And no two forms, in doing this, draw more heavily upon feminist thinking and process. TV movies and talk shows–along with soap operas–are today the premier "women's" forms on television, overwhelmingly addressing women's concerns from a woman's angle. (Indeed, it is arguable that the sneering dismissal these forms receive from critics is in major part a matter of sexist prejudice against things so clearly and unapologetically "female" [Rapping 1994]).

But what is most remarkable about these forms, given their "feminization," is their ascent to positions of central importance in society generally, as more than mere "women's" culture. There have always been "women's"

movies, books, magazines, and other cultural artifacts, of course. But none
has had so visible and influential a place in the dominant culture. Critically
acclaimed or not, these shows garner huge ratings and have an enormous
impact on public debate and consciousness, far beyond the ghettoized "back
pages" of traditional female culture. The impact of *The Burning Bed* on public awareness of domestic violence, for example, or of *Something About Ame-
lia* on public awareness of incest, has been enormous and salutary. And they
are only a few of the many TV movies—from *Roe v. Wade*, about reproductive rights, to *A Case of Rape* and *When He's Not a Stranger*—about rape and
date rape—which have called national attention to important women's issues
in a way that more "serious" media could not have done.

To grasp the significance of the impact of these docudramas, we need
only look, comparatively, at the immediate generic precursor of the TV
movie for women, the Hollywood "weepie," which, while strikingly similar,
plays a much less central role in American cultural history. From the 1930s
Stella Dallas, about a woman who gives up her child, to the 1950s *Peyton
Place*, about the crisis-ridden lives of a small town community, the weepie
dramatized the clashes between women's sexuality and maternal responsibilities, the push and pull between love and money in choosing—as was necessary for survival—a lifetime mate, and other pressures of family life, which
thwarted women's desires for fulfillment (Haskell 1974).

But there was a difference. The weepie did not take itself seriously as social commentary, as today's video versions do. It was never as doctrinaire or
preachy about women's issues, or as eager to help viewers sort them out. And
most notably, it never insisted upon a happy ending for its protagonists—
achieved through the proper practice of socially authorized techniques—as
TV movies today so overbearingly do. On the contrary, the weepies—hence
their nickname—were likely to give tragic endings to their stories of female
strivings against the limits of sexist society. Women went; women wept;
women were duly warned against foolish fancies of escape from their lots.
And women were sent home to their traditional, unfulfilling lives, glad to be
safe and alive.[6]

The TV movie, which replaced this female genre, is a very different matter, socially and emotionally. Typically, a two-hour drama explicitly made
for television, rather than the theater, and structured to accommodate commercial and other interruptions, the TV movie has become familiar to viewers, if only through the endless promotional clips the networks run to
promote and publicize them. It has become, through the careful molding of
the powers that be in mass media, a formulaic, often dramatically powerful

but incessantly ideological form. No more the "read it and weep" lesson for unhappy housewives. Today women's films tell us that our problems do indeed matter, that they are being attended to, and that, if only we heed the word of the producers, silver linings will replace the clouds. And by the late 1980s, the most common formula for achieving the silver lining was a 12 Step group.

Having found its formula, the TV movie came to fill an important social and economic place in TV programming. The networks, bound by the FCC to provide a certain amount of public interest/public service programming, and by sponsors to attract women, saw the form as potentially invaluable, and they were right. As a "long form" dramatic genre, on which a single issue could be elaborately laid out and analyzed in ways which series shows could not manage, the docudrama became a showcase genre in which the networks could prove their "serious," "socially responsible" intentions by doing "good works" in the interest of social welfare and family stability (Gomery 1983; Gitlin 1986; Rapping 1994). As a commercially sponsored effort, the docudrama became a ready-made advertisement for how well the traditional American lifestyle–as pushed on commercials–could be made to work, no matter how hard things might seem.

TV movies and miniseries–from *Roots* to *The Burning Bed* to *The Day After*–have become television's special events. They are public rituals in which serious concerns of the day are presented in ways both entertaining and preachy, dramatic and instructional. Their narrative structures work to tie up the loose ends the real world leaves ragged and bloody. In the process they offer support, advice, book titles, phone numbers, and addresses to those suffering from–usually–the very troubles addressed by 12 Step groups across the country. TV, through the docudrama, tells us it understands our troubles. It hears us crying, sees us bleeding, and knows a guy we can call who will fix us right up in a way which will not–and this is central–upset the apple cart of state and commerce.

Over 50 percent of these movies involve female protagonists dealing with gender-inflected issues, broadly defined (Marill 1987). In the most impressive, the most vexed and crucial family and gender issues are raised and resolved in ways which do in fact suggest–through narrative structure and character development–that women can empower themselves, change the conditions of their lives, and even–it is occasionally hinted–create a better world for other women. *The Burning Bed* (about domestic violence) and *Lois Gibbs and the Love Canal* (about corporate pollution) are only two of the praiseworthy examples in which feminism is the implicit driving force around which all the heroine's, and other characters', actions are understood.

But while it is remarkable that such movies were made at all, let alone that they became popular and influential, they were, even in the 1970s, a relatively minor subgenre of what was rapidly developing into the "real" classic TV movie aimed at women viewers: the family-based "social issue movie" in which the heroine, always a mother, handles and heals a family crisis indicative of profound social upheaval.

Families, in the seventies and early eighties, were increasingly "troubled" by all sorts of social, sexual, emotional, and economic disasters. And insofar as these movies addressed women, it was primarily as the traditional socializers and nurturers we were still assumed to be. Indeed, in these movies—and there are still many of them being made—the "woman's angle" is the way in which women are approached. "This is what the problem is," the movies tell us in a "Can we talk?" tone of respect and seriousness. "This is what you've got to do about it." These movies pay more respect to women's intelligence and importance than other forms do, but only in our capacities as mothers and wives.

These movies assume a seventies, liberal-style approach to social issues. Families are pictured as upper middle class in lifestyle, and social agencies and therapists (often explicitly AA-based, but sometimes not) are shown as liberal institutions capable of keeping our families functioning, even as the world turns on its head all around them. Movies like *Consenting Adults*, in which a family comes to terms with a gay child, and *Another Woman's Child*, which deals with step-parenting problems, are among the many TV movies that work hard to educate and encourage women viewers in their efforts to adjust to changing family norms without giving up on the family itself. They are hopeful and upbeat, socially and economically (Rapping 1994, pp. 148–55).

It is this trend in the woman-oriented docudrama form that ultimately lent itself most neatly and successfully to the 1980s recovery movement rhetoric. In these movies, and their underlying philosophies, we see the seeds of much of the thinking of 1980s recovery theory. They suggest that all personal problems should be viewed as mental health problems to be solved therapeutically by a therapist or social worker, privately or in group treatment; and that individual and family "disease" and "dysfunction," rather than social forces, should be seen as the causes of all such problems. Indeed, these movies were ready-made for a recovery-style updating of seventies liberalism in the Reagan/Bush eighties—which is what they often got. As the liberal worldview of progress through reason and benevolent government gave way to a darker, economically downscale, law-and-order view of how to combat "evil," more family crisis movies ended with the (always benevolent) courts and police intervening and ordering mandatory attendance at various–free–12 Step programs.

To see how this happened, and how the growing problem of women's addiction was gradually incorporated–with the help of feminism–into TV's standard approach, we need to look at the way in which addiction as a female problem has traditionally been handled, in theatrical films, and how television diverged from, and built upon, that tradition.

HOLLYWOOD'S DRUNKS VS. TV'S ADDICTS

The first thing one notes in looking back at old movies about alcoholism, especially classic women's genres, is the way in which alcohol or drugs, in and of themselves, are rarely presented as the main issues (Denzin 1984; Room 1983). Where, in today's TV culture, addiction serves as the *causal* factor in problem films, Hollywood has been more imaginative in analyzing the circumstances that lead to "substance abuse." In 1936, for example, before AA was even established, Bette Davis played an alcoholic in a movie called *Dangerous* which was not about alcoholism as a disease, or even a problem, at all. Davis played a tragic heroine who loses her lover in grand style. Her drinking is largely incidental to the plot structure, an excuse for putting her in the situation in which her tragedy occurs. It does not, however, figure as a sign of her weakness or flawed character. This, from today's viewpoint, is quite remarkable.

The women's "problem drinking" film, influenced by AA's propaganda about alcoholism as a disease, emerges a bit later and is, again, primarily used in tragic movies about truly extraordinary women–often stars like Lillian Roth in *I'll Cry Tomorrow,* for example. In these movies, celebrity, not drinking, is presented as the hard-to-handle critical issue which leads these women to drink as a way of handling their impossible situations. Women in the limelight, pushed and pulled by the needs of success and love, are seen to sink ever deeper into addiction, from which they either emerge victorious or die tragically. This genre remained popular into the seventies, after which the recovery movement's influence in Hollywood probably made its non-ideological, old-fashioned approach to addiction problematic.

In 1972, for example, *Lady Sings the Blues,* among the best of this long-standing Hollywood star bio genre, showed how the pressures of racism, sexism, and stardom all combined to drive Billie Holliday to heroin. That such social issues as race and gender should be so prominently featured, while heroin itself figures only as the logical, because most easily available, escape, in Billie Holiday's movie biography, points to the very different concerns of feature filmmakers and TV producers working in the same era.

In the very same year, for example, the TV movie *Sarah T: Portrait of a Teenage Alcoholic* treated the issues of women's addiction very differently. Beginning with a documentary lead-in filled with horrifying statistics about the epidemic of teen drinking, it proceeded to lay out, in a predictable format, the progress of the disease of alcoholism in a troubled young girl who cannot adapt to her parents' divorce and her mother's remarriage. Sarah's father is presented as an irresponsible dreamer and drinker. Her stepfather, a responsible business type, is far more stable. Sarah is seen to drink secretly as a way of handling adolescent awkwardness, shyness in a new school, and the problems in the new family situation. Soon she is in deep trouble. She is nearly raped by a group of thugs to whom she offers "anything you want" if they will buy her liquor, and then she is nearly killed in a traffic accident.

It is only when Sarah's mother faces her responsibility, through the help of therapy, of course, for not recognizing Sarah's unhealthy attachment to her alcoholic father that Sarah's drinking problem is acknowledged for what it is, and she is sent to an AA group (which, remarkably, has many members under the age of twelve). The doctrinaire, preachy tone of this often moving film is apparent. The disease model and 12 Step cure are clearly major concerns of the producers—as they certainly are not in the Billie Holiday theatrical film of the same year.

Even codependency, or coaddiction, as it is sometimes called, received very different treatment in the classic women's films of the fifties. *The Country Girl*, a 1954 movie starring Grace Kelly, portrayed the problem of alcoholism in a performer, this time from his wife's point of view. The movie, based on a play by Clifford Odets, shows how Kelly's spouse keeps her with him (as an "enabler" in today's terms) by manipulating her sympathy for his tragic condition. Finally she does break free, with the help of an outside agent. It is not however a therapist who saves her; it is a new lover, with whom she lives happily ever after, as she deserves.

This movie is remarkable for its emotional honesty about the twisted interdependencies that keep women in destructive relationships. It is a precursor to Robin Norwood, in that respect. Its ending, however, couldn't be more different than the Norwood model. The woman, way back in the fifties, is allowed to leave her very unsympathetic mate and find romantic, guilt-free happiness for herself by leaving her emotionally crippled husband behind. She is not, as she would certainly be today, labeled a codependent and sent off to a treatment group or center.

In today's TV movies of codependency and enabling within married couples, things work out far less romantically and more dogmatically. In the award-winning movie *Shattered Spirits*, Martin Sheen plays the addict–and he is very definitely a classic addict. He begins as a social drinker. His family is seen to ignore his behavior, cover for him, lie to each other and to others. His children suffer horrible indignities of embarrassment and humiliation. His daughter becomes the surrogate mother as his wife works harder and harder to please and nurture him, in the false hope of helping him stop.

Things, of course, go from bad to worse as Sheen loses his job and is arrested. As in movies like *The Burning Bed*, the legal and other institutional procedures by which society handles such cases are shown in detail. But where that movie critiques the sexism of the institutions, this one applauds their coercive, ideological methods. Sheen, for example, is forced to go to AA by court order; this saves his life. The children are taken from home and steered similarly into a group meeting sponsored by the National Association of Children of Alcoholics (NACA), another 12 Step–based program also touted in the credits. And the therapist the family consults, of course, is herself a recovering alcoholic. When Sheen admits, before his group meeting, that he too is "an alcoholic," the happy ending is guaranteed and the family is reunited. Neatly labeled and categorized, each character is sent off to her or his proper meeting, given her proper reading matter, and taught his proper slogans and chants. The credits then roll, followed by news followups about the issue, and then a list of addresses, book titles, and phone numbers for more help and information.

Society–it must be stressed again–does not change in any way at all in this TV movie; nor is it seen to need changing. This, in spite of the obvious miseries of this family in their personal and–for Sheen, a Willy Lomanesque salesman in constant fear for his livelihood–work lives. The wife's dependency is never analyzed in terms of patriarchy, nor are the children's sex-stereotyped relations with their parents and each other so analyzed, although sexism and inappropriate gender power relations are rampant throughout. The daughter, for example, is made to do household chores while the son is endlessly being told how to "be the man of the family" when his dad is "not feeling well."

Shattered Spirits does a superb job of gratifying its producers and its viewers. It is indeed intelligent and helpful. It gives a sensible dose of understanding and advice. And it keeps the increasingly troubled and disintegrating American family on the track to rejuvenation and reintegration.

Nonetheless, the profound difference between its worldview and the Hollywood version of the story–even Hollywood back in the fifties–says volumes about the way in which television has been put to the service, first, of the therapeutic worldview, and second, of the recovery movement worldview, in constructing a social model where addiction takes precedence over character, work, even fate in explaining our lives to ourselves. No more classic tragic or comic narratives of heroes confronting fate. Today we are offered a thinner narrative gruel, supplemented, like mass-produced white bread, with ideological chemicals and vitamins to replace what's been lost in human complexity, ambiguity, and emotional texture.

THE CRISIS DEEPENS:
WOMEN AS BIG-TIME ADDICTS ON THE SMALL SCREEN

Which brings me to the most recent, and most significant, trend, for women, in this genre–the "woman in recovery" movie which has, since about 1986, been a clear trendsetter on the networks. Undoubtedly, a sign of the growing difficulties in resolving the conflicts in women's lives brought on by feminism and postfeminism is the decision by producers of TV movies in the last few years to present more and more feature-length dramas about women in the throes of their own very serious kinds of addictions. In these movies women are not presented as care-givers and problem-solvers, and the preservation of the family–unless the husband is willing to take it on as *his* job–is not placed first on the narrative agenda.

The image of the typical American family, in classic family crisis movies, has begun to look increasingly unrealistic by today's standards. The families in these movies–made in the days of the *Dallas* and *Dynasty* television series–all were startlingly prosperous and luxury-laden. The men were all successful businessmen and professionals, and the women were all able to stay home and cope with personal matters full-time. But the prevailing image of the strong, stable woman, steering the ship of hearth and home to health and happiness, was not long for this world. It was based on a myth–long proven absurd–about women in middle-class families being able and willing to devote their entire lives to family harmony.

The economic crisis of the eighties and nineties made this image problematic. Indeed, the plush parlors, restaurants, and boutiques which served as settings where the women of the seventies and early eighties TV movies met and discussed their family problems have given way, these days, to far less affluent settings for the typical troubled family or, if luxury still prevails, to a harried career woman/wife who is—and here comes the female addiction movie—herself frazzled and frantic. By the mid-eighties and nineties a whole new subgenre of addiction films emerged in which women were indeed—as the large recovery movement was making clear to everyone—seen to be addicted to all sorts of things, among which alcohol was the least interesting since, after all, it had been done to death.

Two very typical TV movies—*Kate's Secret*, about bulimia, and *House of Secrets*, about codependency—made respectively in 1986 and 1992 reveal the ways in which the recovery movement, as it has increasingly addressed and reached women, has grown in importance as a theme for TV movies about women as well. In fact, 1986, the year *Shattered Spirits* was also made, saw many more movies about women and their intriguing new addictions than the more standard dramas about men and alcohol.

Both *Kate's Secret* and *House of Secrets* present their women addicts as troubled wives in whose lives many of the most typical conflicts of our post-feminist age figure: career/family conflicts; anxiety about appearance in an age of media pressure to look younger and more glamorous while doing way too many jobs at once; self-esteem issues in a world in which one's social standing still, very often, depends upon one's mate; and struggles with male anxieties and hostilities toward successful women.

Kate, the bulimic, is a full-time housewife terrified of losing her husband to his gorgeous, successful law partner. This movie is unusual in still presenting upper-middle-class family life, in which women do not work, as an option. The script, however, makes clear that it is just this lack of career that is a major source of Kate's low self-esteem. The idea that full-time housework—so unrealistically glorified before—has now, somehow, become demeaning and embarrassing enough to lead to addiction in women is clearly a new wrinkle in the family crisis movie.

Susan, the codependent wife in *House of Secrets*, is, more typically for these recent movies, a very successful TV producer married to an also successful, although insecure, attorney who is himself a sex addict, and whose infidelities obsess and terrify her as much as Kate's husband's imagined misdeeds do her. In both cases, we see the addictive behavior of the women, as classically spelled out in the literature of Overeaters Anonymous (OA) and Codependents Anonymous (CODA), progress to crisis levels in which their very lives are endangered.

Kate binges and purges, works outs compulsively, and hides her eating from everyone. She avoids sex with her husband because of her growing addictive compulsions. When her weight fluctuates a pound or two, she rushes to the gym. When her anxieties about her role as hostess cause her to crave food, she sends her amorous husband off on an errand, so she can binge and purge in privacy. The scenes of binging and purging, as well as the precipitating causes, are portrayed here in horrifying accuracy of detail.

Susan's behavior is equally predictable, dramatic, and believable. She frantically searches her husband's clothing for signs of infidelity. She turns down promotions when he shows signs of hostility toward her success. Her work goes downhill as her panic and obsessiveness grow. Finally, like Kate, who collapses from weakness, Susan's addiction almost kills her. She becomes so self-destructive–she nearly kills her husband by running her car into his in a fit of hysterical rage–that, like Kate, she is forced to seek help. It is not surprising that, by 1992, when the notion of cross-addiction has so pervaded recovery talk, Susan's addiction is discovered by a woman suffering from a different addiction, a former prostitute and sex addict whom Susan is interviewing. This woman picks up on Susan's codependency–from which she also suffers–and points it out to her. Cross-addiction–addiction to more than one thing–is a big part of the analysis in this movie. All roads, after all, lead to the 12 Steps.

Both these movies are exemplary in many ways. Like their feminist precursors–most obviously *The Burning Bed*, in which a wife kills her abusive husband and is acquitted–they lay out in clear, accurate terms the problems that lead women to engage in, or put up with, destructive behavior patterns. They make especially clear the ways in which sexism (although the term never comes up, of course) and women's difficult life problems are causal factors. The men in these movies are either typically insensitive and blind or downright vicious in classically sexist ways. And the ways in which family backgrounds, work environments, and media play into the women's problems are spelled out. So far, so good.

There is an important difference, however. In *The Burning Bed* Francine Hughes's abusive treatment by her husband and the support he receives from everyone else stand as justification for her rebellion–even when it leads to murder. *Kate's Secret* and *House of Secrets* allow for no such radical, empowering solutions. These films–unlike the earlier addiction films we looked at–do not necessarily save the family, or if they do, it is not the heroine's role to manage the salvation. Nonetheless, even though the heroine is not tending to the family, it is never empowerment, but rather rehabilitation, that she triumphantly seeks and achieves.

Kate does save her marriage, but that is almost incidental to the story. It is Kate's therapy and the support network she finds with other women food addicts who understand her problems and keep her on her program that save her. Susan's marriage ends, since her husband will not accept his addiction and enter recovery. But it is not her release from this marriage that offers her salvation. That comes through the recovery movement itself and the other women she finds to support and understand her.

In these two movies, we see the clever and effective way in which TV movies for women have incorporated elements of both the better, more feminist-informed classics and the more troubling, family-systems varieties. Women are taken seriously in *Kate's Secret* and *House of Secrets*, as are their addictions and the life problems that cause them (or at least trigger them). But, while these moves acknowledge the social, sexist roots of the heroines' problems—indeed they fairly scream them out—the solutions they offer virtually deny that these women are the victims of sexism. Instead, as in the recovery movement generally, a classic disease/addiction analysis is offered in which Kate and Susan have no reason to be angry or rebellious at their social conditions since their problems are internal. They are diagnosed as victims of a progressive disease they have somehow caught while hanging out in their homes and offices and malls. And, having found this disease, of course, they are led to group meetings in which they recite many sins and failings and humiliations, admit they are powerless over their disease, and begin to work a program.

VARIATIONS ON THE RECOVERY THEME: THE TALK SHOW CURES

I have dealt with TV movies in some detail because, like the classic texts of the recovery movement, they provide—for a larger, more general audience—the dramatized master narratives by which all of us, but especially women, are being taught how to analyze and take action upon our most troubling personal and social sorrows. Other TV shows—from dramatic series like *LA Law* to family sitcoms like *Growing Pains*—have devoted segments to issues of addiction. In these shows, however, the problem is more or less named and dealt with in a matter of minutes. Nor are the sufferers, usually at least, the central characters. A client, or a child's friend, will be seen to "have an addiction." And then the principal characters will figure out, through therapy, the law, whatever, how to help them. The TV movie, on the other hand, centers its tale on the addict herself, and seriously leads us though the routes by which—we are informed—one becomes addicted, nearly dies, and then finds "recovery."

The repetitive formula by which these steps are taken, no matter what the issue or movie, has a great social effect on all of us, even when we insist that we never watch these movies. For watch them or not, we are aware of them. They are the grand sociological myths of our day whose virtue is to incorporate, in a single, simplistic narrative, the key points of a worldview gleaned from the main experts and organizational literature of the movement, creating a story whose melodramatic appeal is its truthfulness about so many experiences so many of us really do share.

But if TV movies present the narratives and their lessons in classic, dramatic form, it is daytime talk shows—which air continuously, if you channel hop, from nine in the morning until six in the evening—that provide the endless snippets and variations and versions of those narratives which we hear even in our sleep at times, in an endless, propagandistic drone.[7] The E! network airs a show called *Talk Soup* each day, in which highlights of the day's talk shows, picked from twenty daily shows, are shown—and there are even more they do not monitor.

In a casual survey of the titles listed in the multiple subject indexes of Journal Graphics—the company that sells transcripts of talk shows and public interest programs—on the topics of Alcoholism, Addiction, Psychology, and Mental health, I quickly found titles of hundreds of programs which addressed addiction issues and featured recovery movement authors and therapists. And each year the number of such shows listed in the annual index increases.

Looking more closely at twenty-five talk shows which I selected for study—half on the basis of their titles and half on blind hunches that "recovery talk" would come up—supplemented of course by my own continuous monitoring of current shows—I found a prevalent use of addiction and recovery language and concepts in statements by guests, hosts, and experts. Shows about violence against women, for example, more often than not included statements from victims in which comments like "I was hooked on him, I guess," "I just couldn't leave him," "I was always rescuing him," and "It was like an addiction; I felt like I needed him to survive," are used to describe emotional relationships and other kinds of behavior.

The growing prevalence of this kind of language on talk shows is the dynamic that works most profoundly to establish the recovery movement as a kind of common sense religion. Here, on these shows, women's problems—problems first raised and enunciated by feminists and later redefined and redirected by the 12 Step movements—are seriously and endlessly presented and discussed. And these shows, I believe—against the grain of critical dismissal—like the recovery movement itself, do in fact most seriously offer help and insight to the many women who are finding life in postfeminist times increasingly difficult to maneuver.

While most people seem cynically to assume that people must be paid, or coerced in some way, to appear on these shows, the truth is quite different. There are long waiting lists of people who are dying (sometimes literally) to get on and discuss their problems. And there are hordes of people—mostly women—who stand in line for hours to be in the audiences. In fact, there are many groups of women in New York (and in the many other cities where local talk shows exist) who regularly attend and discuss the shows together, much as women attend 12 Step groups, and as they used to attend consciousness-raising groups in the 1960s. I learned about this phenomenon first on a segment of *Sally Jessy Raphael* (which might have been called "Women Who Love Talk Shows Too Much") and have since spoken with two of the regular audience members.

The fervor with which people seek out these shows, as guests and observers, is in keeping with my views about the recovery movement generally. Like the groups, and the books, these shows provide a sense of community sharing, and a source of information and even hope, for the many people—especially women—for whom modern life has become a mystery and a trauma. I was told by a staff person on *Geraldo* that the show receives 1500 calls a day from people who want to go on the show to talk about their problems. And the main reasons given for wanting publicly to reveal the greatest shames and humiliations of life are that people—sufferers and perpetrators alike—want help in solving their problems and do not have access to any other source.

Understandably, it is mostly less educated, poorer people who actually go on these shows, or even talk publicly about watching and visiting them. But it is a far larger, more homogeneous group—protestations to the contrary notwithstanding—who participate in these shows as viewers. Of course most of us watch. For one thing, these shows are visible in bars, airports, hospital waiting rooms, department store showrooms, and elsewhere. But more than that, talk television is quite often irresistible. We come upon an argument between lovers, perhaps, as we channel surf, we are struck by something we see or hear that intrigues or rings a bell; and we stop to watch for a while, sometimes a long while. And why not? Daytime talk shows, raise—often in the most extreme and bizarre form—the very issues we all worry about and find hardest to discuss in respectable circles. Talk show topics, after all, are some of the most vexed issues of the day and we are invested in them even if they do not directly affect our own lives.

The issues they raise are only very common ones; they are rooted in the very social and gender upheavals of our day. Women do, indeed, sleep with their daughters' and mothers' boyfriends; bear their best friends' children; find themselves married to bisexuals who suddenly decide to come out; intermarry racially with both happy and sad results. Or perhaps women always made these choices but only now feel safe enough to talk about them or sophisticated enough to understand that they are engaging in behaviors which are socially significant. Whatever the explanation, these issues have social resonance and so these shows hold our interest. On one level, after all, gossip is sociology.

That the status of talk shows, as culturally "declassé" pastimes, keeps them from being taken seriously in more respectable places, is actually a plus for embarrassed viewers. The less we admit openly to *seriously* (as opposed to mockingly) watching them, the easier it is to ride the fine line between private and public, secret and open, that these shows demarcate. They are at once our "guilty pleasures," hidden from view and separate from our public personae, and our entrée into a very public sphere, created electronically, in which we join a community–half visible, half invisible–which provides space for truths not yet acceptable elsewhere.

If docudramas are public rituals, serving, in a sense, the role that Greek tragedy played at that time, for that culture, then talk shows are our electronic town meetings and gabfests. On one level, they approximate media representation of the 12 Step groups I visited in which truly unspeakable, still socially hidden things are spoken. They create a pseudo-public version of these meetings in which we can all participate without leaving home or being seen. Talk shows also incorporate aspects of the feminist consciousness-raising groups of the sixties, in which things common to all of us, but never before admitted publicly, are shared in ways which may facilitate personal, if not social, change. In this, they are perfect models for the premise of this book: they work magically to interweave feminist analyses with recovery solutions in ways which, even as they acknowledge the crisis of gender and family issues today, reduce them to a common, apolitical level of addictive disorders and point us toward personal rather than social cures.[8]

That talk shows are inherently feminine, and even feminist-derived, in nature is seen in their structure as well as their subject matter. Unlike the more traditional discussion shows on television, in which male hosts run things and orchestrate what is said and by whom about topics designated "public" and "serious" by tradition, these shows follow a much different structure and criteria for both topics and "expertise." Unlike the hierarchy of classic "male" media, in which host and experts sit up front before the camera and audiences are invisible, these shows—like consciousness-raising groups and 12 Step meetings—arrange guests, audience, and host in a circle, equalizing everyone's position. Even the host participates as a "regular person" by sharing her or his own experiences and problems with the guests and viewers.

It is no surprise that Oprah Winfrey and Geraldo Rivera, two people whose past experiences as victims, sufferers, and perpetrators of abuse are widely known and often invoked on their shows (she has survived childhood rape, while he has recently published a memoir chronicling his former sex addiction), are the most popular of talk show hosts (Masciarotte 1991). The ease with which these two negotiate discussions in which viewers, callers, guests, host, and even experts themselves seem to shift roles and share in the uneasy equality represented in each show's structure makes for a very comfortable situation in which—it seems—raw experience and spontaneous opinion are being expressed.

Like the 12 Step meetings, talk shows allow us all to share painful experiences and have them heard and addressed by caring "friends." Guests and audience members—even the host—will offer words of comfort that bring tears to the eyes of others. Often male guests will be chastised and shamed by women who are irate over their sexist acts. Rage, shame, even sisterhood at times, does occur on these shows.

That this is a mere "image" and not therefore "real" community is the usual assumption made by those for whom such shows are seen as wholly "exploitative" of guests. But this charge, while valid in many ways, is overly simplistic and reductive. To the extent that we all do share a common experience of television viewing—commercialized, commodified, and state-regulated as it is—the meaning of the word "real" becomes less clear. Television is indeed real; it does indeed constitute a kind of public community space. And if it is not the ideal community Thomas Jefferson might have wished for, it is, nonetheless, the only one we have today that manages to penetrate and bring together the various arenas of our lives often kept separate by the structures of our social and work lives.

In creating space for open, somewhat free and spontaneous discussion of things the respectable, male-dominated media do not allow—not only sexual but also social matters—daytime talk shows have actually inserted themselves into serious public discourse in ways which are even becoming apparent to media pundits (Katz 1993). By providing opportunities for average people who are never seen or heard on the news or *Meet the Press—*

people who do in fact look and talk and think like most Americans–to be heard and seen, and to contest official positions and myths, they have called attention to the growing crisis of credibility and authority in the more "respectable" news media.

This credibility crisis was made clear in the 1992 presidential campaign when candidates chose to appear on *Donahue*, MTV, and *Arsenio Hall*. Talk shows and other popular formats are taken *more* seriously than *Nightline* and *Meet the Press* by voters who feel the latter exclude them or lie and condescend to them. And their popularity is dramatic evidence that the old formats, with their neat splits between public and private, important and "trivial," areas of life, no longer work or make sense. The personal is indeed political today–as feminists were the first to announce–and if Ted Koppel and Dan Rather are not up to the job of handling this explosive situation, well, Oprah and Phil and Geraldo certainly are.

Rather than focusing on the "low-class" or "trashy" aspects of the form, then, we might more usefully look at its serious role in the world of public discourse. The talk show, as Wayne Munson (1993)[9] asserts, is a form made-to-order for a media-driven society built, in theory if not practice, upon the ideals of participatory democracy. Structured to mimic the ideal of the town meeting, the talk show inserts "the oral tradition of the village into mass communications and the nation state" (p. 155). Following cultural scholar James Carey (1989) Munson reminds us that Thomas Jefferson's idea of democracy, from the start, depended upon a "vision of expanded communication" in which discourse and debate among large numbers of citizens might be accomplished through new media (p. 154). This is indeed what television has done, what it was set up to do. And talk shows–sometimes for better, often for worse–are where television most effectively accomplishes this job today. The commercial, state-regulated nature of the medium, of course, ensures that the debates will be kept within strict social and ideological limits. But such, again, are the contradictions of all our official institutions.

Like the recovery movement, talk shows are at once highly reactionary and, at times, surprisingly progressive. That their subject matter edges dangerously toward the borders of acceptable taste and opinion is what makes them, at least potentially, transgressive. At times they verge upon exposure of the key myths and hypocrisies upon which established society stands. People who boldly defy sexual and moral norms are given space and, surprisingly often, even audience and host support in their wayward habits and beliefs. There is an "Oh yeah? Says who?" quality to much of the dialogue and debate, often energizing in its bravado. "Who are you to say that bisexuality, or interracial dating, or lesbian marriage are wrong?" is the constant challenge of guests on these shows to audiences—in the studio and at home. And there is something dangerous and refreshing about this kind of provocation on a medium known for its conservative conformity.

The threat to convention is never quite as real as it seems, however, for reasons which owe much to the recovery movement's focus on addiction. Also talk shows are national public forums, not "anonymous" meetings, and are far more carefully and forcefully controlled than the proceedings I witnessed in meetings of 12 Step groups like Adult Children of Alcoholics and Codependents Anonymous. Indeed, the similarities and differences between these meetings and talk shows are worth considering for a moment because they help to clarify the disparate ways in which groups and mass media serve the large recovery agenda.

While sitting in on 12 Step meetings like CODA and ACOA (Adult Children of Alcoholics), I often felt as though I were listening to talk show confessions of the more bizarre kind. The sense of shock and exposure, of the speakers' often nervous bravado and wariness of hostile responses, of being privy to things I perhaps should not be hearing, would perhaps rather not be hearing, were common to both. But the meetings, while loosely held together by an adherence to the broad assumptions of recovery, were nonetheless much more chaotic and unsettling in effect. For unlike talk shows (and more traditional AA groups), they offered no sense of ongoing, predictable coherence and closure. The 12 Step rules of order were always more or less enforced. The terms of the standard discourse were invoked regularly enough to position even the most bizarre utterances within the context of the family-dysfunction-as-disease ideology which is the mainstay of the group rhetoric. And members clearly felt relief—even life-saving relief—at having a safe space to blurt out their horrors.

But despite what I came to see as their important social function for *certain* select people, there was no sense of group assessment or agreement upon any course of action. It was all right—even necessary—to leave many things, especially the most bizarre and upsetting things, hanging in the air, in these looser 12 Step groups, because it was not action, but a more general way of thinking and feeling, which was being shared.

Indeed, in these groups, (again, as opposed to traditional AA) the matter of "addiction" as behavior was not necessarily touched upon directly. Rather, it was the idea—and it is a most important idea—of addiction as a social identity, based on common labels and attitudes about family and interpersonal relations, which was being shared and validated and reinforced. No matter how amazing, how rambling, how emotionally charged, a personal confession, or "share," might be, there was a tacit sense within the group that its source was the universal one: toxic family dynamics caused by, and causing (whether mentioned at the time or not) addictive behavior. But the idea that one would leave the meeting with a mandate to do something to correct, reverse, or alleviate the situation that caused the addiction was rarely if ever suggested.

Talk shows about addiction never leave things hanging. They work—and here they are like the more programmatic self-help books which provide many rules and exercises, sometimes even charts and worksheets—toward hour's end to bring out, insist upon, and reinforce through "expert" testimony by therapists and authors, the ultimate solution to all personal problems: the recovery movement as doctrine and practice. Sometimes hosts will actually insist, at program's end, that guests agree to attend groups or therapy and, in some cases, even offer to pay for it. Results matter here, and the preferred result is that those most confused and unstable be routed to the official place of treatment: the 12 Step movement. Thus, "action" seems to have been taken, although, once one gets to a meeting, little else may change.

Talk shows sent you home not just in one piece, as many 12 Step meetings do, but with a plan—one suited to specific social ends and not others. In true confessional form, they manage, in the very process of allowing the hidden to appear, to immediately "commodify" and transform it into a prepackaged, institutionalized message, which is spelled out explicitly and predictably at the end of each and every segment, lest anyone miss the sponsor's and network's ultimate "position" on human suffering, what it means, and how it gets fixed. The lesson may well be to attend a meeting, but ironically enough, once one gets that message and begins attending, the ideological overkill is in fact loosened a bit. One has, after all, been convinced to join the movement and learn its ways and words—from TV more than likely. And that is enough to keep one off the streets and out of more socially problematic or progressive forms of trouble.

TODAY ON OPRAH—WOMEN WHO GET BAMBOOZLED

To see how talk shows work as propaganda for the recovery movement, let's look at a few examples of how issues—not necessarily tagged as addictions—were presented on daytime talk in ways which managed at once to acknowledge and then distort their larger social meanings, in the interests of a kind of social programming. On a typical and particularly revealing segment of *Oprah* in 1992, for example, the topic was predictably odd, at least as presented. The guests assembled had all had a common childhood experience which left them scarred for life. They had been ridiculed by other children. This may not seem a particularly terrible experience, but there was no question, in watching these now middle-aged, respectable looking guests, that it had created a lasting impression on all of them. Indeed, the very effort to recall the childhood ridicule was impossible for any of them to accomplish without tearing up and, in one case, sobbing.

It is this kind of public emotional display that brings charges of sensationalism and exploitation to these shows. And yet, there was no question that the guests' stories were being taken very seriously by Oprah and her audience, many of whom recounted similar experiences that had created lasting scars. Nor was there any doubt that the guests were relieved to have these memories examined and analyzed by concerned others who understood them.

What was most interesting about this particular show, however, was that, in the course of the free-for-all style discussion which such shows allow, the real cause was revealed to be class-based. The epithets hurled at these people had been terms like "white trash" and were always related to the fact that they were poor. They had the wrong clothes, lived on the wrong side of the tracks, had the wrong kinds of fathers and mothers who did the wrong kinds of work, or were on welfare.

More amazing yet, Oprah had managed to get the perpetrators of this ridicule, thirty years after the fact, to come to the show and sit in the audience, where they were confronted by their victims as well as other audience members and callers, and called to account. And their honest expressions of remorse and apology were indeed moving and gratifying.

Had this been a feminist consciousness-raising meeting, and had the stories told been about gender rather than class oppression and shame, the whole proceeding would have been radically different. The meeting would have moved toward an analysis of the bases of this humiliation in the built-in sexism of our schools, churches, and family ideologies.

But that was then and this is now. Oprah did indeed move the discussion toward an analysis which would explain the problem, but it was not a social analysis. It was a spiritual and psychological one, in which *internal* wounds were all seen as important and *external* causes were ignored. In the first segment of the hour, an expert was brought on camera to negotiate the confrontation between victims and perpetrators and to offer advice and help. No, she did not suggest that we give up our class-based snobbery. No, she did not even suggest that the materialist, consumerist values by which children are shamed for not having the "right things" be rejected, even on moral or spiritual grounds. Instead–and this was a tough one, even for Oprah and her ready stash of recovery gurus–she managed to redefine the problem in terms of the ideas she had come to espouse, ideas which were, of course, in her own book on "wounded inner children" and their need for "recovery." What was important, in her view, was that each person "own" her or his pain and anger and allow her or his inner child to "feel the sorrow" and "allow" her/himself to "cry for that sad and hurting little person."

So quick was this sleight of hand, by which economic and class bigotry was converted into the victim's internal problem, that I did a double take. But yes, I heard right. The expert did indeed advise these people to "work on healing [their] inner children" by finding an ACOA group to attend. The audience perpetrators were similarly instructed, since their own cruelty must too have been based upon inner child wounds suffered in *their* families of origin, to seek out ACOA groups.

I can readily imagine the result if they acted upon this advice, having attended such meetings. Their experiences, told in sobs, would be heard and acknowledged and tacitly sympathized with. Inner child wounds of all kinds, in ACOA after all, are readily recognized and grieved over. The unhealthy, unjust, cruel interpersonal dynamics—based on dysfunctional family norms to begin with, it is universally assumed—which cause inner child wounds that don't heal are shared by all of us. And it is soothing—and I can attest to this—to be allowed to repeat these things, knowing that everyone in the room, unlike your previous perpetrators, and most of the rest of your associates, can relate and sympathize.

I use this *Oprah* segment as my first example because, although it did not actually deal with the concept of addiction, it was particularly revealing of the political subtext of talk show strategy and discourse. But most talk shows, even when they deal with issues as unrelated to addiction as this one, usually do manage to bring in addiction, whether or not the host has planned to introduce it or has invited a recovery "expert" to attend. I have seen any number of shows about sexual harassment, incest, and parental neglect in which guests were led to connect their emotional pain with subsequent addictive disorders–usually centered on food or sexuality. In these shows, in part because audience members bring up the subject, but usually because of the presence of recovery experts, the issues of addiction and recovery soon become the main focus of the show.

Even when, as happens on shows at times, feminist insights are expressed by the audience and sometimes by the hosts, they are invariably diverted into addiction discussions because of the agendas of the producers who have planned the show around a certain expert and her/his message, as well as the by-now programmed responses of most audience members and callers. The host, for example, will turn to the expert author or therapist for a comment when an audience member or caller raises a political point, thereby leading the program back onto its preplanned track. On a segment of *The Jane Whitney Show,* for example, an audience member suggested that eating disorders were different from cancer, a biological disease which one did in fact "just get," as she put it, rather than a form of behavior we learn. The furor this observation unleashed from the audience and the pain it caused the suffering guests were extreme. "How can you question this woman's suffering?" said many participants, in one way or another. As though the idea that eating was not an addiction or disease somehow was a way of "blaming the victim" for her pain. "Of course she has a disease," said one and all in support of the distressed guest. While it was, in this case, the audience that led the show back to addiction theories, the very readiness with which members of the audience leapt to this tack and resisted an alternate reading is at least in part a result of the familiarity of addiction ideas to those who regularly watch these shows.

The effects of this kind of exchange are complex. The speaker, in the show's context, does seem to be questioning the real pain of the guests (which, indeed, she may have been doing). In this case, however, the speaker was attempting to lead the participants to an analysis of eating disorders which pointed toward the role of sexist media. She was trying to suggest that it was sexism that led to an unhealthy concern with body weight, and that the guests, perhaps, should stop hating themselves for their size and begin hating the media. The audience and guests were so offended by her apparent "meanness" that this point could not easily be heard or fit into the broader discussion. The dominance of addiction theory thus works as an automatic censoring mechanism, making it difficult for any other way of thinking—even a feminist counter-agenda–to be credited. In this way, these shows—and television generally, to the extent that it follows this dominant format–become increasingly over time an agent of a kind of propaganda which is universal and irrefutable, to most people.

Given this dynamic, it is not surprising that most talk shows, most of the time, have no trouble at all fitting any and all behavior into the addiction mold and blindly ignoring other obvious factors such as race, class, gender, and the state. A look at five randomly selected talk shows–gleaned from the files of *Donahue, Sally Jessy Raphael,* and *Jane Whitney*–underscores this point. The titles of the shows are typical: "Addicted to Addiction," "I'm Sorry for What My Addiction Did to You," "Women Who Love Sex Addicts," "Shop Till You Drop But Feel Compelled to Buy More: Shopaholics," "I Gambled My Life Away," and "Actress Mariette Hartley" (which I chose on a hunch because I knew of her previously publicized emotional problems). The process by which addiction is approached and defined in each show seems perfectly obvious on the surface, but is in fact accomplished in devious and coercive ways.

Each of these shows, except the celebrity interview, also featured a well-known therapist and author. "Addicted to Addiction" was capped off by a visit from Ann Wilson Schaef, the author of several of the most influential recovery self-help books. Her agenda was quite obvious—to sell her latest book and her many commercial services. The guests on the show suffered from a variety of compulsions—shopping, relationship addiction, compulsive escape from intimacy, workaholism, and self-abuse. (These labels were given on the transcript cover based on the label bars for each guest.) But whether the behavior was "banging my head against the wall" or bilking and betraying women, Dr. Schaef was able to explain it in terms of "our addictive society." The entire show, as Schaef orchestrated it, revolved around the theme of "lying" as a "symptom of addiction," which was the theme she clearly planned to push, no matter what, since it was central to the new book she was selling.

Lying, at least as I understand it, has many different uses and meanings, many of which were apparent in the testimony of all the guests, and most of which were not as obviously related to addiction as Schaef insisted. Lying, for example, is a form of power play in which one may seek to gain something from another person by withholding or fabricating information. Men who lie to women about their sexual habits, work life, and intentions, for example, as one guest admitted doing compulsively, are exercising power over them, in a context of sexist cultural norms in gender relations. While men who lie in public office, for related but different reasons, are engaging in very different kinds of power plays in the public sphere, bolstered by different cultural traditions.

But Schaef, of course, denied this difference. Even the self-abuser, it turned out, was using her "addictive behavior" in order to lie *to herself* about her failures. "Hurting myself" she had learned was a way of not facing problems, of "lying to myself and my husband and my boss" about "why I wasn't doing what I was supposed to do." Indeed, at Schaef's prodding, each and every one of these people admitted that lying and dishonesty—clear signs of addiction of course—were their real issues and that telling the truth, publicly, in a safe group setting was the cure for their problems. This line of reasoning leads to the conclusion that even the politician who lies needs to be in a group, rather than, say, in jail.

The tangled ways in which talk show discussions are reduced to such simplistic solutions for people whose positions in life, problems, and life situations are so radically different is one of the more annoying things about recovery discourse. Political power, gender power, and self-hatred born of abusive parenting (as the self-abuser soon confided) are widely different problems based on widely different social positions and experiences. Even the audience members found Schaef's approach troubling, as their questions made clear. "Maybe I'm a little confused about the difference between addiction and control," said an audience member, helpfully. "I see the first man's problem as a need to control another human being, a woman . . . Is this really an addiction or is it a control problem?" Good question, I thought. One that might lead nicely to gender relations and inequalities which are culturally enforced. But Dr. Schaef was ahead of me. She had a different answer of course, one in which "control" itself was always a mere "illusion" and, you guessed it, "one of the main characteristics of addiction." That "control," in the sense that compulsive people seek to exercise it, is an illusion, of course, has nothing to do with the very real fact of control as an aspect of *real* power in the social and political sense. Politicians do indeed have power over their lives and those of others, as compulsive head-bangers surely do not.

Many of the shows I've watched do present moving, healthy encounters between abusers and abused, in which parents and spouses and children apologize and take responsibility for the pain they have caused. To hear an alcoholic father apologize to his neglected, abused children is useful as well as moving, since it models new forms of male behavior which are based on feminist ideas about men needing to take responsibility for their emotional relationships, take parenting seriously, and admit that their traditionally acceptable male behaviors were wrong and hurtful.

Even here though, the dread issue of power as a *political* issue is neatly elided by the expert guests. Several father/daughter TV reconciliations I've seen lead to "recovery" for both parties. Both parent and child in these sex abuse cases are seen as equally diseased and damaged. Rage and retribution, much less social change, are not allowed to come up. And these are the most positive incidents of the media-zation of sex abuse as "diseased" relationship. Far more often, even these potentially healthy exchanges get hopelessly twisted by the glib, increasingly bizarre uses to which recovery dogma is put by hosts and experts far less adept than Oprah or Dr. Schaef.

On the *Sally Jessy Raphael* show called "I'm Sorry for What My Addiction Did to You," for example, a woman identified as a "sex addict" begged her mother for forgiveness for the embarrassment she caused her by wearing sexy clothes and engaging in promiscuous relations. In the course of the hour, however, it became clear—to me at least—that the mother should have been the one apologizing. She had chastized her daughter for her healthy desire for pretty clothes and found shame with her for wanting normal dating experiences through her rigid, puritanical religious rules. But since the daughter was the self-identified "addict," not the mother, and since addiction and recovery were the themes, the mother's failures—largely those of the larger sexist culture that socialized her—were not relevant. And since the host, audience, and the "addict" herself all accepted the disease model of sexual excess in which the daughter was the "patient," everything she said was tinged with the mark of illness and deviance.

Much that the daughter said—about her experience of prostitution, for example—was predictably met with hoots and expressions of outrage from one and all. Prostitution after all is a form of "acting out" (in recovery talk) which is understandably common among female "sex addicts." But in this case the "acting out" was at least as plausibly seen as a rebellion against the sexist and sexual repression of women's upbringing and socialization which, in this case, was extreme. And in many cases—those of most of the female prostitutes who appear on talk shows regularly to discuss various aspects of their lives, as a matter of fact—such "acting out" is not acting out at all but a perhaps rational, if unfortunate, economic decision, based on the paucity of options for many women in a sexist economic system. Needless to say none of these possibilities—sexist economics, sexist culture, sexist religion—is ever recognized as a serious factor or possibility in these shows. Addiction and disease are the discourses of choice precisely because they allow so easily for the masking of these other, more dangerous factors.

The sordid sufferings of prostitutes and other "riff raff" is of course common on talk shows. But if they were the only ones willing to come on and admit to "addictions," the recovery movement would not be as successful at using TV as propaganda as it clearly is. It is the more celebrated and glamorous of the self-identified addicts, the movie stars, athletes, and rock stars, that have done most to ensure that addiction is an equal opportunity disease and recovery a panacea which crosses class lines to offer help to one and all, no matter how high or low in station. That's why I made sure to order several transcripts of celebrity interview segments of talk shows, even if the titles did not indicate addiction would come up.

I selected the Mariette Hartley transcript because, as I said, I had reason to suspect she would be a celebrity who would choose addiction confession as a mode of presenting herself to the public. Celebrity guest appearances on talk shows by, for example, Elizabeth Taylor, Liza Minelli, Kitty Dukakis—whether to sell books, promote movies or records, or simply keep themselves in the public eye—more and more often involve the celebrity's confession to an addiction and report on her or his recovery. Hartley offered up the same kind of recovery truths told in other talk shows and celebrity/expert advice on how to make your life picture perfect. Celebrities' stories always have happier endings than those of regular addicts for the obvious reason that they are constructed by public relations people and reflect the position of people with more money and power than the average person. Hartley survived the suicide of her father, her own drinking, drug, and food addictions and more. But even as she told her horrible, humiliating tales, there she was, the picture of perfection and bliss, a true role model for the rest of us lesser beings to emulate.

Her secret? ACOA and John Bradshaw, of course, whose teachings about dysfunctional families and wounded inner children had made Hartley's transformation possible. It's really easy, she insisted. You must learn that "as Bradshaw says, we bring that kid [one's inner child] with us wherever we go. And until we attend to that kid and the needs of that kid, it's going to rule us till the day we die." So much for everything else that molded Hartley, much less everything else that differentiated her from the rest of us less fortunate sons and daughters of dysfunction. The implication is that one need only buy a book, or watch the Bradshaw series on PBS, or perhaps, if one is wealthy enough, go on one of his Recovery Cruises to turn out just like Hartley. But the implication of course is not only misleading but cruel.

Surveying these shows, in their tamest most sensational modes, is fascinating and revealing. Day and night, whenever we turn on the TV, this talk is available—ostensibly not to be taken seriously or acknowledged, and yet watched and digested with relish and even hope. To pretend that its prevalence is inconsequential, and that shows like *Nightline*—where sex addicts, to my knowledge, have not yet been featured—are the only important or serious things on TV is to delude ourselves about what most Americans think, and "know," and care about. America—as feminists have long known—is a nation of secret and not-so-secret sufferers at the mercy of a system in which harmful family dynamics merely reflect and reinforce the perils of the broader society in all its institutions. And it is woman-oriented television—especially talk and docudrama—that most dramatically clarifies these perils to anyone who's watching and paying attention.

The woman-oriented television of the 1990s is not the same as the "family viewing" of the 1950s and 1960s, which was also geared to a largely female audience of mother/housewife/consumers. It has been overhauled and lubricated extensively to fit the more complicated, challenging, and perilous times in which women now live. Two major mass movements—1960s second wave feminism and 1980s recovery-thought—have contributed most to the transformation of society that the television programs of today reflect.

The rest of this book will trace the process by which so much of our culture has come under the influence of the far-reaching recovery movement. I'll begin by looking briefly at the beginnings of second wave feminism and at some of the parallel ideas and processes that link that 1960s movement to the 1980s recovery movement.

✦

CHAPTER TWO

Personal Politics:
The Feminist Roots of Recovery

Anyone who doubts that second wave feminism did indeed change the world will do well to take a quick excursion down memory lane and recall the bad old days when polarizing, demeaning gender norms and stereotypes really did hold sway over almost everyone's heart and mind. The generation of men and women raised in the post–World War II 1950s were the first Americans for whom home TV was a constant, socializing presence. Through its constant barrage of endlessly reproduced and circulated images of docile housewives, ditzy airheads, coy sex kittens, evil femmes fatales, and pathetic spinsters, the new medium seemed to be working hard to ensure that such tough 1940s role models as Eleanor Roosevelt and Rosie the Riveter would soon be lost to memory.

Every middle-class girl who grew up in those years will remember the mixture of desire and vague anxiety which these images and messages–echoed in every textbook, women's magazine, and movie–aroused. The pristine kitchens in which smiling, shirt-waisted "homemakers" stood proudly before a gleaming backdrop of avocado-green appliances at once tantalized and warned us of the delights–and the limits–of our fates. "The girl that I marry will have to be / As soft and as pink as a nursery" went one of the songs of the day. And the movies made clear the consequences of not buying the image. Pert and perky Debbie Reynolds always ended up smiling, of course. And so, eventually, did Katharine Hepburn, once she got her female priorities straight, forgot about being president, and learned to settle for love and marriage. But Barbara Stanwyck and Joan Crawford and Bette Davis generally did a lot less well for themselves, and their tragic downfalls haunted the dreams of every young girl who imagined, even for a moment, that careers, sexual adventures, or any other form of freedom from the feminine ideal, would bring anything but heartache and tragedy.

Volumes of feminist scholarship and reportage have been written to document, from any number of disciplinary and political perspectives, what these times were like for women, and what the coming of feminism did to change them.[1] Perhaps even more moving are the many wonderful novels written by women whose lives were radically changed—as indeed was mine—by the coming of second wave feminism. These novels—Marilyn French's *The Women's Room*, Marge Piercy's *Small Changes*, Alix Kates Shulman's *Memoirs of an Ex-Prom Queen* are among the best—chronicle, in rich detail, what it felt like to move, like the child in *The Secret Garden*, from a world of shadowy blacks and whites, of imprisoning walls and depressing dead ends, to one filled, as if by miracle, with bright new paths and vistas, offering the possibility of miraculous new life. These books dramatically bring to life the emotional and political conditions of women's lives in the fifties, and the joy and excitement that hit so many of us when, suddenly, the women's movement entered our lives.

I do not intend in this chapter to rework, or even to summarize, this well-known and well-documented chapter of American and feminist history. I wish instead to draw upon this work, and on my own experiences and those of the many women I knew in the sixties and met and interviewed while working on the book, to create a sketch of those aspects of the movement and its history—political, personal, procedural—which are most relevant to my own story and argument. I want to recall some of the relevant historic and social highpoints of a movement whose effects are now, perhaps, so familiar as to be taken for granted, and remind the reader of how truly radical their content, and the feelings they engendered, really were, in a world unprepared for them.[2]

THE PERSONAL IS POLITICAL: AN IDEA FOR OUR AGE

What most united the particular mélange of ideas and methods that made up "second wave" feminism of the 1960s and 1970s was their emphasis on the personal and emotional as socially determinant and central to life. Born in the 1960s, and very much a child of its era, second wave feminism brought to the world a particular emphasis on personal and emotional experience which changed the very definition of "politics" by bringing to public awareness a whole set of experiences and interactions that had previously been deemed irrelevant to public life and theory.

Interestingly enough, the contemporary recovery movement owes least to the brand of feminism which probably is most associated, in the popular imagination, with the term "feminism"–the liberal feminism of the National Organization for Women. NOW was formed in the sixties–its founding conference took place in 1966 (Davis 1991, p. 56)–and, eventually, it did incorporate many of the features and ideas first developed by more radical groups (Evans 1979, p. 19). NOW certainly was responsible for much of the media attention which feminism attracted, at least that part of it which gave the movement credibility and respectability (Davis 1991, pp. 49–69). Nonetheless, its political traditions and its original methods and agendas were quite different, culturally and politically, from the ones I am primarily focusing on here.

I recall vividly my own early forays into feminism when, having been startled into awareness by Doris Lessing, I began searching for other women with whom to share my newfound, troubling consciousness. Stumbling timidly into a NOW meeting, in the mid-1960s, I recall sitting silently and nervously, in a conference room of a downtown bank, listening to high-powered, professionally dressed women, most much older than I and certainly more poised and established in life, efficiently and rigidly plan a variety of campaigns and events and legal battles around issues that seemed foreign, even incomprehensible, to me.

Hands went up, Roberts Rules were smoothly imposed, lists and tasks and moneys were drawn up and collected and assigned, as I sat in bewilderment, with nothing to offer and no one to ask for guidance. When the meeting adjourned I left and never returned. What had any of this to do with the profound shock of recognition I had felt reading *The Golden Notebook* and discussing it with my friend, I wondered? These were women whose hearts and minds and problems–I imagined–were entirely different from the problems that had sent me searching for a group of women to talk to.

These women of NOW seemed (indeed they were) exceptional, in that they had already done, personally, a lot of what the coming mass women's movement would be working to make possible for many more women to achieve. They were pioneers who, to their credit–and unlike the more typical "token" successful women of the day–were committed to working for political change for women generally. They were visionaries who early saw the need for a political movement to advance the cause of women's rights and create opportunities for all women. But for me, at that time a thoroughly apolitical housewife and student with two babies and a traditional, overpowering husband, and living in a world which I "knew" was "normal," but which nonetheless bored and enraged me in ways I had no language or space to articulate, the things NOW was doing and saying seemed to come from another planet.

Shortly after that meeting, I attended my first Women's Liberation Union meeting at the university I was then attending as a graduate student. I knew I had found what I was looking for. This meeting, of women who were mostly younger, not older than I, was as informal, personal, and emotional as the NOW meeting had been businesslike. And the issues being discussed, the actions being planned, made as much sense to me as the NOW meeting had left me baffled. Women in these meetings were angry at things that were happening every day in their personal lives. Sexist comments by professors, the absence of female authors on reading lists, of female administrators and professors anywhere, of child care facilities for staff and students; these were the topics of the day, topics which were expressed in emotional tones and met with equally passionate responses. And unlike the women in the NOW meeting, the women in these meetings were insisting that their raw emotion—which I recognized as my own inchoate rage—should not be suppressed but loudly and publicly vented; that it was, indeed, what politics should be about.

It was here that I got my earliest political education about sexist culture and the male power structure, in terms I could understand and relate to personally. It was here that I came to understand why the scene in *The Golden Notebook* in which the man insists upon sex when the woman has household tasks to perform so moved and angered me. It was because Lessing had hit upon what we were all, in this wonderful university classroom, learning: that the smallest things that happened to us, that kept us confused and frightened and self-contemptuous, were part of a social system which—it suddenly became infuriatingly clear—had no regard for our needs and desires whatever, because we were "only" women.

From such insights as these came the idea, which proved to be so powerful, that "the personal is political"; that what we feel and do in every detail of our lives is *not* trivial at all, because it is all, every cliché and ritual of it, produced by a social institution or idea developed by men to serve their interests. And as dogmatic and even dated as such words now sound, they were utterly earth-shattering to those of us who first spoke them out loud and wrote and distributed them in mimeographed leaflets and pamphlets.

As women we were used to being ignored in class, used to deferring to our fathers and brothers and boyfriends and professors in every aspect of life. And as women we were used to accepting the ideas and stories and theories which men found "true" and "important" and "great"—in which women were mostly demeaned and exploited—as worthy of scholarship and attention, while the stories and ideas and theories of women (what few we were aware of) were deemed inferior, less true and beautiful.

But here, in this classroom from which men were barred, all of this suddenly seemed ridiculous, even insane. Here, the theories and tastes and whims of the men in our lives—human and textual—were critiqued from a whole new vantage point and found wanting in every way. Here, the ideas and songs and stories we ourselves often secretly loved—from Jane Austen and Anaïs Nin to Wonder Woman and Nancy Drew—were similarly reassessed and found, to our mutual agreement, to be unbelievably wonderful and deserving of respect.

Here in this room silent women suddenly erupted in outbursts of brilliance and rage; sweet-faced women suddenly "spoke bitterness"; isolated, shame-filled women suddenly felt a unity based on shared experiences spoken out loud, for the first time, and—miraculously—understood and agreed to by us all. In this room rigid male-defined rules and structures, based on the workings of the public realm where men ruled, gave way to spontaneity and feeling and laughter and tears, from women previously silent and timid. And as we planned our outrageous attacks on established cultural institutions—Miss America qualifiers, ROTC privileges and rituals, male-defined literary canons and social science theories which taught us that *The Golden Notebook* was "bad" literature while Herman Melville and Charles Dickens were geniuses—we came to understand how thoroughly we had been divided against each other and brainwashed into subservience and self-loathing.

These meetings were wildly different from my first NOW meeting and, indeed, from the classes (where professors separated "men from boys") and PTA meetings and women's auxiliaries and Girl Scout groups which, until then, were the most usual gathering places for women. They made of emotional and cultural experience a basis for political theory and action of a new kind, not only for women but for the world. And, although we certainly could not have guessed it at the time, these new ways of theorizing and organizing were destined to make history.

Within that first feminist organization I made friends with a few other women who, like me, were married, had small children, and were struggling—against the grain of family, husband, and academic pressures—to get Ph.D.'s and build academic careers. I joined my first consciousness-raising group and discovered an even more profound feeling of sisterhood and mutual rage at the subtle, deeply internalized, assumptions and feelings which kept us all guilty and scared about every step we tried to take for ourselves, about every idea or feeling or action which did not serve our husbands or children or did not meet with the approval of our mothers and teachers and bosses.

This smaller, more intimate subset of the larger group, made up of a self-selected group of married women, met in members' living rooms. There we found a place of refuge in which things that were not so funny or joyful or easily organized against could be spoken and heard and considered. While our group had its own characteristics, rituals, and purposes—there was a lot of variety among groups depending upon many factors—we shared with the hundreds of thousands of groups then forming and meeting across the nation a common general structure and process.[3] Consciousness-raising (or "CR") groups generally had anywhere between four or five and perhaps fifteen or twenty members. Some groups were quite political in focus while others—probably the majority—were concerned with the politics of personal life. Some groups chose topics for the evening and stayed with them, even regulating the number of times and for how long each member was allowed to speak. Others were more free-floating, following the inclinations and often urgent needs of members as they arose. But all groups shared a common goal: to develop an analysis, through comparing and sharing details of personal experience, of the sexist culture which was dictating the patterns of our lives as women.

My first group (I participated in five or six CR groups in all, as my own problems and circumstances changed during this highly charged period) was fairly unstructured and fraught with the passion and intensity of the newly converted. Here we talked—à la Lessing—about our confusing, often unsatisfying sex lives; our "irrational" and "selfish" anger at husbands and children; our past experiences of sexual abuse and exploitation and more. No issue seemed too trivial to raise and analyze and fit into the larger worldview we were developing in our readings of exciting new feminist tracts and pamphlets coming from similar groups all over the nation. The pink and blue blankets given infants in hospitals were as likely to fuel our rage as the foot-binding rituals and clitoridectomies of the third world. And as we discussed our humiliation and shame at early sexual experiences, at having worn the wrong clothes in high school, at having the wrong size or shape breasts, at ruining the boeuf bourguignon again and again, we came to an even greater understanding of our political situations.

In these meetings, lives were transformed, quickly (sometimes too quickly), once and forever. Women who hated their marriages divorced.

Women who hated sex with men entered joyful, frightening relations with other women. Women who had never spoken back to a man in their lives began making demands on their husbands and children and–with the support of the group–stuck to those demands until, amazingly, they were met!

These two strains of second wave feminist practice–CR and women's liberation action groups–were the main features of the feminist paradigm that I later frequently saw at work in the recovery movement. Both features distinguish the newer 12 Step groups from traditional AA which does not usually deal with details of personal and emotional experience, but rather focuses exclusively on problem drinking and how to stop it.[4] In contrast, CR and women's liberation action groups both started with minute details of personal and emotional experience and built from these details of female experience the broader generalizations on which theories about the ultimate causes and patterns of our pain and unease could be raised.

CR groups, developed and institutionalized by radical feminists, boldly articulated rules and methods whereby the principles of the new feminist insights into gender relations could be codified and circulated to women everywhere, as a way of building a movement based on the idea that the personal was political. They set guidelines for sharing and generalizing about our experiences so that action could be taken–individually and collectively–to change our circumstances. The idea was that individual, private relationships and dynamics parallel collective, public ones. And with each step a woman took to free herself from the psychological and material bonds that held her down in her personal relationships, it was argued, she would also be empowering herself for the larger, related struggle–this one collective and organized–to change social power structures and dynamics (Echols 1989, pp. 83–88, 140–43).

CR, like the newer kinds of recovery theories, ultimately builds a worldview which is powerful in its all-inclusiveness and ability to explain and integrate many phenomena. It posits a simple, common set of root causes for almost all gender experiences and behavior which, it is assumed, affect all members identically. It holds a lantern to all gender relations, previously assumed to be "natural," and exposes their origins in social and economic structures far beyond the immediate sites of the behavior examined. It was generally agreed, for example, that male behavior–as we were coming to understand it–followed increasingly recognizable patterns, which all of our fathers, brothers, lovers, and bosses exhibited. And the vast majority of our experiences did indeed bear this out, to our mutual amazement and delight. The common "error"–made at times by most of us–of insisting that one's own man was different, exceptional, not really sexist at all, was quickly corrected and shown to be a matter of "false consciousness" which the group would help a woman to overcome.

I am here painting a picture of the CR movement at its best, a picture which masks the important differences between CR and recovery groups and the forces that ultimately made the former very short-lived while the latter belong to a movement that shows no signs of faltering or ending its expansion. CR groups very often, and sometimes fatally, failed to live up to the utopian expectations of their theories and rules. There were horror stories of conflict and pain and anger (Echols 1989, pp. 203–81). Groups split and disbanded because the guidelines for political and emotional process were both philosophically problematic and impossible for many women, socialized to act and feel very differently about each other, to live up to.

The problem for a political movement like the second wave, it soon became clear, was that the assumptions upon which CR rules of discourse were based–the ones which gained their theoretical and procedural power by insisting upon the uniformity of all female experience–were too overly simplified, reductive, and dogmatic to survive as anything but a limiting and politically regressive imperative. Based as they were on the limited experiences of a very narrow segment of the female population–the white, middle-class educated, young–they soon became impediments to the growth of the movement, to its implicit mandate to reach all women everywhere.

It was not long before the limits of our own class and race experiences became problematic, as we realized that many of things we found "universal" to male and female experience were in fact limited to our own narrow circles and those of the mass media which tended, generally, to reflect and reproduce the norms of the white middle class. And it was not long after that that even our own white middle-class "universals"–based as they were on some of the most superficial markings of sexist culture–were called into question by many women whose growing confidence allowed them to admit, even within their women's groups, that they did not always feel exactly the same way as the others about everything discussed. As Echols reports, this growing awareness of the political naiveté and oversimplification of much of CR's dogma led to much of the discord and confusion that eventually destroyed the CR movement. Nonetheless, there is no way to overestimate the power and impact of those first dramatic insights into dominant, previously unrecognized patterns of gender relations. Limited and doctrinaire as the teachings of the second wave were, they opened up a world of insight, analysis, and passion for social change among women which is still shaking and reshaping the world.

PERSONAL POLITICS BRANCHES OUT

The radicalism of second wave feminism's slogans and strategies is largely forgotten today. The days of visible mass political movement are over now, and, in the media versions most familiar to us, feminism (and here is one reason so many women are uncomfortable with the word) is presented as a rather exclusive clique of upscale, personally ambitious and successful white professional women out to get what they can in a system they have no interest in changing. To make things more confusing, much of what was most radical in CR and the rest of the second wave movement has, as I said, come into the public domain in ways which mask its original, revolutionary context.

Nonetheless, CR was indeed born of a revolutionary program to change the world, and insofar as many of its teachings and demands have been taken up and realized, by so many people and in so many ways, it has succeeded. For in forcing the world to recognize the clear links between what goes on in families, on dates, on movie screens, in sports arenas, and in all-male social gatherings, with what goes on in the highest, most public arenas of wealth and power, feminists forced the issue of gender and emotional nuance into places from which the male power structure had always worked hard to exclude them.

But the radicalism of second wave feminism went far beyond simple matters of gender relation and theory. In fact, a full understanding of the complex ways in which feminism came to influence the recovery movement requires that we look at the women's movement in the broader context of the historic period in which it grew up. For CR and women's liberation were not the only political activities feminists were involved in. This was after all "The Sixties," and we were—as white, middle-class educated women—squarely in the midst of a much larger political and cultural period in which the very kinds of social and economic injustices we were discovering and protesting about in women's lives were also being discovered and addressed by others in other arenas, including the civil rights and anti-war movements.[5]

Moreover, as CR groups, women's liberation unions, and broader political developments like the civil rights, antiwar, and New Left movements began to interact and cross-fertilize, in membership as well as thinking, they all, inevitably, influenced each other. Some women came from these other movements into feminism. Others moved in the opposite direction, becoming feminists first and then broadening their range of activities. Most were involved in various shifting projects and groups over the period of time in which New Left and counterculture institutions thrived. (The joke about socialist-feminists at the time, for example, was that they were distinguished by having to attend twice as many meetings as everyone else.)

Out of this cross-fertilization came even more political conflict and sectarian splits and fights. But on another level, the cross-fertilization was healthy. It led women to a broader grasp of how various social and political problems grew from the same root causes. And traditional male-led groups were led into confrontation with the increasingly angry, sophisticated, and powerful feminist contingents who were, everywhere, bringing a militant agenda and presence to meetings and conferences.

All of this political activity came together in a cataclysmic uproar against the established power structure, attacking its every cultural, political, military, intellectual, and economic manifestation. Feminism was only a part of this wider struggle for political and cultural change, but it was a particularly important and unique part, without which "The Sixties" would not have taken the same form nor had the same impact. For it was the radicalism of the CR movement's procedures and its way of linking small personal details with much larger public phenomena that most mark feminism's contribution to the entire gestalt of the 1960s. And just as feminist concern with the politics of daily life, of gender relations, of the links between emotional and material issues gradually worked its way into the framework of all the political and social movements of the day—and indeed of our own day—its concerns and mandates have also been the driving forces behind the transformation of the traditional AA-based 12 Step movement, and the broader, more woman-centered recovery movement of the 1980s and 1990s. For it is just this feminist concern for targeting emotional and relational dynamics, generally routed in the structures and dynamics of the nuclear family, that distinguishes feminism from other 1960s movements, and later, the recovery movement from traditional AA.

FROM REVOLUTION TO REACTION: HARD TIMES FOR WOMEN

But I am getting a bit ahead of myself. Between the glory days of radical feminism and the rise of the recovery movement came the depressing 1970s—a time of great confusion and readjustment. The promise of feminism and of the idealistic, utopian social visions presented by all the social and culture movements of the day, did not so easily or quickly come to fruition. The very people who developed and fought for these things aged and matured, as indeed, did the world generally, and a period of reaction, predictably enough, followed the euphoria of the sixties. In some ways, perhaps, we scared ourselves and the world to death with our radical, transgressive actions and slogans and attitudes. Most people do not take eagerly to the kind of overhauling the youth culture of the day was demanding and expecting, and in such short order.

The figures on the participation of women in feminist organizations in those years are dramatic and depressing. In 1973, according to Anita Shreve,[6] there were at least 100,000 women actively involved in CR groups all over the country. And of these women, many were also active–along with thousands of others–in the hundreds of women's liberation groups engaged in political agitation of so many kinds in so many sites and arenas, as to constitute a mass movement of women heretofore unheard of in America. But by 1975, according to Flora Davis, "most of the women's liberation groups had vanished" (Davis 1991, p. 138).

"How could they achieve so much and then just disappear?" she asks, as we ourselves may well ask. One part of the answer is that they did not really die, at least in spirit. But that is a too easy and glib response. Certainly, feminism's impact on American society has been profound and permanent. And certainly, in recent years, grass roots activism has begun to revive and reappear (or perhaps more accurately, to regain the attention of the mass media). But there is no question that the generation of women that made up the second wave, the generation that ultimately found its way, in increasing numbers, into the recovery movement, met with increasing political disillusionment in the years between 1982 and 1992 and saw the decline of the radical visions and beliefs which had characterized the years between 1965 and 1975.

The second wave was a movement of young women, largely privileged and economically well off. It centered in the university at a time when the American economy was flourishing and it was possible, as it has certainly not been since, for young people to live reasonably well by taking odd jobs and leaning on friends and relatives. It was a time when divorce–the economic and emotional ramifications of which were not yet well known or felt–seemed an easy solution to personal unhappiness, even when one had children, because, for many white middle-class feminists, economic hardship did not seem a possibility. Jobs were plentiful; education was a ticket to economic well-being beyond one's mother's dreams; and unemployment was not the issue it has been ever since. And—unbelievable as it seems to-day—I can attest that youthful activists of the time were indeed idealistic and naive enough, very often, to believe that their revolutionary plans to tear down the old structures and build a democratic, utopian land of plenty were just around the corner.

What actually happened was quite different, and for many of us shock-ing, personally and socially. For one thing, the demands and responsibilities of age—marriage, children, jobs—cramped our political and personal style more than we had figured. Many women found themselves emotionally and economically strapped and stressed. There was little time for the kind of endless social and political meetings which organizing and consciousness raising demanded. Nor were the men we had been trying with so much en-ergy and rage to change quite so far along as we had hoped they would be-come in their awareness of, and willingness to deal with, their sexist flaws and privileges. Such a widespread, radical transformation in gender rela-tions, as we now know all too well, was going to take many decades at least, even for the most elementary changes.

Even the gains we did achieve through feminist agitation often seemed less than blessings. Ironically, the aspects of feminism that did survive into the 1970s and beyond were those which were least in tune with the spirit and soul of the second wave as I've been describing it. To our chagrin, attention now focused on a version of feminism which was unrecognizable to former radicals; a version tailor-made by media and corporate professionals to fit easily into their own economic and cultural game plans. Suddenly feminist ideas and slogans were being tagged onto media campaigns meant to glam-orize and encourage consumerism and individualist career ambition. Glitzy new magazines and exercise programs and expensive home and child care services for the fortunate few token women rising in the traditional male bastions of power appeared on every TV screen and newstand, urging us to become even more productive or impossibly gorgeous than ever, in the name of feminism and "The New Woman."

Far from helping women, these images and lures served to further in-crease women's low self-esteem and self-doubt, and to make the better world we had dreamed of seem even further out of our reach and beyond our abili-ties and energies. For behind these mocking images and lures, the truth about most women's social and economic situations was very grim indeed. The economy was shrinking. The government and public opinion, in reac-tion, were moving to the right. And the women who had divorced, the women who had been living on social welfare programs now being gutted, the women who were entering shrinking job markets–most women, that is–were feeling the economic pinch of what came to be called "the feminization of poverty," as women and children filled the growing ranks of the hungry and homeless and hopeless.

It was not surprising, in such a climate of disillusionment and backtracking, that women cut back on organizing. It was hard to find the time, or the energy, or–to be honest–the faith or optimism to keep up the fight for a social transformation which now seemed to most people to have been a pipe dream, a fantasy concocted by a bunch of rich, spoiled, self-indulgent kids. And as individual hardship and social disillusionment rose, it is hardly surprising that personal problems and anxieties grew, as did the turn to unhealthy and artificial activities and substances, as escape and relief from the pressures and problems of an ever-darkening reality.

THE RECOVERY CURE AND ITS SIDE EFFECTS

And so we see the rise of the recovery movement, in the early 1980s, as an understandably appealing development, offering comfort in a world that had become, very suddenly, very difficult and confusing. The recovery movement, with its rapidly expanding menu of support groups and methods, promising to help women with every conceivable kind of difficulty–from addiction to hopelessly sexist men to compulsive spending habits born in economically healthier times–offered shelter from the storm of despair and anxiety and self-doubt which the post-feminist years brought to most women. It suggested that the many problems and pains of female existence, of sexual and family relationships, were, after all, within our individual control. Such problems were not–as feminists had believed–socially determined after all; rather, they were the result of personal, internal flaws of character, of a disease called "addiction" which could be treated (although never cured) by programs and methods of the spiritual, therapeutic 12 Step programs which formed the core units of the movements.

The recovery movement's leaders and gurus–Beattie, Bradshaw, Norwood–preached to a generation of women understandably turned off by political solutions to personal and financial problems that political activities were indeed dead ends because the root causes of unhappiness and failure– in every arena of life–were not structural or economic but addictive, even genetic. And it offered, to all those suffering from confusion and cynicism and pain, a refuge at once familiar and strange–as I discovered in my early visits to OA meetings–in which many of the best and most effective aspects and ideas of feminist and New Left thought and behavior were once again available, while the more utopian, social aspects—which now seemed to have been so misleading in their promises—were replaced by spiritual rewards and visions.

In that first OA meeting, I sensed that feminism itself had been responsible for much of the newly felt confusion and despair of women somehow stuck between two worlds. Indeed, I believe this confusion is true of the entire culture—men, women, and children—in ways directly related to the ideas and gains of second wave 1960s feminism. For feminism—in the days of consciousness raising and organizing for changes in media, workplaces, families, therapists' offices, academic curricula, the courts, and other institutions which determined the conditions of our lives as women—changed the way an entire society now must think about and deal with emotional and family and personal relations as a whole, not only at home, but everywhere.

Indeed, feminism at its most powerful takes a set a values traditionally applied only to private life and insists they be applied to public life as well; insists, further, that private life *is* political, and political life, personal. For when feminists back in the sixties said that "the personal is political," they brought out into the open, and gave political visibility and identity to, a host of injustices and abuses—between men and women, gays and straights, children and parents, lawmakers and citizens, employees and employers—that had previously been kept hidden from public view because they were considered "merely personal." The list of now crucial political and legal matters—domestic violence, incest, date rape, sexual harassment, women and gays in the military, and on and on—wracking this country with confusion and conflict are all on the table these days *because* feminism put them there. And as a result, the world we inhabit as citizens and workers, as well as parents, spouses and children, will never be the same.

When women insist that sex be on their terms; that emotional nuances and differences be brought into the open and considered in all negotiations; that fathers and husbands be held accountable, in the courts, for their power abuses within their own homes; that gay and lesbian relationships, which don't reproduce, but rather challenge, male-dominated family norms, be accepted as normal; you have what amounts to a small revolution in the ways we think and behave at virtually every moment of our lives. And since the schools and churches and legislatures and courts are not traditionally built to handle such matters, there is a massive breakdown in the authority and credibility of institutions, and in people's faith in their own common sense and instincts about their lives.

Moreover, feminist ideas about life and relationships did not affect women only. Increasingly, in the 12 Step meetings dealing with sexual and emotional problems, in the workplaces forced to deal with issues like "diversity" and "sensitivity," in the emotional and substance abuse problems of growing numbers of male employees, and in the challenges to tradition within families, schools, and the military, we find boys and men being affected by feminist ideas and actions, and feeling as confused and anxious about it all as the women.

To attribute all our current social unrest and challenging of authority to feminism may seem overly bold. But second wave feminism was not merely about equal rights, or a bigger piece of the pie. It was, as I have been saying, an outgrowth–a rebellious outgrowth–of the entire cultural and political gestalt of the sixties, a time of enormous and broad social upheaval, in the name of radical cultural and political democracy. The effects of this upheaval may seem at times to be minimal, even cancelled out, by the rise of right-wing forces of reaction and backlash in the eighties, as I myself believe the recovery movement to be. But this is a short-sighted vision of society and of history. The truth is more complicated. What we have, I would argue, is a social and cultural revolution in the making, halfway home, getting tired and doubtful, confused and scared. And the effects of this stress and confusion are both positive and negative, causing "dysfunction" and social chaos, on one hand, and ever more rebellious demands for further change on the other. The recovery movement comes on the scene at just this critical point in our development, as a community and culture. It has come, indeed, to play a major role in helping us to negotiate this stormy period. And it has borrowed tools from feminist thought and practice to keep us afloat. In what follows, the recovery movement and its social role will be described and evaluated.

CHAPTER THREE

Recovery, Inc: The Marketing of "Addiction"

The incorporation of feminist ideas and processes into the Anonymous and 12 Step programs makes for a wonderful social metaphor of a grand, dynastic marriage between an aging, somewhat anxious, but still hopeful bride—second wave feminism—and a powerful, long-standing, very much set in its ways, patriarchal household—pre-1980s Alcoholics Anonymous, or AA.

Feminism grew up in times of prosperity, hope, and idealistic agitation against the existing order. It was a movement of young women determined to change the world. AA's founders, as we shall see, were losers, victims of forces of social upheaval and "progress" which had left them unmoored and reeling, emotionally and materially. They were men who had "bottomed out" in their efforts to run with the tide of social and economic change and who had turned to alcohol as a way of escaping their sense of pain and failure in a world gone too far too fast for them to keep up.

Given these vast differences, it is not surprising that the informing goals and perspectives of these two social movements should be diametrically opposed. What is more surprising, perhaps, is that they should find their way to each other at all. To understand how this improbable marriage came about, we need to explore the intellectual roots and institutional workings of Alcoholics Anonymous.[1] This chapter covers a lot of territory—the social context and birth of the 12 Step movement; the ideological, moral, and political bases of its traditions and methods; the vast and Byzantine economic and institutional workings of the contemporary recovery movement—before returning to the specific question of how women and feminism fit into the scheme of things.

Feminism, as I argued in the previous chapter, is not merely about women and gender. It is—like the 12 Step programs we are now examining—a movement which presents a worldview, an approach to life as a whole, which has implications for, and impacts upon, the entire society and all its people. Just as feminism, in hurling its new ideas and demands and attitudes into the middle of American life, caused the world to shift its focus and alter its habits and structures, so did AA hurl its 12 Step process into the midst of American life and change it. For just as feminism is about more than gender, AA is about much more than "addiction."

Indeed, the very concept of "addiction" is no more than a metaphor itself for a much larger human and social problem that began to plague American life as one of many side effects of industrialization. And in switching focus from "sexism"–or for that matter any of the other "isms" which construct human suffering in political terms–to "addiction" in thinking about what hurts us, we are shifting our focus on human issues generally in a paradigmatic way.

BILL W. AND DR. BOB'S EXCELLENT IDEA

For all the differences between feminism's history and direction and AA's, there are certain profound similarities in their developments. Like feminism–and unlike more traditionally political movements–AA grew up in response to certain ongoing, ever-increasing flaws and glitches in the personal, daily lives of growing numbers of Americans. It was, like feminism, initially and most obviously, a response to emotional difficulties and frustrations.

AA was founded in 1935 by Bill Wilson, a stockbroker, and Dr. Robert Holbrook Smith, a physician. Both men had battled their chronic drinking problems for years with no success and with increasing damage to their health, personal lives, and careers. When they met and began sharing their stories they came to see the value of the mutual support and empathy which only other sufferers of their affliction and history could give each other. "Bill W.," as he is universally called, had by then been influenced by the Oxford Group, a "fellowship" of men who believed in returning to the simple teachings of the early Christians, and shared a nonjudgmental view of drinking and a belief in seeking out and helping the unfortunate. During one of his stays in the hospital, perhaps as a result of alcohol withdrawal, Wilson experienced a religious conversion: an hallucinatory sense of exaltation in which he believed he was in the presence of God. From that point on, with the help of the Oxford Group, he began to devote himself to seeking out and "recruiting" other alcoholics to his newly formed religious approach to sobriety. During that hospital stay, Bill W. also encountered a doctor who told him of a new theory of alcoholism as an "allergy" which certain people simply "caught" like the flu. This theory–the basis of the "disease model" of addiction as a physiological condition–combined with the religious fervor and mission to recruit and save others formed the core of what would become AA.

When Bill W. met Dr. Holbrook, widely known in 12 Step circles as "Dr. Bob," and recruited him to his beliefs, the two–finding so much strength and support in their regular, mutual sharings–developed the meeting procedures which would become AA. Step by step, literally, they codified each of the beliefs and methods which they had learned, from experience, were useful in stopping alcohol abuse and staying sober. The idea was that one "worked" the program of 12 Steps, one by one, moving from the first–"we admitted that we were powerless over alcohol–that our lives had become unmanageable"–to the last–"Having had a spiritual awakening as a result of these steps, we tried to carry this message to alcoholics and to practice these principles in all our affairs."[2] Step 2, we "Came to believe that a Power greater than ourselves could restore us to sanity," and Step 3, we "Made a decision to turn our will and our lives over to the care of God *as we understood him*," enforce the traditional religious underpinning of the movement. The next steps require "a searching and fearless moral inventory of ourselves," the admission "to God, to ourselves, and to another human being the exact nature of our wrongs" and a willingness "to have God remove our shortcomings." Other steps involve making reparations to those the addict has hurt, practicing prayer and discipline, and spreading the word to other sufferers and helping them to embark on the program of recovery.

In AA, as Bill W. and Dr. Bob developed it, meetings begin by repeating these 12 Steps and the 12 Traditions of AA which expand upon the meaning of the 12 Steps and offer guidance in various public and private matters. They include the confessional "sharing" of past abuses by members who identify themselves as alcoholics, the announcing and praising of milestones in abstinence, and the supportive encouragement of those who confess to having relapsed. Members are encouraged to seek out a sponsor, an older member to whom one may turn at all hours of the day or night for help in abstaining from drink, and veterans are encouraged, as part of the service that keeps one practicing the program, to seek out new members and offer sponsorship. In the beginning, members are asked to attend a meeting a day. Later, the number of meetings is a matter of personal choice. But it is assumed that one will continue to attend, at least on a somewhat regular basis, for one's entire lifetime, since the disease, being incurable, must be constantly treated.

Today AA is a massive international network of groups, centralized in New York City. There are said to be two million members in 63,000 groups in 114 countries, all holding free meetings in donated spaces. AA upholds the rule of anonymity, refrains from taking public positions on any issue, produces and distributes the official literature of the movement, and oversees the workings of the local fellowships. It survives more or less ideologically intact. But it has gradually spawned variations on its major themes over the years. Its methods and doctrines have been adapted, over the years, to fit the dimensions of a variety of compulsive behaviors which seem, on the surface, to mimic alcoholism in the difficulty sufferers experience when they try to stop.

Anonymous fellowships to help people end drug abuse emerged in the 1960s, as did Overeaters Anonymous, one of the first fellowships to attract large numbers of women. But the greatest upsurge in numbers of new fellowships and recruits came in the 1980s, with the publication of the many best-selling self-help books theorizing a variety of emotional problems as classic "addictions" and offering the 12 Step model of abstinence and fellowship as cures. Robin Norwood's *Women Who Love Too Much* and Melody Beattie's *Codependent No More,* both huge best-sellers, began the movement to create more and more 12 Step fellowships. Today, there are estimated to be at least five hundred different groups. They range from groups like Shoppers Anonymous, whose specific goal is limited and clearly behavioral, to those like Emotions Anonymous, whose goals are far more vaguely and generally defined. Each of these groups is affiliated with central AA and adopts and adapts AA's Steps, Traditions, and other materials. But each new fellowship produces its own specific version of the literature and maintains its own central offices—often no more than a phone with an answering machine in someone's home, giving times and locations for local meetings which take place in members' homes, or in churches, hospitals, schools, and other public meeting rooms donated by local institutions.

The enormous growth of AA and its offshoots, and the spread of its ideology and structure since its birth in 1935, have been phenomenal. Its success in rooting itself so deeply in American culture can perhaps best be understood by analyzing the key elements of its process and thought and placing them in the social and historic context in which they developed. Bill W.'s happening upon the Oxford Group, which routed him back to a Christianity he had long ago abandoned, and his fortuitous introduction to the "allergy" theory of alcoholism were the two central elements in his success in developing and spreading AA so quickly and so far. For both the Christian and "allergy" features of AA turned out to be happily suited to the needs of various social and professional organizations and leaders who were already becoming alarmed by the growth in alcohol abuse and its social costs.

Indeed as early as the 1940s, when AA had been around for only a few years, it had already carved out a niche for itself which allowed for acceptance within the medical and religious establishments as well as by the general population (Peele 1989, pp. 45–48). This was because the roots of its doctrines were so in keeping with dominant ideas and interests of the day. AA was developed by two middle-class, white, Protestant, professional gentlemen, one a doctor and one a stockbroker, which meant that, unlike cults and religions more on the fringe, AA's attitudes and style meshed with mainstream ideas and rituals. The Christianity it espoused was in keeping with middle American Protestantism.

Even more important, the ideas AA developed about the causes and cures of alcoholism were compatible with the values and goals of the medical profession. Doctors understandably didn't know how to "cure" alcoholism. At the same time, they were increasingly confronted by patients for whom alcoholism, as the cause of great number of physical and emotional troubles, was a key issue. The "disease model" of alcoholism popularized by AA was a godsend for medical practitioners unwilling to consider the emotional and social bases of physical ailments. It assumed that alcoholism was caused by a physiological condition which was thought to be "like an allergy," in that it seemed only to affect certain drinkers (Peele 1989, pp. 116–21). This meant that no matter how successful AA was in controlling the disease, it could never eradicate alcoholism. People would continue to fall off their wagons and resume their health-destroying patterns. Neither AA nor medical science, then, would ever be put out of business by being too successful. Nor would anyone need to look further–to social conditions–for other possible causal factors.

At the time of its adoption by AA the disease model seemed perfectly suited to the interests of those most concerned about alcoholism. It made alcoholism a medical problem and gave the powerful medical establishment reason to welcome AA, rather than fear it, as they would have had AA's methods been strictly based on spirituality.

But the disease model had yet another great benefit which emerged over time. The biologically deterministic explanation for why some people cannot handle liquor while others, it seems, can–an explanation fully integrated into our common sense thinking today–in fact comes and goes, predictably, as society comes to find *certain kinds* of indulgence, favored by *certain kinds* of population segments, anxiety provoking. The model offers a means of directing attention away from the social context in which deviant behavior occurs and from the social causes which contribute to *certain* groups, at *certain* times, behaving in unacceptable ways. Instead, the disease model–with its corollary, genetic determinism–poses the problem of drinking, or any other troubling behavior, as an inherent, biologically determined feature of the stigmatized group, much as women are seen, in sexist societies, as having biologically inherent qualities which make them socially inferior (Nadelmann 1992b, pp. 90–1).

In fact, over time, estimates of the number of people who apparently had "caught" or been born with the disease of addiction would expand to include nearly everyone, as the idea of what the "disease" actually was expanded to fit so many different kinds of problematic behavior as to become nearly meaningless. The recent term "addictive personality," implicitly based on AA's idea of genetic predisposition, allows the idea of addiction to be used to describe every conceivable kind of excessive behavior, from shopping to dieting (Peele 1989, pp. 11–14). That these behaviors, in today's world, do indeed reflect the growing self-destructiveness of people trying desperately to keep up and succeed in a competitive, market-driven world is masked in public discourse by the idea that "addictive disorders" are genetically–not socially–engendered.

Over time, as the definition of addiction broadened and the problem it masked deepened, other tenets of AA would similarly be altered by those in the medical and therapeutic professions for whom the rise in the number of patients and clients with self-destructive, compulsive behavior patterns created a diagnostic nightmare. Through a combination of expediency and what may well have seemed to be common sense, these people, helped along by members of the insurance industry and law enforcement agencies, turned to addiction discourse and its ways of analyzing and treating such problems for help. The program seemed to work–at least better than anything else known to these institutions and professionals–and the idea of sending more and more people into "treatment," by coercion if necessary, and whether or not they had "bottomed out" or considered themselves addicts, made therapeutic sense. There is a subtle kind of social control at work in this gradual broadening of the definitions and rules governing addiction and recovery, one which, often with the best of intentions on the part of law enforcement and mental health workers, has had profound, not always salutary, effects on public thought and policy concerning social ills. For the form of social control offered, as we shall see, in so many new 12 Step groups, is far less a matter of changing behavior than of changing *ideas* about why one is unhappy and how one's suffering can be assuaged (Schlesinger and Dorwart 1992, pp. 196–97).[3]

But for now, we need to return to the social setting in which AA took root and analyze the particular nature of the soil in which it flourished. AA came upon the American scene in the 1930s, at a time when the prospects for economic, political, and psychological survival were worsening for growing numbers of white, middle-class and working-class males. The causes of this crisis were indeed social and political, but not in the traditional sense that chroniclers of political rebellions and of social swings to left and right use these terms, for the economic roots of the crisis were not obvious to anyone.

THE SOCIAL CONSTRUCTION OF A NATIONAL DISEASE

To say that AA arose out of daily life crises rather than economic or political ones is not to say that the root causes of these crises were not inherently political and economic. They certainly were. But where political and economic uprisings—and the repression that follows them—tend to come and go cyclically, the kind of malaise that leads to depression, anxiety, and addictive habits does not have the same dramatic ups and downs. It is progressive, not cyclical, because it runs parallel to the ongoing rise of certain elementary patterns in American social and economic life which have never significantly changed, no matter the political climate.

The reason for the progressive rise in drinking (as well as for—in very different ways, of course—the massive female unhappiness that led to the feminist movement) a generation later was the rise, growth, and expansion of an industrial, consumer society and the kind of work and home patterns and routines and feelings it engendered and demanded of Americans. In the 1930s, as industrialism and the corporate/consumerist life-style it produced spread and intensified, male workers were increasingly stressed by the conditions and rewards of their lives. Our social and economic system has—from the start—fostered an emotional and spiritual "dis-ease" and angst that leads to self-destructive habits. The values of the industrial and corporate workplace—the need for ever more regimented, often dehumanizing routines and ever more competitive, anxiety-provoking, often meaningless activities—took its toll on the spirit. So did the demands and values of the consumer marketplace with its ever-increasing pressure to consume, to strive for unattainable images of happiness and success. And the stresses of work and marketplace were reflected, in subtle ways, in the private sphere of home and family.

It is easy to see, today, what the results of such a process have been. But the seeds of the current malaise were visible way back in the early nineteenth century, when the "problem" of alcohol was first observed. Indeed it is important to realize that the idea of mind-altering substance use – especially drinking – as a *problem* is socially and historically rooted.[4] There is nothing obvious or "natural" about the idea that drinking, even getting drunk, is a bad thing. Societies of all kinds, from ancient Greece to contemporary Europe, have, in general, had much more tolerant, even positive, attitudes about such behavior. And even in the United States, attitudes and policies toward drugs and alcohol have tended to swing back and forth, from "left" to "right" if you will, according to the social and political tenor of the times (Meacham 1992, p. 26).

Indeed, public drinking, even drunkenness, was not considered either socially or personally dangerous or problematic until quite recently in American history. In the early colonial years, there was no stigma attached to drinking or even public rowdiness (at least for men, of course). Before 1785, "drunkenness was not seen as the *cause* of deviant social behavior" (Levine 1978, p. 152). In the late eighteenth century, however, when national unrest due to massive social change was experienced, the idea that alcohol was "evil" and could "enslave a person against his will" (ibid., p. 167) – an early theoretical precursor of the "disease model" – was first advanced by Benjamin Rush, a physician and signer of the Declaration of Independence.

This tendency to clamp down upon drinking during periods of social and political unrest has, since the late eighteenth century, occurred somewhat cyclically, as indeed have periods of radical unrest and agitation. As has been widely observed (Musto 1987; Nadelmann 1992a and 1992b), repressive attitudes toward drink and drugs tend to coincide with periods of political unrest and reflect a need, on the part of government, to repress behavior seen to encourage rebelliousness. The 1960s certainly bear this out. But every period of extreme political unrest reveals a similar pattern (Musto 1987, p. 8).

Political responses to problem drinking varied, but after each cyclical, conservative effort to crack down on drink and drugs, the problem itself remained, and indeed, even intensified over time, as industrialism and postindustrialism themselves progressed. In the century and a half between 1789, when the first wave of immigrants entered the nation and the first linking of alcohol with "evil" and "sin" occurred, and 1935, when AA was inaugurated, for example, there were periodic crackdowns upon drinking – the Prohibition laws of 1919 are the most obvious example – which coincided with times of political turmoil. (Musto 1987, pp. 1–22). But each successive antidrinking campaign was forced to be more intense and wide-ranging than the last because the real and incessantly intensified problem–stresses produced by our consumer society–continued to plague Americans no matter what the political scene.

Finally, in the early 1940s, in the years just after AA was formed, the need for a permanent, institutional structure to combat what had become–obviously–a permanent social problem, with devastating social costs, was apparent. The recognition and adoption of AA by schools, churches, hospitals, insurance companies, private corporations, government agencies–all major institutions of American society–marks the point when the cyclical, politically charged crackdowns on drinking, especially among dissidents and other social undesirables, gave way to an admission that alcoholism itself was a problem so severe and so socially costly as to warrant constant attention. And with the development in the 1980s of the much broader recovery movement, to treat ever broader kinds of problems and sufferers–especially women, who had never before been targeted for such attention–this policy has reached a new level of effectiveness.

That problems with addictions now suddenly seem to affect women more and more, and that public attention is now being drawn more and more to women's sufferings and dysfunction, are of course related to the effects of feminism on women's consciousness and the influx of women into the work force. Indeed, in the beginning, AA did not appeal to, or even allow, women as members (Robertson 1988). It was established at a time when social unrest and economic upheaval most urgently affected males in the work force, and their instability was the prime focus of the antidrinking forces. True, women did also work in factories and work at home, and they did have drinking problems (Bauer 1982; Sandmaier 1992). But when AA was first formed the number of women drinkers was not linked to serious industrial dysfuntion, as, increasingly, was the case with male drinkers.

Among its many effects, industrialism challenged and eroded many of the most important features of patriarchal privilege for the many men who went to work in the factories and offices of the day. The late nineteenth and early twentieth centuries was a time when industrialization increasingly took men away from their previous lives as self-sufficient property owners and managers, on small farms and in family businesses of which they were sole masters and turned them into wage-earners (Ewen 1976, pp. 151–59). Where previously male heads of families did have authority and control over their livelihoods, and children could see the fruits of their fathers' labor and its direct relationship to their very survival and security, now men went off to work for a wage, doing bits and pieces of larger jobs, the end results of which were not always clear. When they returned home, their wives and children saw only a paycheck—not field plowed and planted, no road or bridge or house built, no book whose binding is hand sewn—no evidence of their fathers' labor, talent, or significance.

It is important to realize then that AA—so traditionally white, middle-class, and masculinist in its assumptions—was the perfect organization for the times precisely because it did focus primarily upon the segment of the population, white Christian males, whose traditional roles and perquisites were being most severely challenged and usurped, but upon whom the new system nonetheless depended. AA was understandably concerned with preserving and bolstering male authority. And it desperately needed to enlist women in its quest not only to keep male workers functional and sober, but also, and relatedly, to preserve and bolster male self-esteem. From the beginning, those concerned with implementing the new industrial economic order understood the need, in the words of Barbara Ehrenreich and Deirdre English, to "bring the home into harmony with industrial conditions" (1979, p. 211), in any number of ways. As drinking became a serious impediment to the functioning of the workforce itself, AA became an increasingly important part of that project.

Originally, the members of AA were all male, and the wives of the founders were instrumental—in traditional female ways—in keeping it going. They opened their homes to the many derelicts and dysfuntionals recruited by the founders from hospitals and jails, many of whom were actually dangerous at times (Robertson 1988, pp. 46–51). They served and nursed and mothered these men selflessly, as part of their own marriage agreements, and the economic contract of codependency upon which it was based. In this way, AA reproduced the basic structures of patriarchal family life, at a time when its economic foundations were shifting and failing for many men.

AA was for obvious reasons a godsend to social conservatives. It offered an ideological and structural way of containing the excesses of self-indulgence that had become a permanent fixture of modern life, as it rocked and rolled its way toward the rapidly evolving future. Unlike the less sophisticated and unworkable legal approach of Prohibition, AA offered more than a simple injunction to "say no." It presented those in pain from the stresses of their daily lives with a way of thinking which worked not only to regulate drinking itself—not in fact the most serious issue—but to reformulate and reinvent rituals and values and community for a newly uprooted group of people. The idea of sponsorship and the tradition of inviting

(sometimes dragging) drunks home to be cared for and supported in a traditional family environment was culturally and emotionally central to AA's
program of rehabilitation. Even for those less drastically in need of help, the
meetings provided a structured, emotionally intimate and supportive environment for those uprooted from their traditional homes or suffering the
stress of the new economic order. The "shares," the sense of churchlike religious ritual, the reinforcement of "good behavior" and encouragement to
overcome "bad" by a group of familiars all served to provide a new version
of the old stabilizing forces and traditions which many urban dwellers and
workers missed.

The group–really a little community or family unit–was there to help
and support the male members, to get them out of bed, off to work, off the
streets and out of the bars and jails, so to speak, in a world now filled with
anxieties and seductive distractions. Like the recovery movement of today,
and its far broader population, AA offered something amazingly well suited
to the times, a new institutional structure whereby the "values" of conservative WASP America could be shored up.

FEMINISM AND THE 12 STEPS: SIMILAR BUT DIFFERENT

For all the differences between feminism's history and direction and those of
AA, there are profound similarities in their developments. Like feminism–
and unlike more traditionally political movements–AA grew up in response
to certain ongoing, ever-increasing flaws and glitches in the personal, daily
lives of growing numbers of Americans. Like feminism, the movement
was initially and most obviously a response to *emotional* difficulties and
frustrations.

Feminism begins with the acknowledgement of what Betty Friedan
called "the problem that has no name," the problem of female malaise and
depression. It spoke to a growing sense among American women that old
masculinist way of negotiating emotional and domestic matters were not
working for growing numbers of women. AA, when it began, spoke to a similar sense of unhappiness and dysfunction among growing numbers of
Americans, this time, primarily, working and professional males.

But the similarities end there. For the approaches–theoretical and procedural–to solving these problems were wildly at odds. The key idea of AA
dogma is that alcohol abuse is a progressive and incurable "disease." This is
the most important feature of the 12 Step movement as a whole, and what
most distinguishes it from movements like feminism, which assume that all
significant social behaviors are learned and rooted in social causes.[5] When

women, in the 1960s, came into consciousness-raising (CR) groups and recognized their common pain and anger, they immediately grabbed onto the idea that this shared pain and anger was socially constructed and could therefore be changed. When the men who formed AA first came together to share *their* common pain, they immediately assumed something quite opposite: that they must have contracted a disease.

The reasons for the different assumptions are easy to guess. Young women in CR were for the first time realizing that they *were* in pain, unhappy. The alcoholics in AA, on the other hand, came together at the tail end of their endlessly unsuccessful struggle to change their condition and were, by then, so beaten and despondent about their failures that they could not imagine that they had it in their power to change. Indeed, the word "power" is central to both traditions. Women saw that they were powerless against male society and determined to empower themselves and fight back. Men in AA saw that they "were powerless" (as Step 1 goes) against alcohol and determined to give up their lives to a "Higher Power," often a very traditional Christian God, whom they asked to help them get by, one day at a time.

Here, in this first assumption of "disease" and disavowal of "power," is the heart of AA and the key to its enormous success in helping society help those who are in pain to the point of dysfunction to resume their lives. Resuming, not changing, one's life is the point here. And "gratitude" for the ability to function, diseased as one now knows oneself to be, is a central aspect of 12 Step ideology. Melody Beattie, in the depths of her addiction and despair, when her life was in shambles, tells of getting on her knees and "practicing gratitude"–giving thanks to God for her terrible life. And from there she began to improve, she says (Beattie 1987, p. 37). That such an approach to problem solving tends to support the social status quo, where feminism's very different assumptions tend to disrupt and threaten it, is undeniable.

That Beattie, whose "addictions" included alcohol and drugs, should have become famous and influential for her books on the disease of "codependency"–a nonchemical condition affecting women in relationships primarily–is an indication of how smoothly the doctrines of AA, developed to deal with chemical dependencies, have been enlisted in the service of emotional stresses and behaviors which, increasingly, have troubled women in a postfeminist age. To call a dependent relationship with an unsuitable male an "addiction" rather than a function of sexist conditioning, and to suggest that one seek help in detaching oneself from this relationship in a "Higher Power," is a far cry from feminism, one which could only have occurred to Beattie through her own experiences in 12 Step programs for chemical abusers. And those experiences were made possible–indeed, by the 1980s, had become the inevitable route for problem drinkers and drug users–because of the amazing success of AA in promoting its ideas about "disease" as the root of emotional dysfunctions which lead to compulsive behavior.

CONSCIOUSNESS-RAISING AND CONFESSION: AA's MORAL AGENDA

Where the 12 Step process clearly if superficially resembles feminist consciousness raising structurally is in the meetings themselves, which employ a confessional mode of presentation to address personal hurt. But where feminist CR works to free women from the constraints of traditional mores and ethics, AA works to reinforce traditional ideology. While the repressive aspects of 12 Step thinking are far more pronounced in classic AA meetings, where the entreaties to Higher Powers to help one fight off wayward impulses are important, than in the newer, more female-oriented programs, the subtle ramifications of this puritanical strain of AA are nonetheless important even in groups like Codependents Anonymous (CODA) and certainly Overeaters Anonymous (OA). For in merely talking about oneself as "addicted" and looking to spiritual sources for help, one does indeed internalize a way of thinking and feeling which places blame on one's failings and seeks help in improving *oneself* rather than the world.

In AA, one is encouraged to confess, publicly, to one's drinking behavior. One comes into the movement fearful and in a state of shame and self-loathing. One hears others testify to their similar states and give narratives of hope and healing in which their lives are seen to miraculously improve. And one is encouraged, moved, to testify oneself.

"Hi, my name is Jane and I am an alcoholic" is the first thing one learns to say in AA. And it is a confession at once liberating and very doctrinaire and controlling. For in adopting this label of disease, one begins–is forced–to alter one's sense of identity in a way which puts this single aspect of one's life and behavior foremost in one's mind as an identifying feature. One is *in essence* an alcoholic, from that day forward. In OA and CODA, as we shall see, the emphasis on behavioral change is far less prominent, if it exists at all, than this emphasis on changing one's sense of identity. The opening salvo– "Hi, I'm Judy and I'm a codependent " or "an adult child" or "a compulsive shopper"–and the ritual readings of the 12 Steps and Traditions, even when they are not referred to much as the meeting goes on, have the effect of identifying one as a member of an official group of "addicts" committed to a set of beliefs and actions which are imposed from above–literally–and unquestioningly accepted.

One must admit, in Step 1, that one is "powerless" over alcohol–or food, or shopping, or whatever–and give oneself up to a "Higher Power" to whom one entrusts one's life. And each further Step–read at every meeting–similarly charts a predetermined, restrictive course of thinking and feeling whereby one, again and again, identifies oneself as a diseased person, and admits, publicly, to one's many weaknesses and failings and sins against others. This ritual, no matter how weak is its actual ability to enforce behavior changes, colors and controls the entire process and one's way of relating to one's life.

There is, to be sure, a great relief, a sense of peace and freedom, in being able, finally, to rid oneself of the dark secret of one's abuse. But the cost of this "freedom" makes questionable the very use of this word. And this is especially true when, as has now become the case, the dogma to which one submits has become a near-universal way of thinking about human troubles in the larger society and has, indeed, become widely sanctioned and invoked by the media and other social institutions, from the medical to the religious to the corporate.

It is not surprising that the recovery movement's message should have taken hold so easily during the Reagan/Bush years, when conservative ideology was in greater favor than it had been for a very long time. For the recovery movement–with its insistence on imposing order upon wayward, morally weak, and diseased souls and its use of a confessional process which is itself at least somewhat coercive–has many features which fit very well with the most repressive and regressive political and moral attitudes in the American political spectrum.

As Foucault explains in *The History of Sexuality* (and as we shall more completely see in the next chapter), public confession has always been a subtle form of social control. One believes one is finally revealing one's true self, speaking from one's deepest center at last, after being silenced by the rituals of impersonal, alienating social life. But in fact, by publicly "confessing" one is more deeply binding oneself to the rule of repressive public discourse. "The confession has spread its effects far and wide," says Foucault;

> it plays a part in justice, medicine, education, family relationships and love relations, in the most ordinary affairs of everyday life and in the most solemn rites. One confesses one's crimes, one's sins, one's thoughts and desires, one's illnesses and troubles; one goes about tell-

ing, with the greatest precision, whatever is most difficult to tell. One
confesses in public and private, to one's parents, one's educators, one's
doctor, to those one loves; one admits to oneself, in pleasure and in
pain, things it would be impossible to tell anyone else, the things people
write books about. One confesses—or is forced to confess."

For, as he comments further in the same passage,

the confession . . . is a ritual that unfolds within a power relationship,
for one does not confess without the presence of a partner who is . . . the
authority who requires the confession, prescribes and appreciates it,
and intervenes in order to judge, punish, forgive, console, and recon-
cile. . . . It exonerates, redeems and purifies [the confessor], it unbur-
dens him of his wrongs, liberates him, and promises him salvation."
(1990, pp. 59–62)

Foucault might have been describing a 12 Step meeting when he wrote these
words, so exact is his description of the way in which the public context of
the personal narratives presented so emotionally by members transforms
the utterances from the merely personal into the inherently social utterances
of an official doctrine within an institutional setting endowed with the
power to validate them as "true" and "right."

On the surface, much of this confessional process resembles feminist
consciousness-raising. Here too one learns that each emotion, each learned,
self-destructive action, is rooted in a deeper pattern of behavior. The source
here is "addiction" rather than social or political forces, of course. But the
ways of overcoming the pain and self-destruction are eerily similar. There
are guidelines one can easily understand and follow. And there is a group of
sister sufferers who are there to lend support and understanding.

In my many visits to 12 Step meetings, I saw and heard, again and again,
things I had earlier learned to say and depend upon in CR groups. In CR
groups, as in CODA and OA and the like, everyone is listened to; everyone
has a chance to speak. In both CR and recovery groups there are sometimes
rigid, but clever, methods of enforcing this principle developed and used nationally, to insure that each woman can be heard, that no woman speaks at
too great a length or too often, that no woman's contribution is ridiculed or
discounted. Timekeepers and markers, for example, are often used in both
arenas to ensure that turns and time are democratically allotted.

There are similarities in the content of what is said in both groups as well,
and how the content is regulated. CR groups, like recovery groups, insisted
that women focus on concrete personal experiences. Leaders passed out
readings and lists of generalizations by which the concrete details of what

was shared could be shown to fit within the theoretical overview of female experience which had been developed from what had already been learned from previous such meetings.

In these meetings, as in 12 Step groups, members often nodded in agreement and responded with the kind of supportive clichés – "I can really relate to what you're saying" – that built unity and emotional safety for those all too used to hearing and feeling hostility, scorn, and contempt. Week after week, one heard stories of small successes and failures, emotional ups and downs, in the members' various efforts to understand and change their personal and social relationships and feelings. And – as in 12 Step meetings – members who had "been there" offered words of encouragement and nods of empathy to those who were not doing so well.[6]

But there are profound differences between 12 Step confessional processes and those of CR. CR was an oppositional movement and doctrine, radical in its challenge to every tenet of sexist life. The use of confession was never validated by any official "listener" as in AA, where an implicit "Higher Power" is always spoken to and felt to be present and all-powerful. Nor were the members ever "anonymous" in the political sense. Its purpose was clearly to challenge and change orthodoxy, and there was no contradiction in its workings.

AA's very different use of confession involves – whatever else it contains – at least, a strong element of social control. To the extent that AA is a publicly sanctioned and endorsed institution preaching a doctrine which is now codified and incorporated into our institutions of work and law and education, it clearly works to enforce, subtly but coercively, a unitary, official doctrine. I am not, of course, suggesting that AA is a planned out conspiracy of control and indoctrination. But as AA and its philosophy and teachings have been circulated and adopted and repeated and employed in the policies and doctrines of more and more social institutions, and as these teachings have come to be instinctively invoked and adhered to as "common sense" in more and more social, work, school, family, church, and medical settings as the obvious, only, way to address "addictive" problems, they take on a hegemonic authority which is hard to resist. It is in this sense that I speak of the recovery movement as a loose, uncodified, but nonetheless effective means of social control. Its very expansion and endless variation and repetition, in insurance policies, in social service treatment centers, in the laws governing parole and sentencing of criminals of all kinds,[7] gives it an authority which renders its ideas and rules of conduct a kind of universal set of guidelines for proper living which – for better or worse, and I think there are elements of both—works to keep society and its members functioning in an orderly manner. That this doctrine and set of rules and guidelines for living are based on ideas of human weakness and disease and religious ideas of salvation through confession, makes them—whatever their positive effects—morally and politically problematic to say the least (Foucault 1990, p. 62).

I am not overlooking the very real service performed by 12 Step groups, especially AA, in helping many to survive. The point is, however, that the focus on ideas of disease and addiction—whether in talking about drugs or anorexia or battered women syndrome—is dangerously misleading. It takes attention away from the *why* of the epidemics and their consequences, the reasons and causes for so much misery. Why are we hurting so much? Why are we turning to drugs and others forms of self-destruction to function? Why are we in need of so many, more powerful crutches to get through a day of life in America? I believe the reason is not "addictive personalities" today any more than it was alcohol during the days of Prohibition.

But we can "come to believe" that addictive personalities do cause our distress, personal and social. If we can further "come to believe" that our compulsive attraction to food, shopping, or abusive mates is rooted in diseases and allergies, which can be sometimes, partly, controlled by a spiritual, confessional group process which can be extended and enforced throughout society, we are on the road to a massive system of social control—from church basements to prison wards—in which actual social problems are made invisible and things, somehow, keep getting worse. My long months of visiting and interviewing those who maintain this now vast system of institutions and policies based upon 12 Step thinking and practice—an empire of medical/religious/health professionals and entrepreneurs now so massive and influential as to boggle the mind—convinced me we are well on our way down that road.

SEND LAWYERS, GUNS, AND MONEY:
AA AS POSTMODERN PHENOMENON

I am going to take you through this system, as I traveled through it in interviews, conferences, and meetings, and give you a sense of the thinking and the rules that govern it. Who makes drug policy? Who runs the burgeoning treatment industry and its many hospitals and treatment centers? How are the publicity and advertising for the movement handled? Who lobbies Congress for public financing of treatment and education and for legislation which will be informed by and sympathetic to the claims and goals of the movement? Who decides, in today's playing field, what kinds of "addictions" and treatments are important enough for support and funding? How, in a time of great economic recession, is the whole thing kept afloat? And how, finally, do women's pain and suffering fit in? These may seem like odd questions to be asking about addiction issues. But they are crucial to a real understanding of how we, as a society, have come to adopt certain beliefs and practices and not others in our efforts to improve our lives.

One reason these questions may seem odd is that the recovery movement has been so successful in creating an image of itself as a purely personal and voluntary phenomenon, a counter, if you will, to the anxiety-provoking, addiction-inducing conditions of American life, in its public manifestations. This view is easy to maintain since most of us who have any direct or casual contact with the movement do indeed experience it as a merely personal or cultural phenomenon. Our friends attend meetings and come home to rave about the 12 Step "cure." We watch a daytime talk show and see and hear more such personal experiences. But this is only the tip of the recovery iceberg. Beneath the surface are aspects of the movement that are themselves part and parcel of the very economic and bureaucratic structures which so often contribute to our "addictive" problems. Also hidden from sight are the ideological and religious features of the movement—those we have just examined—which work to control and redirect impulses toward political change, so that the offending social forces will not be pressured to reform themselves.

To see this "submerged" aspect of the movement, let's look at a few more startling figures about addiction and recovery. Epidemiologist Robin Room claims that between 1942 and 1976 the number of alcoholics in treatment in the United States multiplied twentyfold (Room 1980). In the decade between 1977 and 1987, the period that saw the expansion of the movement to include emotional addictions, AA membership—now a major conduit into other 12 Step fellowships—doubled according to Stanton Peele (1989, p. 49). And during that time, in the years between 1978 and 1984, the number of for-profit residential addiction treatment centers increased by 350 percent and their caseloads by 400 percent (Room and Weisner 1984). By the mid-eighties, the addiction treatment industry had become a two-billion-dollar enterprise, while private treatment hospitals alone earned one billion dollars annually. Nor are alcohol and drug abuse the only sources of these profits. Overeating, now called and addiction, generates several million dollars a year. And some of that money also goes to private treatment centers. Nor is this the extent of what hospital administrators and professional groups foresee for the future of the industry and its growth.

How did we reach this point of massive economic and ideological investment in 12 Step ideas and techniques? Why was the disease idea so appealing as time went on? Why, according to Peele, by 1987, did 90 percent of all Americans believe that alcohol use–an accepted part of social life in most civilizations–is a disease over which millions upon millions have no control; for which there is no cure; which progresses to worse and worse stages, like a cancer, unless absolute abstinence is practiced (Peele, 1989, p. 73)? The answers lie in the often invisible ways in which this nonprofit, spiritual organization has over the years become deeply involved in economic and political movements contradictory to its public image.

AA itself, as a self-help network, has a separate institutional structure which abides by rules of anonymity and nonprofit. I am not suggesting otherwise. When one goes to a fellowship meeting at a local church, one is indeed safely entering a free, trustworthy, voluntary "fellowship" of like sufferers whose only interest is achieving sobriety through service and obedience to the program.

But there is more to the 12 Step movement these days than the groups alone. Ever since their formation in the early 1940s, the highly influential Yale Center of Alcohol Studies and the National Council on Alcoholism have endorsed and promoted the disease theory and the 12 Step method and fostered the spread of their influence throughout wider and wider arcs of society. At the same time that the 12 Step method has grown more popular, its program and its ideology have changed in dramatic ways. Because most of us–viewing the recovery movement through the glass of media and propaganda distortion–focus all our attention on individual suffering and recovery, we are understandably inclined to see the movement simply as a voluntary self-help movement which hurting, desperate souls decide to enter after having surveyed their choices–free-market–style–and determined that this is their best option. But there is no such free market of possible "cures" for today's suffering. There is instead a single, almost universally accepted "cure" for America's spiritual troubles, the recovery movement, to which most institutions now send emotionally troubled people of all kinds.

Most of what goes on in the self-help groups–the aspect of the movement with which most people are most familiar–has no direct economic or legal link to the recovery movement structures I observed that are now integral to our criminal justice and education and medical treatment systems. The majority of women who are "coming to believe" that they are "addicts" and that their various troubles are caused by a "disease" are not and will not be participants in these structures. Rather, they are turning, by the millions, to recovery groups and books and seminars and cruises and even TV talk shows about addiction and recovery to help them manage the traumas of postfeminism.

Nonetheless, it is important to understand the links between these economic and social structures and the broader, more amorphous culture of recovery to which so many women are drawn in more or less ongoing, life-changing ways. For the ideology that filters down into women's lives these days, through TV, through friends, through magazines and bookstore displays, through advice from therapists and physicians, through classroom lectures and educational media, is indeed funded by and integrally connected to economic and social structures from which most women may indeed feel and be quite divorced.

It may be only the most extremely dysfunctional and out of control–or wealthy–that end up in jails and hospitals for serious drug and alcohol and emotional problems, but the thinking and values of those who establish drug and criminal justice policy, who run teaching and treatment hospitals and other education programs, do indeed push the ideas first established within AA as a worldview, a way of thinking and handling all the social stresses of contemporary life. The more powerful and expansive these policy makers become in this mission, the more their ways of handling crime and drug abuse and emotional collapse come to be accepted–enforced really–as the only possible ways of thinking about any emotional problem.

Therapists–even progressive and feminist therapists–now readily send clients to OA, CODA, ACOA, and many other groups as a kind of support system as they undergo private treatment, for example. The experience of being in a group with other sufferers is thought to be therapeutically helpful, and with good reason (as the example of second wave CR and other self-help projects proved). And while the groups do not involve money, hospitalization, or incarceration for any but the most marginal (or wealthy) members, they do indeed reproduce (as CR certainly did not) the ideology that leads, eventually, to a way of thinking and feeling that feeds into the universe of recovery doctrine. The women in the looser, newer groups we will be meeting in chapter 4 are very much a part of the larger economic and social structures which we are examining here, and they would not be hearing about, much less visiting, these groups, had the economic and ideological power of early AA and its 12 Step program not been so forcefully and successfully enlisted in the service of the representatives of these larger structures: doctors, judges, corporate managers, educators, and anti-drug activists.

One of the most important factors in building this crucial, if invisible, bridge between the medical and criminal justice structures and groups like Overeaters Anonymous and Codependents Anonymous has been the gradual revision of the doctrine of addiction to fit the economic and social interests of those who run hospitals, courts, and prisons (Peele 1989, pp. 40–58, 125–38). The most significant change has been in the identification of "addicts" and the process of entry into programs. Originally, it was believed that an addict could be identified from the first drink, that there was an experiential difference between those born with the "allergy" to drink and those who could safely imbibe. And even those born addicts usually had to "hit bottom" before voluntarily entering groups, thus reinforcing the self-identification–"I'm John and I'm an alcoholic"–requirement for effective treatment.

In the 1970s, the idea that people were identifiable as addicts from their first drink and the notion of a benefit derived from voluntarily entering treatment gave way to the idea of "denial." Suddenly it became necessary to convince addicts of what was not as obvious. Many drunks, it is now believed, do not in fact realize immediately that they are "different" from social drinkers but continue, throughout their lives even, to consider themselves nonaddicts, to function at work and socially, and to suffer none of the dramatic symptoms that characterized the often criminally dangerous recruits of Bill W. and Dr. Bob.

What to do about these "denial addicts" is a question asked and answered intriguingly by the current leaders of the recovery movement. We must, they have determined, find objective–not subjective–standards for identifying and defining addiction, even when the "patient" herself does not in any way experience the problem or believe herself to be ill. For if the recovery system is to expand and prosper–as it is doing very nicely–there must be ways to insure a regular influx of new consumers, ever eager to find and buy the movement's products and services. This turn from traditional AA thinking is profound in its implications.

At a conference I attended of the National Treatment Consortium (essentially a lobbying group for addiction treatment centers) in August 1992, the central issue in virtually every session was the problem of "national standards." Speakers from Employee Assistance Programs (EAPs, divisions maintained by private corporations to identify employees who are addicts and route them into treatment programs), hospital administrations, and insurance companies discussed ways to garner highly competitive medical research funding for addiction medicine. They worked together to come up with commonly agreed upon definitions of addiction as well as hard statistics "proving" that certain kinds of people are verifiably "ill" and that certain kinds of treatments can be proven to "work," by scientific standards of testing. This is no small task, obviously, and the level of anxiety and frustration at this conference was palpable. But once it is accomplished—and the conference evidenced the determination of all concerned to succeed—the channeling of more and more people into treatment via "addiction" diagnoses will undoubtedly increase. If money can be found to warrant it, more and more treatment centers will be working hard to convince therapists and clients that every kind of addiction now addressed in the newer self-help groups, such as OA and CODA (which, it's worth noting, are frequented largely by women), should be targeted for residential treatment as well.

It is clear that, in the process of discussing these matters and developing policies to help in the search for money, treatment center officials have already rationalized just this kind of expansion of residential treatment for women. For example, there is already an understanding among treatment center officials that certain kinds of recovery jargon and methodology are not suitable for insurance and government funding applications. One EAP officer on a panel I observed on standards and definitions advised the group, for example, to downplay "vague and fuzzy" terms for addiction and to avoid the overuse of "spirituality language" and "oddball" techniques, such as subliminal tape recordings, which insurers will easily dismiss. The idea, accepted by everyone, was that scientifically verifiable definitions and statistical results must be agreed upon and universally adopted in order for this new professional network and its institutional affiliates to gain their rightful place in the managed care complex within which government, hospitals, and corporations negotiate payment plans and rules.

While, on the one hand, this trend may seem to threaten many of the hallowed spiritual ideas of 12 Step thinking, in fact it will actually work to structure and rationalize the huge addiction empire. The adoption of scientifically verifiable national standards will create a clearly defined division of labor and services in the addiction industry, and help practitioners to identify their appropriate market segment and establish the appropriate rules and terms for that subsection of the now multi-faceted industry.

Self-help books, for example, can be as spiritual and novelty-laden as they like since their advertising and distribution methods are strictly commercial and their intended market is private, mostly middle-class female consumers. Hospital brochures, on the other hand, must rigidly conform to the far more conservative terms and requirements of medical/scientific/government regulatory discourse.

In the end, of course, all these markets feed upon and support each other. People who enter or visit treatment centers will, for example, be steered toward gift shops which carry all the "softer" private consumer–oriented books and trinkets and tapes which bear the slogans of the more New Age, less scientific elements of the recovery movement. Like the world of Gulf & Western media products or Kellogg's cereal, all the items are produced and sold by the same centralized industry and the illusion of "choice" is stylistically superficial. Granola for baby boomers, Cap'n Crunch for tots, oatmeal for Grandma. "Seinfeld" for baby boomers, "Ninja Turtles" for tots, and "Golden Girls" for Grandma.

The bottom line is that the entire structure stands on the ideology and practice of the 12 Step movement, just as Kellogg's cereals are made from the same grains and by the same machines. Whether it's Hazelden, a Bradshaw cruise, a prison program, or public school "drug education" seminar, the treatment method provided is the AA 12 Step model. There is almost no discussion of alternatives. At every conference I attended in writing this book, and at every interview I conducted with therapists, EAP professionals, law enforcers, and hospital administrators, the idea that another system might be considered was met with confusion and disbelief, as though I were really too ignorant to be writing a book about addiction. The idea, for example, that women in particular might be suffering from the increased stresses of the "double day"–the need to work outside the home while also raising a family and caring for a home–and thus becoming more prone to tranquilizing drug use as a way of coping, rather than as an addiction, was summarily dismissed many times by many interviewees. The idea that regular drug use, no matter how recent or how clearly (to me) situationally engendered, might be anything but a sign of addiction was simply not considered possible by these people, so convinced were they that addiction was the explanation for all such sudden turns to chemical "life supports," no matter how late in life the occurrence.

The centralized workings of this diverse group of agencies and individuals within the context of a common, core philosophy of "treatment" which announces itself unable to "cure" is intriguing. Everyone agrees, today, that whatever the problem, wherever it emerges and whoever catches it, the central route toward recovery is the 12 Step group process. As Peele notes, for example, "the main source of referrals for alcoholism treatment is drunk driving arrests" (1989, p. 127). And that treatment, it is always taken for granted, will be AA. It is now common for law enforcement agencies to require DUI arrestees to attend AA meetings as a way of staying out of jail.

Many of these arrests involve young males who are, if funds are available, routed into 12 Step–based treatment centers like the CompCare and Fair Oaks hospital chains. Between 1980 and 1984 there was a 350 percent jump in the hospitalization of teenagers for emotional problems in which some drug or alcohol use was apparent (Peele 1989, p. 70). CompCare, and its successful imitators, have made inroads into the school system where they train guidance counselors to identify and refer problem youths. And their massive, expensive advertising campaigns, seen on television and in other media venues, also reach parents of male youths who are independently wealthy enough, or well-insured enough, to pay their own way into these centers.

On another front, corporations, with their EAPs and drug-testing professionals in place, play a similar role of steering all sorts of people into the treatment industry at the expense of employers. Indeed, one of the most intriguing analyses of the politics of drug testing–itself a growing, profitable industry of drug professionals–is that it has perfected a "good cop/bad cop" technique for channeling people from one set of institutional walls to another, all of which are linked by their dependence on 12 Step thinking (O'Malley and Mugford 1991, p. 64). Whether you are at work, at school, in the booking room, or at Bellevue, the "bad cop" arrests you and the "good cop"–teacher, social worker, or EAP officer–offers you a deal. "You need not suffer the humiliation and trauma of being fired or turned over to the law, or interred in jail," he informs you. Instead you will be given "help" in the form of mandatory treatment.

Here too we see the Foucaultian logic of this system: while apparently "freeing" you from the grip of addiction, it actually works to lock you more firmly in the grip of institutional and discursive control. As Zimring and Hawkins put it, "the mixed motives of [EAPs] that have been established to discover and facilitate the treatment of employees with drug- and alcohol-abuse behaviors" are double-edged. "Unlike screening programs that operate prior to the establishment of such employment relationships," these programs "are usually premised" on the idea of "employee entitlement" (1991, pp. 118–19). Yet, the "right" of workers to the fringe benefit of (mandatory) "treatment" is inherently repressive and disciplinary. Like the use of "confession" in 12 Step treatment, as a way of speaking from one's deep inner self in a safe space, these apparently benign and individual-oriented practices serve in subtle ways to place the individual in a social and sometimes institutional context in which her needs and problems are defined and controlled by rules and discourses which are, at least in some ways, in the service of repressive and even humiliating social control agencies. A female manager, for example, discovered to be using stimulants or tranquilizers because of un-usual, perhaps temporary, home problems, will be guided toward a 12 Step program in which, indeed, she will find a sympathetic audience for her problems, often problems shared by many other women in similar roles. Rather than addressing the real issues and perhaps coming up with solu-tions–an on-site child care center, for example, or a program based on flex-time–the group will diagnose the woman as an addict suffering from a dis-ease and put her into ongoing "treatment."

The centralized but multi-faceted addiction empire is remarkably inven-tive in its ability to sort out issues of terminology and money in ways which provide ever new ideas about steering people into profitable treatment cen-ters. In fact, in my interviews with treatment professionals, it was generally agreed–and this was not considered "shady" at all, since the ideology is firmly accepted–that while it is still very difficult to get employers to pay for illnesses such as overeating and codependency, once one was in treatment for any addictive disorder–eating, sex, gambling, shoplifting–it was inevi-table that "cross-addictions" would be discovered, one of which, usually de-pression, would qualify the employee for paid treatment under insurance and government regulations. That depression is the most common diagno-sis used, especially for women suffering from eating disorders, "codepen-dent" relationships with abusive men, and general "self-esteem" problems, is understandable. Women suffering from all these troubles do indeed tend to be depressed, often in the most extreme clinical definitions of that term.

Even more promising–and here is where women will clearly be affected in the future–are plans to convince insurers to broaden inclusion on the ba-sis of newly found "diseases." If a woman can get into treatment as a "com-pulsive eater," for example, she need not tortuously twist her symptoms to fit the all-purpose, but emotionally vague, "depression" definition. Indeed, in the October 1992 issue of *Changes*, Jan Marie Werblin, a staff writer for this industry-based publication, documents the steps now being taken to have "binge-eating disorder . . . included in the official manual of psychiatric di-agnoses along with anorexia and bulimia" so that "patients' participation in weight-loss programs could be covered by insurance." Since, she explains, "as many as 30 percent of people who participate in hospital-based weight-reduction programs meet the criteria" for this newly coined "disorder," hav-ing it officially recognized will be a good boon to sufferers and addiction specialists alike (1992b, p. 39). According to Werblin, OA, the 12 Step group most of the targeted new patients now attend, while necessary, may not be "enough help" for many truly "ill" food addicts. And so, the argument goes, medical professionals must convince insurers and employees that these people "have to seek a disorder specialist" working out of a residential treatment center in order to adequately combat their "disease" (ibid., p. 52). As eating disorders go, of course, so will go many other addictive disorders common to women. If "depression" is a universal symptom for all addictions, it will easily be used to pay for treatment of women suffering from everything from nail-biting to shoplifting.

The ways in which money changes hands to support the addiction, treatment, recovery empire are also Byzantine. Corporations, for example, have been convinced to spend money on health insurance programs that include drug and mental health treatment, which in turn is increasingly based on the principles of the 12 Step movement, at great expense. The installation of EAP personnel and departments in corporations is costly and provides jobs for many who find themselves, suddenly, in a new "profession." In a world in which massive layoffs, and the threat of layoffs, produce the kind of anxiety which leads to addiction, it is interesting to note that this very condition is, at least for some, creating new economic opportunities. I spoke to many such "born again" drug professionals, who had previously worked as everything from engineers to stockbrokers to school teachers. There is a growing market for drug treatment experts in a recessionary world in which so a many other "professionals" are finding themselves unemployed.

The treatment centers and the many therapists involved are similarly on the receiving end of a great new windfall. As Peele (1989) points out, one of the most unusual things about the treatment industry is that it employs its own. Virtually all drug counselors and therapists identify themselves as recovering addicts and in many cases this is their primary claim to expertise. Every conference I attended in writing this book provided numerous "meetings" for addicts of every kind, and every meeting was filled. The injunction "Physician heal thyself" is taken very literally in this growing field.

Insurance agencies and governmental regulatory agencies—the institutions that make policies and decisions about how much money should be spent in what ways and who should be on the receiving end of how much of each kind of "approved" expenditure—also constitute a bureaucratic work force employing and paying thousands upon thousands of employees. If one considers that the various behaviors now called "addictions" may often arise as a result of the strains of unemployment, an ever more common experience for many workers in an economy constantly in flux and transformation, in which cyclical unemployment is a built-in condition, one can see that the recovery movement's offer, to so many, of new careers, as well as recovery treatment, may well be a factor in its strong ideological and emotional appeal. One needn't be a Marxist to see that people are likely to be sympathetic to a particular ideology if their livelihoods depend upon it. Just as youths are likelier to join the army when other jobs are scarce, so are people likely to join the recovery work force and embrace its dogma when other employment dries up.

Ever new branches of the recovery system are being spawned every day it seems, enlisting ever new members into the professional and volunteer work force of the movement, and insuring that the AA message will be ever more firmly inscribed in the public mind as the sole authoritative answer to the problem of "addiction." Among the most important of these, in terms of public relations, is the burgeoning public interest, grass roots activity—which in other days went to very different issues—which now attracts huge numbers of concerned citizens to lobbying and media campaigns against drugs and alcohol. For they too have been very important in making sure that private and public monies become available to treat addictions. The case of Mothers Against Drunk Driving (MADD) is particularly revealing of how the 12 Step movement gets promoted in other contexts. MADD is a group, organized by the mother of a victim of drunk driving, which grew into a national network of grass roots community organizations. It has been instrumental in changing public perceptions about the social costs of drinking and also in generating money, from private and government sources, for the treatment industry. MADD has also been responsible for the enactment of new drug control laws which not only impose far stricter surveillance of drivers and make the grounds for arrest or license removal more stringent, but also enforce even more coercive laws forcing drivers to attend treatment groups and programs based on the 12 Step model. Of course, the problem of drunk drivers is no small matter, and the efforts to curb such behavior understandable and even laudable. The point is, however, that the enlistment of so many female activists in efforts to get drinkers off the road and into treatment or prison, or both, is a decision—as are most solutions to social problems that rely exclusively on the criminal justice and prison systems—which doesn't address the root causes of alcoholism or of crime in general, but rather reinforces the more punitive, "law and order" approaches to human suffering and dysfunction.

The social and political implications of all of this activity are worth serious consideration. Not the least of these is the rerouting of women activists who would, in earlier days, have been organizing around gender justice issues, into effective, time-consuming organizations which spread a doctrine that turns attention away from social and economic issues and toward the "problem" of "addiction" as the cause of crimes like rape and domestic abuse. Senator Bob Packwood, we know, has been made to attend AA meetings. Feminist education, unfortunately, has not been suggested as a proper way for him to handle his problems with women (Reinarmann 1988).

My cynicism in discussing this aspect of the recovery movement may seem excessive or unfair. After all, as I well realize, many if not most of the therapists and proselytizers of recovery are deeply sincere and decent (if often misguided) people, and also—as I have been trying to keep in mind—they provide a true and useful service to millions upon millions of suffering souls. Nonetheless, the full impact of the recovery movement cannot be gauged without a cautionary look at this other, deeper level of the movement—the level which is so hard for most people, even professionals within it, to see. Looking there, we discover a web of political and economic forces which have found incentives to bolster and encourage recovery in ways which they would never do for feminism, or any other progressive social movement. We must assess their motives and gains, for whatever is good about the 12 Step movement is deeply compromised by the corporate profit agenda of the industry which supports the recovery movement, and that fact casts the entire movement in a new, far less attractive light.

WOMEN: THE NEW ADDICTS

Having said that, it is time to turn to my main concern: the influx of women into recovery programs and the newly coined, often woman-oriented, species of "addiction" which are doing so much to keep the treatment industry growing and thriving. For if women are not the primary inmates in hospital and prison and school addiction programs, they are an increasing percentage of that population. And this percentage will surely grow as new funds and official recognition of new "addictions" develop. Such is the nature of capitalist expansion in any thriving new industry.

But more to the point, the huge influx of women into 12 Step groups in the last decade, and the dramatic shift in the thinking of these groups and their processes as a result of this influx, has had a pronounced effect on the entire philosophy of 12 Step programs, even within the hospital and justice systems. For one thing, women, often as a result of their indoctrination in a nonchemical self-help group, are entering the treatment professions more and more often. These women, and their postfeminist consciousnesses, have had a great impact upon the discourse of the profession. Every women I spoke to in the profession understood the urgent "need" to see that funds are made available for the treatment of emotional disorders–to make sure, in other words, that the profession accept as valid the "diseasing" of female emotional pain. And as more treatment professionals are women themselves, their commitment to 12 Step thinking (and their economic dependence upon it as well) will invariably fuse with their feminist-informed ways of seeing emotional problems in ways which will even more surely being feminist-tinged attitudes and ideas to the male-dominated structures of money and power which are so far reluctant to include them.

AA no longer has a monopoly on the 12 Step program or its thinking. Nor do AA's somewhat dated, masculinist assumptions about what constitutes "addiction" and how to talk about and cure it now dominate the self-help and media arms of the movement. On the contrary, classic AA groups are fast being overtaken by the burgeoning number of "mutant" 12 Step programs, ideologically and procedurally overhauled to adapt to women's ever more serious, socially costly (and, for some, lucrative) addiction problems and to feminism's ever more inclusive and general way of talking about them. The movement still works to preserve and maintain social order by channeling anxieties away from social causes and into spiritual and therapeutic concerns with the individual and her soul. But its language and process have dramatically changed because of feminism and its influence on modern life. Terms like "inner child," "toxic family," "addictive relationship," "codependency," and so many others which describe family and gender "dysfunction" first pointed out by feminists are the most obvious examples. Where AA concerns itself only with the need to stop drinking, these newer groups incorporate elaborate, insightful analyses of what is wrong with our daily lives and relationships, all of which are now seen to be enmeshed in the problems of addiction.

The logic of the expansionist mission of the burgeoning addiction empire is to propagandize for the great and greater inclusion of as many people, wearing as many social and economic hats as possible into the treatment and consumer net. With every advertisement for Ultra-Slim Fast, with every alarming decline in the average body weight of professional models (Wolf 1991), for example, there is a growing tendency for women to become obsessed with their weight, a state of mind leading to potential compulsive and abusive behaviors of many kinds other than, or as well as, food disorders. Amphetamine and cocaine abuse are only the most obvious. (I read recently of a new 12 Step fellowship for women "addicted" to cosmetic surgery.) When you add to the addiction industry's need to expand its power to advertise simultaneously on so many different fronts, you begin to sense its potential for growth. Women are now exposed to ads and public service messages and TV dramas and magazine articles about all kinds of women's "addictive" troubles—codependency, for example, is now commonly given as a factor in the "Battered Wife Syndrome." All of these addiction stories conclude with happy endings engineered by 12 Step methods (or tragic endings for those who didn't recognize or admit their "addiction"), thus promoting the idea of addiction as a primary cause of a wide range of women's problems and the subtle, indirect, but all-pervasive recruiting of women into the recovery movement.

New types of addiction are continually explored in the quest by media producers for ever new material: cosmetic surgery addiction and addiction to the Internet and other computer-based practices are among the most recent of which I am aware. Each new addiction is easier and easier to accept as valid, since compulsive behavior patterns do indeed all feel and look alike. The inability to sever ties to an abusive mate is very much like the inability to stop doing any number of other compulsive acts—gambling, eating, drinking, shopping. In each case, the "empty feeling at the core of one's soul," as I have often heard it described, leads to endless efforts to "fill up the emptiness" with soporifics of choice. Food, like sex and like alcohol, does indeed momentarily ward off the emptiness and panic that are at the root of addictive habits. How could they not, since they are all, as I've been arguing, responses to common emotional and social pressures? And the reality of "cross addiction" in this context, makes it easy to convince women, once they've tried one group or treatment, that they would profit from multiple groups and treatments.

Problems are real; addictive behaviors (or whatever you want to call them) are real. There is indeed a social problem here. But its cause is not an epidemic of "addictions" to more and more things which, in the past, were not harmful. Addiction—no matter what the National Treatment Consortium will try to argue—is not caused by some virus which suddenly and inexplicably appears in ever more powerful and dangerous strains, afflicting more and more of the population, and especially more and more women. Rather, the cause is the reality of women's lives: the disappointments suffered by a generation of women primed for "liberation" and "empowerment" who find themselves poorer and more frustrated instead, and the ever greater pressure on them to enter the work force and perform more and more effectively in jobs which are alienating, ungratifying, and unrewarding. To send women into "recovery" for those problems is absurdly wrong-headed. For it is not the women who are sick; or at least they wouldn't be in a healthy society. But "recovery" is indeed the dominant, official response—even from many who should know better—to women's suffering these days.

For most women, hospitals will not be affordable and jails will not be needed. Privileged women who have private or fringe benefit funds to pay for it will be encouraged to enter treatment, which is often regarded as a vacation at a spa. As the economy rises and falls, more or less such money will be available for different women. The success of the lobbyists and media campaigners will determine what slice of the pie will go for women in residential or outpatient medical treatment.

The way in which most women will be affected, as the idea of women's addictions grows more popular and the treatment industry supporting it expands, is and will continue to be the 12 Step groups that most of us think of as the "real" recovery movement. Here, more and more women will be encouraged to use their spare time participating in free meetings and other activities which identify them, *politically,* as "recovering addicts," as part of a social grouping whose very sense of self, whose very idea of what is constructive behavior, what are constructive ways to spend time, will be defined by the philosophy and processes of the groups.

In these groups, now so strangely informed by so many ideas and attitudes taken from feminism, women will tell each other personal stories in a language culled—inappropriately—from the discourse of addiction and disease and salvation through a male deity. They will be encouraged to "come to believe," as the 12 Steps put it, that their troubles are internal rather than socially determined; that their cures are to be found in private and spiritual, not social or political arenas; and that their time, as parents, friends, wives, lovers, and even workers, is best spent in spreading the word, in sponsoring and supporting more and more hurting people in 12 Step activities.

✦

CHAPTER FOUR

In the Rooms: Learning to Talk the Talk

AA, the first group I attended regularly,[1] is the one that clearly "works" best in some "empirical" observable sense of verifiable behavior change (and shows the least hint of any feminist influence). This is because its members have a limited, behavioral goal in mind which can be monitored and measured. Meetings begin with members being honored for milestones in sobriety marked in number of days of abstinence. The concern here is behavior, and the meetings stick to a single kind of behavior—drinking or drug use—from which clear physical, life-shattering consequences once ensued. Although recovery spokespersons deny this, the ravages of substance abuse on the body, and the physical—as opposed to emotional—need for the harmful substance are qualitatively different from the effects, even, of "addiction" to a substance like food, which, after all, one must have in some amount in order to survive. I heard again and again that food and gambling and other things produce the same "high" as heroin and alcohol and that withdrawal is as physically devastating. Having overeaten my share of Häagen Dazs and Pepperidge Farm, I don't buy it.

The men I met in the AA group I visited most regularly were hard-core drunks whose addiction had caused the loss of jobs, of families and relationships, of health and very nearly, quite often, of life itself. These were men who regularly got blind drunk and frequently found themselves in alleys and hospital emergency rooms. For them, the rituals of recovery were absolute necessities to survival in the most material, bottom-line sense. It was here that I experienced the most camaraderie, the most open, universal offers of help and support, the most real intimacy and group coherence. It was here that I found my position as an "observer only" most awkward and anxiety provoking.

Upon entering my first meeting, I immediately felt an intensity that startled and scared me. The room (a dingy little storefront on the lower east side of Manhattan) was packed and smoky and I had to struggle to a tiny spot on a nearly filled wooden bench, between two large men. (The group was perhaps 85 to 90 percent white male.) As I settled in, my culture shock certainly written on my face, both men patted me supportively, asked if it was my first meeting, assured me that they knew what I was going through and suggested I get the phone number of one of the few women in the room on the way out (since opposite sex sponsorship relationships are wisely frowned upon). I later discovered that this warm reception was far from typical of other kinds of 12 Step groups.

What was clear to me, at once, was that alcoholism was a life and death situation for these people, and AA, a veritable bunker in a war against a mortal enemy. The stories I heard at these meetings (I did of course explain my purpose, after which I was treated gingerly but politely) were harrowing and repeated similar patterns of experience. The loss of jobs and children and wives. The near death experiences in bars and emergency rooms. The almost boastful retelling of war stories and "heroic" escapes. And of course the conversion stories of how these men finally bottomed out and, through luck or the help of a significant stranger, saw the light and joined AA.

Many of the stories were, not surprisingly, of relapse and remorse and the resumption–with the knowing support of the "fellows"–of the recovery ritual, from Step 1. Recidivism is built into these groups. One can never be lost, or be cured; one can only work one's program more or less successfully. All confessions of lapse are met with understanding words of support, never chastisement or blame. This is a hard game they are playing, and no one who comes to a meeting is scorned or accused.

What most marked this meeting–definitely a "good one" by the standards of movement regulars–was its disciplined way of sticking to the point, repeating the same stories and affirmations over and over again, staying close to the material conditions of existence and survival, creating a sense of "them" against "us" in which membership becomes one's primary identity and the outside world is acknowledged as mortally dangerous. There is shared faith in the "miracle" of giving oneself up to, "knowing," one's "Higher Power" which is palpable.

These are men who are emotionally and economically–emotionally *because* economically–close to the edge. They have been absolute losers in every area of life. They are willing to come to each other's rescue at all hours of the day and night, to wake each other up in the morning, and dress, feed, and drive each other to work when—as is common—that is the only way they will ever get there. These are Bill W.'s kind of drunks and they understand his obsessive ardor in building AA. They will indeed die without it.

In this first meeting, there was almost no talk of work or relationships, except in terms of drinking and not drinking. "My Aunt Rose had to get me up and send me home because I was gonna wreck the whole wedding," said one man in explaining how he managed to stay alive, barely, one recent weekend. The shared laughter at such macho antics is always there, making it difficult (in my view) for the few women present to participate as fully as the men. Most of the women spoke softly and were fairly brief and business-like about their failures or successes in the war against drink. When they did offer stories, however, they were invariably less physical and more emotional. "My husband walked out last night and I gotta get sober up or he'll never come back, I know," said one truly desperate woman. While this was met with obvious nods of sympathy, no one picked up on her "share" or "related to it." The next speakers all resumed horror stories of physical danger and havoc.

In this group, there were a few gay men. Their stories too, however, were of physical danger and near-death, albeit in different settings and by different means perhaps. A young lawyer stumbled through his long story of coming to terms with his sexuality though a tortured adolescence, and of turning to drink to blot out his shame and fear, with his eyes down. When he got to the part of the narrative in which his drinking produced blackouts, lost clients, unremembered fistfights in leather bars, and emergency room mornings far from his own neighborhood, he was on firmer ground and his "share" was followed by other such tales by straight, working-class men.

I visited other AA groups, some all professional, some all female, some all gay and/or lesbian, and met with very different atmospheres and stories. In these groups, as in the groups I'll describe later, relationship and career issues and especially matters of spirituality in relation to lifestyle—as opposed to the old-fashioned scripture-driven prayer of the first group—were common. But it was this first group of sink-or-swim tough guys that most impressed me in its urgency and sincerity and most helped me to see what AA actually has done to earn the respect and awe it gets from health and social service professionals. Here I saw people greet each other with an intensity and warmth born of years of common, soul-wrenching struggle to become and stay "human," as they often put it.

Most moving were the tales of recovery. The details of early morning shakes and trips to liquor stores only barely aborted by sheer determination spoke of such courage and tragedy that I was often moved to tears. "I stood outside the store, shaking, barely able to stand up," reported one man. "I watched the guy coming out tear at the bottle cap and I could just about taste that first gulp going down. But I ran, for my life, and called my sponsor the minute I got home. That was close." "I can't tell you the humiliation of turning tricks for old creeps who were willing to buy me booze," one teenage boy told me privately. "I said, the last time, 'Never again, I'd rather walk into moving traffic.' And I came here. It saved my life."

My experiences led me to agree with many professional observers[2] that this classic AA model operates as a cult—a term I use descriptively, not judgmentally—and therein lies the secret of its success. It thrives on exclusivity and social isolation, on rote repetitions of scriptural doctrine, and on a blind faith in an omnipotent "leader" and God. It enforces rigid rules of behavior that virtually program one's every move every day, week, and month. Members who do best tend to break ties with former friends and family and relate only to fellow drunks, often attending meetings every day, sometimes even twice a day. By repetition the Steps and Traditions become so ingrained that all casual conversation comes to include key phrases—"I let go and let God" is a common saying, for example—and the idea that one's Higher Power had a role in virtually every positive moment of one's life is taken for granted here. The members who told the most inspiring tales, moreover, were generally the ones whose every moment was coordinated according to the Steps and Traditions and meeting schedules. Many members speak often of giving up old haunts and friends to stick "close to home" as one put it, and the conversation of members tends to revolve so thoroughly around ideas and activities of recovery that it is probably a relief to old friends when they drift away. There are alcohol-free social clubs where members meet in many cities, and many members carry around AA literature and turn to it whenever they find themselves with nothing to do, for fear they will return to old habits if they relax. "I read the Big Book (the basic text, written by Bill W.) every day, every time I start to feel nervous," one man told me. "It saved me the other day, when I ran into an old drinking buddy on the subway. He took one look at it and split." I had no doubt.

Marc Galanter, a psychiatrist who studies cults, calls AA a "therapeutic cult" and recommends it to his own alcoholic patients. The use of a common, private language, the tendency to form one's entire social life around the group and its members, the demand to confess, to "take a fearless moral inventory" and give oneself up to the guidance of a Higher Power, all make for the kind of "born again" conversion to a new life and a new social identity that characterizes cult behavior (Galanter 1989, pp. 178–83). The Steps, in general, and especially the Twelfth Step–"We tried to carry the message to alcoholics"–seems to endorse the kind of proselytizing and recruitment which AA's official line (contradictorily) prohibits, and gives moral authority to the larger movement's expansion and institutionalization. This sense of moral, evangelical proselytizing was, most definitely, present in the AA meetings I attended, as was the clear pressure–overt and implicit–to drop other friends and associations and spend all your time with members. (It is ironic of course, and indicative of the kind of sexism which informs classic AA doctrine, that wives of alcoholics are admonished never to leave their husbands, while members themselves are admonished to abandon unrepentant partners completely if they refuse to enter recovery.)

To Galanter, AA's "benign" social role, a feature which, he believes, separates it from socially dangerous cults, is based on the fact that it "does not impinge upon the values of the broader society" since "its ideology is compatible with mainstream attitudes and often gets support and encouragement from nonmembers" (p. 176). This is true enough. The observation is only comforting, however, if one is not concerned about social transformation or even reform. For a person so concerned, AA's fit with "mainstream attitudes" raises problems.

Since one may never "cross talk" or raise issues not related to one's addiction, or even talk about the addiction itself in terms other than the Steps prescribe, one is forced, in the interest of one's progress out of addition, to internalize and adopt the implied "mainstream attitudes" fostered by the program. I often observed the subtle effects of this kind of intellectual constraint. The imposition of religious doctrine of a very conservative kind is the most obvious example. It is common for members to begin shares with statements which include phrases like "I'm Sam and I humbly thank my Higher Power that I'm a recovering alcoholic" and offer thanks to one's "Higher Power for His boundless strength and love." Such statements are clearly informed by and saturated with patriarchal Christian sentiment, although that fact is never acknowledged. The actual language of the Third Step, we "Made a decision to turn our will and our lives over to the care of God *as we understood Him*" is meant, as many insisted to me, to take care of this problem since it allows a member to substitute whatever *idea* of a Higher Power she prefers. (I have actually heard about a woman who decided to think of her Higher Power as Marx!) But the language of the Step, the narrowly ritualistic way in which it is invoked and repeated continuously throughout meetings, and the injunction against "cross talk" within meetings, tend, nonetheless, to reinforce the most traditional reading and to make it difficult for those with other versions to easily fit them into the proceedings. What is said out loud, over and over again, in the meetings so strongly reinforces the traditional, patriarchal Christian doctrine and implicitly denies–through the restrictions on speech enforced by the "cross talk" rule–the existence of alternatives that I found it hard, sitting in these meetings, to imagine how one might in fact substitute a concept with radically, or even mildly, different implications without great difficulty.

The political ramifications of this tendency to subtly impose a totalizing ideology on members are easy to see. A lone lesbian in my AA group, for example, who stayed because, she told me, it was "such a good meeting" tended to speak very little and when she did speak, her shares were rarely picked up on, especially when they included mention of "my lover" (as opposed to "boyfriend" or "husband"). Very often, her alcohol problems were related to her sexual orientation. Once, for example, she confessed to me that she was terrified of "relapsing" when her parents, to whom she was not "out," visited. In the meeting proper, however, she merely stated that she was "under stress" and "really working my first three steps like crazy" so as not to succumb to temptation. For this she was offered praise and support. The subtext of this example–that she did not feel free to say much at all about her nonconventional sexual lifestyle but rather, felt compelled to invoke a traditional male deity's help with a generalized "stress"–speaks volumes about the implicit ideology of these meetings, although what it says is never stated or acknowledged within the meetings themselves. As in any kind of hegemonic discourse or ritual, the absence of apparent ideology is itself the most powerful kind of ideology, since it can never be acknowledged or questioned. The political implications of this kind of thinking, this kind of process, are apparent and depressing. This woman, in managing her alcohol problem, had come to endorse an ideology which seemed to condemn her very identity, and to automatically deny, rather than defend, the legitimacy of her sexual orientation and lifestyle.

This reactionary tendency of AA is further bolstered by its tendency to exclude contact with all "outsiders" who may indeed have other ideas about what has caused a member's suffering and what might be done to assuage it. One of the characteristics of cults described by Arthur Deikman (1990) is a tendency to "devalue outsiders" and assume "an attitude of righteousness" about one's own customs and beliefs. In AA and (to a lesser extent) other recovery groups, this takes the form of labeling as "in denial" those who question basic tenets. David Forbes, for example, in a fairly sympathetic analysis by a former participant, reports on his discomfort at "the conformist norm of the language" and the prohibition against the kind of "political and theoretical categories and constructs" he normally used to speak about his life, "especially class and patriarchy." And while he insists that such concerns could be discussed in the socializing time that generally follows meetings, he admits that he "did not find many people who were interested in doing so" (Forbes 1994, p. 244). Nor did I. I did indeed hear a member, a young man, express discomfort about this language in a social gathering after a meeting. He was told by an "old-timer" that he would "get over" his "denial" when he had successfully managed to "do the First Step" and make contact with his own Higher Power. The young man never broached the subject again to my knowledge, but he soon stopped attending meetings.

Those who find the groups most helpful, on the other hand, tend to incorporate the religious and social underpinnings of the movement more and more automatically, internalizing them as unquestioned truths. I heard so many, many people in so many, many groups make statements like this one by a young woman in an OA meeting: "Now that I've learned to trust my Higher Power, I realize that there is joy everywhere and a purpose to everything. Even when I pass by the homeless people who used to make me feel so sad and upset with this society I can feel peace and trust in God's love. There is glory everywhere, I now realize." In fact, so powerful is the rhetoric of recovery and its internal logic that one soon finds oneself unthinkingly mimicking its language and thought, implicitly reinterpreting social issues in quasi-religious terms as one learns to talk the talk of addiction and redemption.

Members of groups devoted to nonchemical forms of addiction are less likely to feel the need to limit their social circles exclusively to other fellowship members because their need to alter behavior radically is generally far less intense and central to their very survival. The cultlike aspects of classic AA, and the repressive, antipolitical and antisocial features of its discourse, are therefore far more pronounced and disturbing.

Nonetheless, it was AA—conventionally religious, socially isolating, and doctrinaire—that most impressed me in its ability to offer real, even lifesaving, help and support to those most seriously hurting and failing in this world, *precisely because of* its cultlike rigidity and insistence upon ideologically limited and repressive ideas and terms and rituals. The men in AA were the very ones who, like Bill W. and Dr. Bob and their friends, were most adrift in the industrial and postindustrial world of work and family, those least capable of adjusting to its demands and accepting the rigors and repressions of its routines and structures. And because they had this place to come to, these fellows to call upon and count on, this world of apolitical, anti-intellectual isolation, dogma, ritual, and religious fanaticism, they were indeed able to make it, one more day at a time. The number of members who attested, publicly and privately, to the lifesaving effects of meetings was impressive. So was the animosity, fueled by fear, I sometimes thought, with which my skeptical reaction to these claims was generally met. "If you had seen me three years ago," or whatever, "you'd understand what AA has done for me," was a common, passionate sentiment expressed by those with whom I tried to debate the program intellectually. "I could never make it without the meetings and my Higher Power," as one man told me. "I'd be back on the streets in a minute. Trust me, I've tried it many times."

This survival, we have to accept, is the benefit of AA, but the cost, intellectually and politically, of this salvation is exorbitant. People in these traditional AA groups do indeed reject their entire previous lives and values and views of reality. They adopt a new identity and community and family in which no extraneous ideas or thoughts or activities are allowed to distract them from a single goal: staying sober. In the looser, more feminized groups, such cultlike rigidity is not necessary, and the discourse and attitude of these meetings is far more politically contradictory, more progressively inflected with feminist values. But what is gained in ideology is lost in programmatic efficacy, as we shall see.

THE FEMINIZATION OF RECOVERY

Before moving to the female-dominated groups, I want to share with you (the language is catching) a most moving and telling moment in my research which occurred at a Sex Addicts Anonymous (SA) meeting. This meeting was the one in which I learned the most about the relationship between the contemporary recovery movement and feminism. Here I met twelve men (and a single, almost always silent woman) in the grip of a compulsion to act out sexually and, in some cases, to do deeds and crimes against women and children, the thoughts of which have struck fear in my heart all my life. And I must confess that I have never felt safer with any group of men in my life; nor have I ever felt such compassion for my "enemy."

These men were, like those in AA, mostly working class and straight. One was actually homeless and so desperate to "recover" from whatever his sexual crime was (they often didn't specify) that he gave up the chance of a job-training program out of town to attend his meeting. These men's stories were similar to those of the male drunks I heard in AA. They had lost jobs, wives, children, been in jail, been beaten and worse in pursuit of their obsessive sexual predations.

And they were determined to stay "sexually sober" with a passion so deep I felt privileged to witness it. Here were men who had hit bottom as surely as any chemically dependent person because of the publicly unsanctioned nature of their habits. Unlike "love" or food addicts, for example, they usually could not act out their compulsions in privacy and safety. Whether they were exhibitionists, voyeurs, compulsive seekers of commercial sex, or rapists and molesters, they were indeed in danger from the law and therefore likely to lose their material base of security and their license to citizenship itself if their behavior continued. So they were scared straight, as the saying goes.

What made these men different from the drunks, however, was that they could not discuss their addictions without discussing their relationships with women and children and their own sex and gender experiences as children. And so, amazingly, I heard these men weep, saw them cling to each other and hold each other up, as they "confessed" their mistreatment of women and the effects it had had on their own lives, as spouses, workers, and fathers. "Hey," said one construction worker, "I figure we're all in this world together, men and women, and we've got to learn to be good to each other. I never realized that before."

A surprising number of these men (four) admitted (in my presence) to being sexually abused by neighbors, priests, and family members as children. No doubt, AA is filled with men who have been sexually abused as children, but you will not hear about it there. In the SA meeting, one man, a bartender, told of his fear that his girlfriend, a former stripper now dancing in a Broadway chorus line, would leave him because she was becoming more successful than he, and how his fear of abandonment led him to abuse other women. One, a traveling salesman who reminded me of Willy Loman, told of feeling lonely and angry during prolonged business trips to dumpy hotels in dumpy little towns. "My worst nightmare," he said, "is to find myself acting out in some Holiday Inn in Altoona," to which is friends in the meeting responded with phone numbers and schedules of when they could all be reached.

The "acting out" of this salesman was very much like the self-destructive drinking of the men in my AA group. Like the hard-core drunks, this man was miserable in his role as a low-level, alienated industrial wage earner. And like them, he found release in behavior which momentarily took him out of himself and offered a kind of false pleasure or power for which he ultimately suffered and potentially could have landed in jail or dead.

But now, it was clear, his response to his work life was also affecting his relations to women and his domestic life (he was divorced and lonely). Nor could this aspect of his problem be ignored, as it was in Bill W.'s day and is still in classic AA. For when he spoke at greater length about his actual form of "addiction," he, like the construction worker and the bartender and the victims of child sex abuse, was forced to confront a set of feelings and attitudes toward women (and sometimes children) which could not be dealt with as simply and apolitically as AA deals with alcoholism, because gender relations could not be ignored. Of course, the ultimate messages of SA dogma are, like AA's, couched in terms of "Higher Powers" and addictive disorders over which one has no control, except through fellowship and God's grace. Nonetheless, it is the unmistakable play of feminist and New Left ideas and attitudes about how one behaves as a man, a lover, a husband, a father—ideas and attitudes which strongly challenge traditional patriarchal norms and which in AA go unquestioned, or at least unmentioned—which makes SA so much more intriguingly contradictory, and even more inspiring, than AA.

In my view, sexual and emotional compulsions are not technically addictions. Whether they are or not is not an issue the addiction industry and the recovery movement professionals care to debate, since they are in the business of recruiting as many souls to their cause as possible. But if the recovery movement is guilty of definitional jumbling, the confusion has a positive side-effect: the cross-fertilization of gender and chemical problems and issues which makes it more and more likely, today, that male addicts of the hard-core variety will find themselves opening up to the awareness of the deeper social and even political meanings of their self-destructive and hostile actions, as I saw the men in the SA meeting do.

To the extent that I heard and saw men in groups like Codependents Anonymous (CODA) and Overeaters Anonymous (OA), they, like most of the men in SA, had come to these groups through initial experiences with chemical dependencies. In the old days, of course (and in the classic, old-fashioned AA meetings which have not incorporated broader ideological elements and discourse, still), sexual and other emotional problems would never have come up or, certainly, not have been linked to the initial presenting problem of substance abuse. That so many men are now coming to see, upon ending chemical abuse, that their problems go deeper, that in fact their primary, causative problems are emotional and relational, not chemical, is a tribute to feminism. Feminists have made it impossible first, to ignore or condone sexual crimes quite so readily as once was the case; and second, to ignore the demands and values of feminists in thinking about these crimes. It is not enough any more simply to lock up Jack the Ripper and call him evil. We must now, increasingly, analyze his crimes in terms of ideas about gender justice and human equality and dignity and compassion, ideas which feminism has brought to the table where sex crimes are now negotiated. True, in the end, the word "addiction" wins out over the more politically useful "sexism." But feminist assumptions and values are decidedly in the mix, nonetheless, as they were not before.

FOOD, LOVE, AND OTHER NEW "FEMININE" ADDICTIONS

For me it is an irony that my most positive experiences of the recovery movement came from the groups peopled by men of a kind I, in my own (relatively privileged) life as an independent middle-class feminist, generally manage to avoid. I was called "Little Lady" and "Honey" more times in AA and SA meetings than in my entire previous life, I think, and I heard of fantasies and actual deeds that made my flesh crawl and my heartbeat quicken. Yet, especially in SA, I felt a profound "fellowship" with these men because they were so determined to become more like I would like men to be – even the mean drunks – even if that only meant a conscious, committed end to violent behavior. And I felt absolutely safe with these men, in spite of the grossly threatening fantasies and impulses they admitted to, because their sense of community, of commitment to keeping themselves and each other from acting out these fantasies, was tangible.

When I began attending OA and CODA – the "girl groups," as I privately thought of them – much of that respect and "fellowship" faded. The marked difference between most of what I saw and heard in OA and CODA and what I felt about AA and SA was dramatic. It was true, of course, that the subject matter itself, and the sensibilities of most members, were far closer to consciousness-raising groups I remembered from the 1960s than anything I heard in AA or SA. Feminist assumptions and attitudes, while never labeled as such, were very much "in the air" in these meetings of mostly women. The idea that relationships within marriage, and child-care responsibilities, should be shared and egalitarian was generally assumed as given. So were certain kinds of attitudes about women in the work place and in dating situations, in which, by and large, women's rights and the appropriateness of female aggressiveness were taken for granted. Such assumptions were hardly apparent among the AA members I met. But the sense of purpose and focus, of seriousness of endeavor and commitment to change, were, with only some exceptions, largely missing in these more feminist-influenced groups, for reasons which are important in understanding the ultimate role of recovery as a social movement, rather than as a strict form of therapy. Indeed, the further I got from physical addiction and the fear of material obliteration, the less the groups seemed to make any sense at all as agents of personal transformation and the more they came to resemble gab sessions of a much looser, if still somehow coherent, kind.

Gradually, I came to see that unlike AA and SA, groups such as OA were not primarily or necessarily agents of direct behavioral change at all, at least not for the most part, for most participants on most days. In fact, it took me a long time to figure out just what the meaning and purpose of these meetings were for participants, since the disciplined commitment to changing behavior was by no means what most members chose to talk about. Instead, problems at work and in relationships and families were the meat of the meetings. "I had a really bad week," someone might begin, and then go on to detail conflicts with bosses and coworkers. Women often told of discipline problems with children and endless hassles with in-laws and even servants. Progress reports were made by some–although hardly most–members at most OA meetings, but much less often if at all at CODA meetings. And there was much less attention paid to these reports in both groups, as though an emphasis upon such accounts might put too much pressure on other members, whose interests and needs, when they spoke, were far afield from such "bean counting" concerns.

But finally, after a few months of visiting both groups, as well as an Adult Children of Alcoholics (ACOA) group which was in many ways different from any of the other groups, I began to see what was happening "in these rooms," as members put it, what exactly they offered that was worth coming back for week after week. As I listened to the endlessly repeated ideas and words and phrases, I saw that the meetings served to ground people in new beliefs and attitudes, and provide a new identity system–personal and social–to replace the ones that no longer work.

The meetings offered "reasons" for why one suffered so in families and other close relationships; and these reasons–often based on feminist assumptions—made more sense, and were more egalitarian and humane, than the traditional, authoritarian religious and patriarchal dogma most of us were raised on. Fathers were seen to be "on power trips" because of "low self-esteem," for example, and a partner's indifference was likely to be ascribed to "fear of intimacy" or "commitment phobia," concepts which focused attention on psychological and emotional difficulties rather than on moral precepts. The language and its ideology came from a variety of sources. The revised 12 Steps adopted by the group often used such language and ideas. But members also brought in their own elaborations of the basic ideology culled from self-help books and therapy sessions—quotes from therapists, themselves steeped in the discourse, were very common—so that the general ideas and terms soon became part of a new member's lingua franca, circulating even more emphatically within—and presumably outside—the group habitually. To shore up these new lessons in life, the groups offered a litany of new labels and affirmations and sayings—much like what one gets in church or in families—to carry around and trade back and forth as a kind of cultural and social currency for buying entrance into what is clearly a new, semi-institutional social world. "Be sure he's 'safe' before you invite him up," women were cautioned. Or, to men with "performance anxiety," "Hey, man, you don't have to be perfect or omnipotent. It's okay to fail and to need help."

What is troubling to me is that the new language is devoid of the kind of political inferences which colored the feminist and New Left ideas from which it ultimately sprung. "Dysfunctional" replaces "patriarchal"; "toxic" replaces "oppressive"; and so on. And all the ways feminists have taught the world to judge sexist acts and thoughts are here incorporated in ways which take out the political sting and demand for change, and replace them with ideas about "addiction" and "disease" and "giving oneself up to a Higher Power" who will make things right if we only believe. Thus, male sexual offenses—from sexist verbal insults to incestuous assaults—are interpreted as acts of a "diseased" person, or a person in "denial," while the victim herself is seen as a "wounded inner child" or an "addicted codependent" rather than as an object of political oppression or crime who has a right to demand political redress and justice, in the form of changes in institutions and laws.

Nonetheless, there is no question that the new language and its ways of altering our views of how parents should treat children, how men should treat women, how bosses should treat employees, are infinitely more democratic and humane and justice-serving than the religious and legal and patriarchal ones they replace. And most important, the "feeling" groups, especially ACOA, provide a space in which the most hidden, forbidden unspeakable crimes and sorrows of our common world and experience can be spoken, shared, and so made officially "true" and "real," if only for brief moments, among strangers. Indeed, my experience in ACOA (at least in the group I attended regularly; some ACOA groups were far less serious) was as moving and enlightening as my visits to SA, and as reminiscent of the countercultural, feminist sixties—if for different reasons.

ACOA is the only group I visited in which no response was ever expected of anyone. At times, the silence was so nerve-wracking that I felt all eyes upon me, the ever silent presence, to finally speak. When I began to explain myself, however, I was quickly hushed by the leader, who assured me no explanation or response whatever was required of me no matter how long I attended meetings. The utter relief of having nothing whatever expected of one, of having permission to sink totally into oneself, oblivious to social reality, was a unique feeling even for me. (Only visits to my massage therapist and, once, being marooned in Disney World for several days, have offered such complete permission to escape the world.)

The members of my home group were a bizarre lot behaviorally, although, by appearance, they were conventional and respectable. A sixty-ish man in expensive business attire came each day to rant about his arguments with his invalid father, with whom he still lived. One day the issue was shoveling the walk (a task, it soon became clear, which was done by the building staff, and which, in any event, was a minor problem on that particular day). Nonetheless, the intensity of the rage, the power struggle between these two, father and son, whatever the current issues, was so real that the threat of physical violence was obvious.

Other members of this group—there were about ten women and four men—were apparently even more out of control, unable to handle the emotionally charged, unresolved feelings of childhood, for reasons that were sometimes explained—incest and physical torture—and sometimes hard to figure out at all. A young man who came each day with a bag full of stuffed animals would inevitably set them up in front of him, close his eyes, and begin a rambling, inchoate chant of pain, rage, and humiliation concerning food, obesity, and physical revulsion toward his sexually abusive father. "Kale, spinach, a leaf of lettuce, food in, food out, health," he would mutter. And then, in raised voice, "Ugly, fat, I hate you, scum, scum scum!!! . . ." and on and on. Unlike other fellowships, this one had no time limits on shares, and this young man generally went on for many minutes. No one responded to such utterances. If they had, he would have been distressed, I suspect. The next speaker simply began her/his own confession.

The group included a young woman raised in a cult. Her descriptions of her relationships with her mother and with the male cult leader (who, among other things, had sexually abused all the female children), and later, with peers, did not sound nearly as crazy as what I heard from many others, raised in "normal" families. She was in many ways (except for unfashionable, inappropriate dress) the most unremarkable and socially agreeable member. I could not help but feel, listening to her, that a case could be made for the argument that we are all brought up in "cults" of one kind or another; that is the real meaning of the theory that most families are "dysfunctional." For nothing she said about the rules of the cult could not plausibly have been said about many apparently "normal" families—certainly my own—in which rules and traditions might seem somewhat odd to outsiders but were taken for granted by the members and simply kept from friends and associates.

Her problem, what brought her to ACOA, was her inability to "fit in" anywhere or establish a stable relationship with a man. (She was grappling with the possibility that she was a lesbian.) She automatically assumed an oppositional attitude toward every group belief, in every group she entered, and her need to question everything she heard was so aggressive as to be alienating and frightening to others.

But I have known many people like this woman whose upbringings have been so oppressive, so thwarting of independent thought and action as to produce natural "rebels." Some have become political activists of the most heroic kind; others have become obnoxious creeps. And the differences sometimes have depended upon the historic and political age in which they were born. (Jerry Rubin's childishly rebellious injunction to "kill your parents," after all, was taken as acceptable, if metaphoric, social thought for a generation who did not "trust anyone over thirty" for sound political reasons.)

This young woman, of whom I grew fond, could easily have fit into the radical, iconoclastic culture of early feminism (which attracted many social misfits after all). But she had instead, in 1993, drifted into the recovery movement and, in ACOA, finally found a place where she could relax, where she could feel "at home" knowing she would not, ultimately, frighten and alienate others. Here, as in radical consciousness-raising groups, everyone understood how oppressive and unfair had been her "family" relations, and how healthy her need to rebel, to find a new "family" and a new set of ideas about relationship and selfhood. And everyone understood the language she used to describe her feelings—"Ghan's (the cult leader's) presence was so toxic," she would often say; "And there were no boundaries at all in that house, which is why I have such serious boundary issues now." All the women in the room (the majority of members) understood about "toxic" male family heads who do not respect or allow for personal "boundaries," but since the language was purely interpersonal, based on notions of toxicity and disease, or spirituality, there were no political overtones, and, as a result, no talk of changing things. Instead, the woman gradually came to identify more and more with the community and language of recovery and–as I was leaving the group–began training to be a substance abuse counselor in a treatment center.

Most members simply came in, yelled, whimpered, or blankly recited their deepest, most publicly controlled, secret anguish, usually in terms learned in recovery literature and meetings, inflected, subtly, with gender politics, and then left. A young woman, a successful advertising executive who had been put in the role of caretaker and her father and brothers because her mother was always "sick," could not resolve a dilemma she had over getting a dog. "I can't choose one without feeling guilty about rejecting the others," she said. "I'm such a rescuer; it's my main addiction." And so, each day, she went to the pet shop and stood paralyzed and in anguish until she finally was forced to leave.

A young man, handsome and stylish, was convinced that other men were laughing at him everywhere he went because he "wasn't really a man; didn't know how to be a man." (It came out, indirectly, in one meeting, that his father suspected him of being gay.) He had been going to men's movement meetings but the other men, so glib and sure of themselves, terrified him. He came to ACOA to try to work up the nerve to return to these meetings, to get some sense of "what a man is anyway; what people expect." Only here, he said, did he feel his "nothingness" could be safely exposed.

During my visits to this group, a nationally publicized trial was taking place in New York in which four high school athletes were accused of assaulting and raping a mentally retarded woman. One group member, a businesslike, very beautiful young woman who rarely spoke, suddenly blurted out her experiences of rape and incest as an adolescent and her identification with the retarded girl who had said, the day before, on the witness stand, that she had allowed herself to be abused because she "didn't want to make them feel bad." This testimony, which I too had read about that morning, caused the young ACOA woman to confess, at great length, her "really crazy" feelings about her own abuse and many other abusive experiences she has had since. "I know it's really crazy," she kept repeating, "but I feel exactly that way; and I'm not retarded; I was Phi Beta Kappa! But I can't say no to anyone. I just lie there . . ." And then she was back in her childhood bed reliving her acquiescence to unspeakable acts by her father, and then getting up, sitting through dinner, even reporting on her day at school at her father's insistence.

It was in ACOA, in the group I chose to visit regularly that I heard and observed the most startling, even frightening, utterances and behaviors. And it was in ACOA that I came to see, with amazement, the flip side of AA's more traditional contribution to social stability and order. For it was in ACOA that I observed people dangerously close to the emotional edge–as AA and SA members are close to the physical edge–find the emotional glue, day after day, to stick themselves together and go back out into the world and function.

Here I heard rambling nonsensical wails of pain and confusion from conservatively and expensively dressed people who, very often, would abruptly stop talking, pick up their briefcases and return to their "straight" lives as responsible family and work-force members. And here I saw people nod in profound understanding and empathy at things which, if uttered or done on the streets, or in polite company, might lead to arrest or institutionalization.

ACOA is the fellowship for those whose major problems are most noticeably and dramatically with their families of origin. Its issues run deep, emotionally and in personal history. It is the one fellowship to which virtually everyone who has learned the recovery dogma–based as it is on a critique of the patriarchal family as "dysfunctional"–"belongs."

In my experience, ACOA was the safest place to bring serious disturbances and shame-based feelings, and so it attracted the most desperate emotional sufferers, the ones whose childhood pains were so great, so unresolved, so hyper-present in their conscious daily life as to render them dangerously close to the edge. Incest, rape, paternal bullying and brutality and authoritarianism were the stuff of these recoverers' lives. Indeed, it was my sense that many people I met in these groups would not be functioning in the terrifying outside world into which they tried so valiantly to fit if not for ACOA. Day after day, they came to their meeting, a lunchtime meeting in a plush church in upscale midtown Manhattan, to spend an hour howling, crying, rambling, or sitting silently, eyes closed, in apparent oblivion to the voices of others, and so, apparently, find the strength to return to "normalcy."

What I heard in this group was politically loaded and explosive, had its implications been explored. Indeed, the sheer horror of what I heard here, the foul deeds and the passionate, inchoate responses from those so seriously damaged by it, reached a level of political atrocity, when heard and re-heard, week after week that, had it been couched in activist language, would have demanded radical action of a kind today's world does not make easy to consider.

Had any of these people been a part of the sixties social movements, they would surely have learned to think and talk about their family troubles in terms of sexism and patriarchy and gender oppression; of compulsory het-erosexism, perhaps, as an outgrowth of the patriarchal family norms and values. The first woman might have joined a consciousness-raising group and learned to speak up for herself and demand that her male family mem-bers take care of themselves. The second might have joined a feminist group working to counsel abuse victims and change the laws and structures that permit and condone rape and incest and domestic violence. The man might have encountered a men's rap group, in which—at least back then—patriar-chy and heterosexism would have been condemned and the need to join women in the struggle to end them understood.

But here, in this cloistered, paneled room, no such liberating thoughts or ideas were uttered. Instead, there was recognition of how damaged each was by dysfunctional and toxic families and permission to grieve and heal and recover from the diseases and wounds which now permanently scarred and crippled them. Nothing more, if that much, was ever suggested. Indeed, in many cases, obviously, there was not much more that could have been said or done for these people, so seriously damaged and debilitated were they, psychically and emotionally.

Still, no matter how extreme the utterance and the atrocity—and this is important—each and every story, each and every unspeakable feeling and thought, rang true to me and felt weirdly familiar. After all, the secret of the recovery movement's success is that unhappy American families—from the most criminally mad and bizarre to the most "normally" coercive and op-pressive—are, in many ways, alike. No matter how extreme or minor the gen-der/power wounds we carry, on some core level they feel and sound the same. And that's because, as I am arguing, all the family wounds we carry, from the most mild to the most odious, have been suffered in the family's service to the needs of an industrial society out of control and increasingly dependent upon the men and women who head families to conform to its ever more rigorous and stressful demands.

Men act out their humiliations and alienations in the privacy of their homes because they can't safely do so at work or in the streets. (If they can't confine themselves so easily to home, of course, they end up as candidates for AA and SA and Narcotics Anonymous and Gamblers Anonymous.) Women do their best to support and smooth over this socially enforced and condoned male madness because their lives depend upon it. And children grow up mimicking and reacting to these insanities so that they too can survive and, hopefully, prosper in whatever ways they see as viable options.

In the sixties the politics of this kind of family "dysfunction" was better understood and discussed. The work of R. D. Laing[3] on schizophrenia and family dysfunction was very popular among radicals. It was used to bolster the counterculture/left-feminist analysis of how the family works to oppress its members by insisting that secret-telling and truth-telling about systemic madness was itself "mad" so that any member who did indeed reveal, and even utter, the secrets, was deemed "crazy." He argued that "madness" is itself a socially constructed concept used by the powerful to render invisible and impotent the dangerous truths told by those who cannot conform to the oppressive norms of modern family life. When one family member "tells" about the evil and madness within (as incest survivors know well) the entire system breaks down after all. And so, Laing observed, those who cannot keep silent about their experiences at home are institutionalized, and their horror stories are imprisoned in the journals and terms of the psychiatric profession, where their truths are deemed crazy and ignored.

In ACOA, I saw a nineties version of this analysis, stripped of Laing's political context. For Laing, utopian radical that he was, madness, as an escape from family and social oppression, made sense; in some of his writings, he even argued that it was heroic. He hoped that we could hear and learn from the mad, and find ways to change our institutions so that their experiences would not be repeated. It was a tall order which we no longer have the heart or faith, politically, to undertake. We have gotten past such romantic, even idealistic beliefs in the radical, transformative truths and uses of madness.

Today when the culture shocks of the 1960s have so shaken our common social foundations, such public utterances of "family secrets" are perhaps more truly dangerous. When so many people are actually going mad around us and acting out in ways so destructive and self-destructive as to make everyone feel unsafe, we are far less comfortable with the truths of the mad, far less willing to learn from them politically, and far more concerned with hiding and containing them, lest the whole world begin babbling and shouting at random. The recovery movement provides a space for such utterances which does in fact keep them hidden and contained. But it is more concerned with containing than liberating these people. It can only allow the truths and terrors of those most damaged among us to be heard in the repressive language of addiction, disease, and spiritual salvation, for anything more politically descriptive would seriously call into question too many hallowed "truths" of conventional life.

Linda Alcoff and Laura Gray (1993) have written insightfully of the dynamics of the incest survivors' movement in which, as in ACOA, the unspeakable truths of family life are allowed to be spoken and named as crimes. In the meetings they participated in, as survivors, they found that "survivor discourse is closer to the discourse of the mad than the repressed" and, as such, "in direct confrontation with dominant discourse" not over "the determination of truth" but over "the determination of the statable." Reports of sexual abuse, they remind us, have traditionally been met with charges of "delusion, hysteria, madness." But in these groups, as in ACOA, such intolerable socially dangerous truths are uttered, incoherently, wildly, but truly.

Since such truths, Gray and Alcoff argue, are normally censored by social rules of behavior and speech, they are "potentially transgressive" in their power to "disrupt the maintenance and reproduction of dominant discourses." But the survivor groups they describe—which address incest as a crime against children rather than as a manifestation of "disease" or "addiction"—are different from ACOA in one important way: they do not use the language of recovery or 12 Steps in processing the raw material they allow to surface. ACOA, in using this terminology, becomes a more contradictory structure, one which—like the TV talk shows about survival which Alcoff and Gray also describe (pp. 268–69)—works to contain and redirect the emotional distress caused by abuse into "nonthreatening outlets," thus functioning as a subtle form of social control, rather than political liberation.

ANOTHER SIDE OF FAMILY DYSFUNCTION

To go from my ACOA group to my regular CODA group was sometimes like going from Dostoevesky to *The Three Stooges*.[4] Where ACOA attracts those closest to the edge, CODA, which addresses current relationship problems, can attract virtually anyone who wants to "belong" to a new kind of community in which pathological relations and emotions are acknowledged as near-universal, named, and denounced.

There are CODA groups, I am told, in which members are seriously working to free themselves from oppressive partnerships and in which support in doing that is seriously given and effectively used. But while I have read and heard about them, I did not find any in my travels to New York area meetings. What I did find was some variation, in any number of meetings, on what occurred at the group I visited regularly, in an academic, middle-class Manhattan neighborhood.

What I first noted about CODA was that its literature was far lengthier than any I had seen so far, and in it the classic 12 Steps were so overhauled as to be sometimes unrecognizable. For the classic Tenth Step, for example– "We continued to take personal inventory and when we were wrong promptly admitted it"–CODA provides a very long supplementary analysis and set of behavioral guidelines which most of the hard-core drunks I met in AA would find ludicrous. CODA's version of the personal inventory employs a variety of therapeutic/self-help truisms, mostly geared to encouraging one to "take care of oneself" as a way of ending one's "addiction" to others. Many of these lengthy passages sound like reprints from fashion magazine self-improvement articles. Members are told to make "Asset Columns," for example, in which one "jots down" each time one "sets some time aside for [oneself] just to have fun . . ." as a way of recording one's progress toward recovery. The "one day at a time" dictum used to guide AA members to commit themselves each day to abstain from alcohol is here amended to mean one commits "to open my heart and mind, little by little, one day at a time" in order to find "my True Self, mend my relationships, and touch God." Every Step has been similarly revised at length to fit the CODA fellowship, whose most important task seems to be fostering self-love, although what that is and how it can be recognized and achieved is never clarified.

I heard many odd things in the CODA group I attended regularly. As in ACOA, there was little continuity from one speaker to the next. But unlike ACOA, there was no sense that *all* members were listening and empathizing with the speaker, creating a common sense of emotional space and sharing. On the contrary, it often seemed that many members were not paying much attention to the speaker at all, but rather (as in academic meetings quite often) waiting their own turn and planning their own "contributions." A woman in one meeting confessed to suicidal feelings, for example, after catching her husband in her own bed with another woman. She was promptly cut off after three minutes so that the next person could share her joy at defying her husband by buying herself a new outfit "Just for the pleasure of adornment, to please my little inner child." Had this been a consciousness-raising group, such a non sequitur would have been unthinkable. The first woman's problems, after all, were easily addressed in terms of feminist analyses and actions. The second's would have made no sense at all at a political meeting.

But at least these two examples seem to have something to do with solving, or at least talking about, a problem. Some shares went very far afield from any "problem" at all, much less the problem of "codependency." One woman, to cite an intriguing, but characteristic example, chose to tell everyone about a party she and her boyfriend—"my first nonsymbiotic relationship, seven whole weeks!"—attended in honor of Abbie Hoffman's birthday, during which they "realized together" that the work of sixties' activists was important but inadequate; that what was needed now was the "revolution within."

Sometimes speakers would simply get up and shout "Me! me! me! I matter!" to group applause. Other times, long discourses on a member's current reading—usually New Age—were "shared" and others were expected, as most did, to take delight in the speaker's intellectual and spiritual development (I think). Once a man whose management job was in jeopardy related a story about his boss, the point of which was that doing business with people not "in recovery" was a dangerous thing, since most of the people out there are "control freaks in deep denial."

I came to see that problems and problem-solving were not the main point of this group. Analyzing the world in terms that rejected old ideas and values and authorized and reinforced newer, more democratic and humane ones, was. And those terms were often rephrasings—without political inflection and direction—of old feminist and Left ideas from the Sixties. "Denial" is a very safe way to talk about the sins of the capitalist world, when one is oneself trapped within it, dependent upon it. It demands only that we see the offender as a sufferer of a disease he may be convinced to enter "treatment" for. It does not demand that we see the entire enterprise of business as rooted in unhealthy, oppressive relationships and deeds, and work to reform it. Abbie Hoffman's "Smash the state" notions would not go over well here. But others of his ideas, about peace and love as abstractions, states of feeling, do very well indeed here, as long as no one suggests that they might imply more than mere feelings and words.

This kind of rephrasing of feminist and Left ideas in ways which remove the political, activist implications and focus only on good feelings and healthier ways of relating was, in one way or another, what CODA seemed mostly to be about. In a particularly substantive exchange, for example, a member announced that she "no longer felt safe and validated" in the group, to which others nodded supportively. Later, a speaker did return to this woman's "share" to advise her to "ask her inner child" what was scaring her and report back when she found out. She did indeed report back the next week. Her fears, it seems, were caused by the way a new member—male—talked about his old girlfriends. I agreed with her: the man was insensitive and condescending about women. His use of words like "chick" and constant interruptions of women were rude and crude. But while the group did indeed tackle the issue and criticize the man's "rudeness," no mention was ever made of sexism, and the women did not—as they would have in the New Left—band together in a "caucus" to draw up lists of rules and demands based on notions of power imbalances between men and women, in the group and elsewhere. It was all a matter of "two human beings" "honoring each other's uniqueness" and "meeting as two equal souls." People left feeling "heard" and validated," but agreeing to nothing beyond "feeling each other's pain and honoring it."

The sexual dynamics of this group were indeed more comfortable to me than what I experienced in AA and heard about in SA. What seemed to me the clear influence of feminist thinking about gender relations had created a more hospitable environment for women here than in the other groups. But in this group the good feelings this gave me were actually overpowered by my greater sense of annoyance at the whole group. These people were not after all rapists who had never heard of feminism. On the contrary, they were glib and easy with the language of sixties politics, as the Abbie Hoffman "share" indicated. But, as this example further indicates, they were people who were learning and teaching each other to do without the difficult, inconvenient political aspects of a discourse they were quite familiar with, in order to make their quest for "inner peace"—the "revolution within"—easier. The underlying feminist assumptions were there, of course. The very problem of the man's behavior would not have arisen otherwise (indeed did not arise in my AA group, although it would have been appropriate at times). But it was given a new name, based on new language from the recovery lexicon.

That is mostly what I learned from CODA—a new way to talk about old things. Old rules based on institutional power plays and privileges were out; newly self-conscious ways of "sharing" and "caring," of protecting and asserting oneself were in. Rote rules of gender and family life gave way to a kind of self-conscious, "It works for me; does it work for you?" process in which everyone's feelings and priorities were respected and approved, at least rhetorically, and people tried to live their lives in ways which brought self-realization and freedom from being, or making others, crazy.

There is no question that such intense concern with equal, free relations and processes is rooted in the kind of insights about emotional well-being and social ritual–about the "personal" being, if not "political"–for those raised within patriarchal orders, that comes from feminist process and values. You don't find it in AA, and you don't find it in *Father Knows Best.*

Also somewhat encouraging to me was the relative downplaying of Higher Power references and religious talk generally in CODA. But that, again, was because there was so little serious attention paid to how one might actually change one's life. CODA meetings were more like gab fests or kaffee klatsches for people to gripe about their private lives and get agreement and support. They reminded me of the kinds of conversations I would overhear and share in, as a young wife and mother, sitting with other mothers at playgrounds. In those days–before my awakening to feminism–divorce after all did not seem like an option for most women, and resignation to one's private misery seemed necessary. I often sensed that same implicit, almost cozy, resignation to a way of life which irked, but not enough to overthrow it, in CODA meetings. The ways of thinking about conflict and pain may have come from feminism, but the ultimate feeling about the purpose of such discussions was purely idle: "Can we talk?" "I'm so glad that's off my chest." "So what are you making for dinner?"

The women's movement demanded that members indeed consider changing their lives, personally and more broadly. It said "Let's do something about all this," and it checked back next week to see how things were progressing. But groups like CODA have no necessary connection to a program of change, measured and publicly announced each week. The idea is mostly to understand things differently, and while some people are indeed motivated to act and make healthy changes, scores are not kept, as they are in AA. This is perhaps understandable in times like these, when radical social change is clearly not on the immediate agenda. Nonetheless, to me at least, there is something depressing in the total absence of such concern, even in the abstract, in groups like these, which are filled with the very sorts of people who, at least theoretically, have the most concern for progressive causes. "I feel your pain, man," as President Clinton–a true baby boomer and the first to make the rhetoric of recovery pay off politically–might say. And that, it seems these days, is enough to put one on the side of the angels– when it is Newt Gingrich and Bob Dole and Pat Buchanan who represent the alternative. Except, of course, that Gingrich and Dole and Buchanan are indirectly helped by this effete, gabby kind of grouping. For in learning to use the language of disease and addiction and spiritualism—New Age or not—these ex-hippies and protestors are unknowingly buying into an agenda more conservative and repressive than they realize.

FOOD ADDICTION: WHERE FEELINGS AND SUBSTANCES MINGLE

Overeaters Anonymous (OA) represents the link between the "hard" and "soft" groups, the "male" and "female" groups, and so it offers a good picture of precisely how personal change gets separated from social change in recovery. I chose OA as the midpoint of my recovery travels because it seemed so clearly to mix the problems of actual physical dependency with the emotional. While I do not accept the testimony of those who swear that overeating feels the same as taking heroin and has the same aftereffects, I am aware, certainly, that there are measurable changes that can be seen when one changes one's eating habits and there are specific actions one can commit oneself to taking—which again can be reported upon and verified—to achieve these changes. OA's words and injunctions are therefore much more serious—or can be—than CODA's. And the contradictions it embodies—somewhere between AA and CODA—are fascinating and revealing.

The OA group I visited regularly (not of course the original Beginners' meeting) was considered a very "good" one. Perhaps thirty or more people attended regularly and had been doing so for several years, I was told. It met in a Greenwich Village church and attracted a fairly young, rather upscale group of professionals, many of them in media- and art-related fields. I visited many other OA groups in different neighborhoods, of course, to correct for the obvious cultural complexion of my "home group." But while I found great differences in appearance and sophistication, I did not find the substance of the meetings markedly different. My group, oddly enough, was made up of people who were mostly unusually attractive and fashionable. Only a few were obese and many were model- and actress-slim (indeed, many were models and actresses). They came with designer water bottles and duffle bags with workout clothes for their next self-improvement stop.

The women—these groups were invariably almost entirely female—in my group were so good-looking and well-dressed and well-groomed as to be intimidating. There were two or three males, themselves in what Naomi Wolf (1991) calls the display professions, and they too were unusually conscious of, even obsessed by, appearance.

Nonetheless, the meetings were not different in process, content, or group commitment to visible, measurable change, from those in which members were indeed obese, badly groomed, poorer and less educated. In no OA group did I experience a strong sense of group identity, intimacy, solidarity, and mutual support such as I found in the AA and SA groups, no matter the appearance or class make-up.

The regimen in my OA group was far looser than what I experienced in AA and SA (and the Beginner's group I mentioned earlier) but not for the same reasons as in ACOA. In CODA, OA, and other woman-dominated groups like Shoppers Anonymous and Love and Romance Addicts Anonymous, I received a rather cold and distant welcome, relatively speaking. No one rushed to sit near me or touch or reassure me as the "tough" male drunks had done. No one offered a phone number or help in adjusting to the routine. Unlike SA and AA, there was no felt pressure (to my relief) to "share" even after I became a regular. (There is no actual pressure in the male groups either of course; but there is a definite sense that someone is perhaps not serious, perhaps even an outsider with an ulterior motive, if one continuously stays silent. Certainly, I was the cause, several times, for reading the Tradition which prohibits public quoting of the proceedings or dealings with media, to my chagrin.) In fact, I had to approach people who gathered in tight groups, cocktail party–style, before and after meetings to ask such simple questions as how one got a sponsor. The AA rules make sponsorship an absolute obligation for members, and an important part of one's commitment to recovery. But in OA, CODA, and–for different reasons– ACOA, you are on your own, a situation Bill W. would find deplorable.

Once the meetings began, the shares were again surprising to me. There were rarely any announcements of a member's abstinence milestones; in fact very few speakers mentioned abstinence at all. Abstinence–I found out after asking a lot of questions–in OA means something different from AA. Of course one must not starve. Each person must devise her own program (most members keep this secret so even that much help was not provided from old-timers who were supposedly role models) and then stick to it. And while weight gain and loss are noted as signs of recovery, most members do not change their appearance at all.

I returned to my group months after finishing my research to check on this for sure. Everyone looked the same. The young woman who regularly gulped a chocolate croissant outside the building and rushed to the bathroom to purge before entering the meeting–a mere wraith of a child–was still doing so. The woman who complained about her lecherous boss, like the one who complained about her abusive husband, was still at it too, no thinner, no happier, but just as eager to share. In this respect, much of what I heard and saw here was similar to what I experienced in CODA.

There were however inspiring stories here, of a kind I never heard or saw in CODA, because here, at least, there were some people who did indeed "work a program" of controlled eating and spiritual "Steppism" and as a result changed their entire lives, as those in AA and SA do. I saw the transformations occur and was inspired by them here, as in AA and SA. But I was much more critical of the results and much less sanguine about the politics of the change. In SA, after all, feminist input radically humanized male sex criminals. In OA, however, such transformations often meant a devolution of progressive political awareness and concern.

One young woman, for example, had been an aspiring ballet dancer determined to make it in the cutthroat world of dance and married to a dance director who drove her relentlessly toward this goal. In working her program she came to see, however, that this world and its rewards, like her marriage, were unhealthy and repugnant to her and she changed her entire career and identity, divorcing her husband and choosing, in her new life, to use her skills to become a dance therapist, working with women with eating disorders. (It is interesting how many people who do well in recovery become therapists. This is one of the cultlike aspects of the movements, and one of the ways in which the recovery movement alters the economy. People find new professions in this movement, which is a godsend in many cases since the ups and downs of the economy—one of the causes of such widespread addictive abuse—leave so many jobless these days.)

In the progress of this young woman's change, which I followed eagerly, I heard much that was, like so much in my other groups, heartwarming to me as a feminist. Surely the world of media and the arts in New York is filled with the very social and moral flaws feminists and New Leftists were most concerned about. Competitive, cutthroat, individualistic, economically brutal and phony, it was easy to see—especially in relation to dance—how eating disorders and other addictions could arise as byproducts of so heartless and hierarchical a world. What this young woman learned about sexist appearance standards and materialist imperatives and how they contributed to her "addictions" was as powerful as what I saw in consciousness-raising, because, as in those days, I saw someone actually change her life for the better after "learning" a new set of beliefs and values.

Unfortunately, this rare success story scored a point for God not women. As this woman become more and more committed to her program, she also became more and more oblivious to social injustice and more and more smug in her certainty that her Higher Power was responsible for all her new joy in life while the miseries of others were also firmly in His hands and so, somehow, serving His purpose. This was the young woman who learned to disregard the homeless who had previously so bothered her because her new faith in God assured her that all–even their misery–was right with the world.

In every case in which I saw an OA member dramatically "recover," she became radically religious in ways I found disturbing. The women who worked their programs as effectively as the men in AA and SA became as religious and spiritual in their worldviews and activities as these men had become. Only this time much more was lost than was gained, in social terms. To a woman, their recovery meant that spirituality became their entire lives, altering partners, professions, social activities, and–not surprisingly–social and political beliefs in alarmingly reactionary ways.

What members mostly seemed to get from meetings, as in CODA, was a familiar setting in which to share personal ups and downs in work, love, and family. They did indeed know a language and a formula for making sense of what was happening to them. "Toxic" relations, hurt "inner children," false "boundaries" established through weight gain, "addictive" and "codependent" relationships and compulsions to achieve or compete, all were readily and regularly invoked to explain and generalize about the food problems of the group. And their binges, their urges to binge, their purges and fasts, were all explained in this depoliticized, indeed politically regressive, worldview.

TELLING VS. DOING: POLITICS FOR AN APOLITICAL WORLD

OA's interest, like all the "softer" groups, is in developing and retelling classic, mythic "stories" about our pain and learning to relate the common themes and narrative turns to newly coined ways of talking and thinking. One retells an old story of parental abuse. But this time it means something different because the words and feelings have shifted to fit a new paradigm.

This is not a bad, or even a small, thing. In their own way, these groups provide a service to many people in creating and distributing new myths and stories. They form a kind of moral community of souls united in their new, in some ways revolutionary understanding of what is wrong with old "family values." Everyone re-tells a family story which, in the fifties, would mean one thing–"Mom is right and you're weird"–and today means another. This is helpful. The old family norms, in which Dad abuses Mom, Mom abuses the kids, and the kids abuse each other, is oppressive and immoral. It no longer works anyway, since women have stopped agreeing to its terms in such large numbers. And so it's time to find a new set of ideas to live and think and judge by.

But in helping us to make the transition from a modern to a postmodern world, with the help of feminist ideas, the recovery movement also does a dangerous and depressing thing. By using spiritual and disease words, instead of political ones, it encourages us to disregard the economic and political roots and benefits of the system in which we live and distracts us from the possibility that the system itself is flawed.

Feminist therapists Claudia Bepko and Jo-Ann Krestan (1991) have written extensively about addiction and women and have noted, incisively, the way in which the language of the helping professions, now so influenced by recovery theory because of the therapeutic success of AA, tends to depoliticize and de-socialize women's suffering, redefining it in terms of illness rather than oppression. "The increasing tendency to refer to codependent behavior in the context of disease," they write, "speaks to a general social tendency to render behavior that is problematic or confusing a legitimate focus of medical treatment and control" (p. 52). The terms of such discourse, they insist, "are irresponsible and so vague as to be meaningless" (p. 53). They lead to kinds of treatment in which women are subtly coerced into "adjusting" to sexism by changing their own behavior, rather than changing sexist society.

At best, this is what can happen in groups like OA, and it is indeed a funny kind of "best," politically speaking. For whatever positive changes a woman may make in her own life—controlling her weight, perhaps—is, as Bepko and Krestan point out, at the expense of the kind of social changes that might strike at the root causes of the food problem to begin with.

I don't wish to oversimplify. Change, often profound change, does occur in these fellowships. And I am aware that such change does, indeed, often affect social life in subtle and diverse ways. If a woman, through AA, OA, or whatever, leaves an abusive marriage or even takes control of her eating habits there are any number of potentially "feminist" social effects that may ensue. Her children may acquire a politically relevant role model. She may embark on a work project that has some progressive affect, and so on.

Judith Stacey, in her study of "domestic upheaval in the late twentieth century," *Brave New Families* (1990), shows how AA, despite its reactionary theories, did in fact serve to "replace" the feminist activities of some women in the postfeminist 1970s and 1980s in ways which were at worst contradictory and at best useful in empowering them in certain ways. Her observations are in keeping with my own. In a postmodern world, she argues, women are fashioning various politically unorthodox ways of surviving and finding gratification in life within contradictory institutions and rituals. CODA and the other groups provide stopgap ways for women, feminists, to retain and use some of their previous ideas and values under circumstances which make more radical change difficult. In the process of doing this, however, much is ultimately lost, on a broader social and discursive level, which we cannot afford to give up.

Second wave feminism, I could not help but be reminded often in these meetings, had offered a vision of a new world order in which our suffering because of gender inequality and abuse, oppressive standards of beauty, social hypocrisy and double standards, would be done away with, as would any number of related troubles afflicting most men and boys. We didn't achieve that goal, of course at least not entirely. The recovery movement, to the extent that it has a collective, transformative vision, revives the belief in a new world order, not a new political or social order, but a new spiritual order. You can't see it or measure it. Members don't so much share a common set of problems whose solutions require a common set of life changes, as they share a common set of "feelings" and stories and slogans to interpret and do with as they will.

TALES OF ORDER AND MEANING IN WHICH NOTHING HAPPENS

Let me sum up by placing these descriptions of recovery groups and anecdotes of my experiences within them in a larger social perspective. Richard Sennett, in *The Fall of Public Man*,[5] describes many characteristics of modern life which, by elevating private life to public visibility, work to confuse feeling and action, identity and agency. He suggests that our very sense of community—and here the recovery movement is a perfect example—has shifted from an actual geographic place in which we live as physical neighbors to a more general, psychological state of identification with others on the basis of a much less tangible sense of identity, a shared "collective personality" which is not bound by physical place or action, but by shared "imagery" and "feeling." That "what matters is not what you've done but how you feel about it," says Sennett, is a mark of a world in which a pull toward intimacy as the ultimate, desired goal for well-being, replaces the pull toward action and deed as the mark of who one is in the world (pp. 223–63). "I am a codependent" or "an adult child" tells much about how you feel about yourself, think of yourself, but nothing about what you do in life.

This analysis of modernity fits nicely with my sense of the recovery movement as a new kind of community, a postmodern community, in which membership, indeed, is based on repeated affirmations of shared feelings and not on where one lives or how one contributes to that place. To be a feminist in the 1960s and 1970s was to "take responsibility for the world" as Simone de Beauvoir powerfully put it; to do what previously only men had done; to sally forth into the public arena and do battle with the powers that be to effect real change in the institutions responsible for our pain.

To be in recovery, in the emotional groups, is to do no such thing. There is no "world" to take responsibility for. There are no public battles to be waged in the interest of social change. To be sure there is an analysis of institutional injustice as a cause of pain. Families, and in some cases, professional workplaces, are seen to be "toxic" so one must resist and avoid them, must form new patterns, habits, and associations. Well and good. But even at its most efficacious the alterations are at best highly subjective and personal, "spiritual" rather than communal and social, or at best very individual and private.

Entering and immersing oneself in the world of recovery is an experience very different from merely reading or hearing about it through media or personal anecdote. In fact, one of the first things that struck me after visiting only five or six different meetings was the very great amount of variety, even idiosyncrasy, within a movement I had been led to believe by most commentators—whether harsh critics or devout advocates—was homogeneous and uniform in all its manifestations.[6] In spite of all the differences with the recovery culture, I came gradually to feel as I entered each new space, or returned to the several I eventually focused on as my core sources, that I was part of an essentially coherent network of social groupings, unified around a distinct way of thinking and relating, all of which were based on the common stories and storytelling practices of the groups. Even in New York City, an often threatening, culturally diverse, urban sprawl, marked by its dramatic contrasts, from block to block, of extreme wealth and poverty, cultivation and brutality, the recovery network—an invisible plane hovering somewhere between the traditional dualities of "private" and "public," "personal" and "political"—seems to form a web of cohesive social interactions informed by a common, easily recognized set of beliefs and rituals. Its activities are constant and ubiquitous, if invisible to the uninitiated. And these continuous, rotating sites of "re-education and re-socialization"—as I came to think of them—serve as a socially mediating force, helping the frazzled and frightened and frustrated to defuse their inner tensions and find new words and stories and habits by which to reenter the world that has so defeated them.

Nor does the movement, in its entirety, confine itself to physical geographic space. It exists in many other arenas. One can encounter recovery gurus and "meetings" in print, on TV, and even in cyberspace. There are now, for example, a burgeoning number of online newsgroups, mailing lists, and relay chat forums on the Internet in which recovery meetings and dialogues, among people living in different parts of the globe, take place continuously. The movement has thus become a kind of postmodern "space" constructed of "meeting rooms" all over the world to which one travels by air, by subway, by car, by books and television shows and computer modems, and then returns to one's physical "home" which is not one; to one's family, which is not one; to one's colleagues in work, who are not that either. One's true identity, one's true belief system, is rooted in a sense of space which is now psychological and spiritual; which requires only that one *say* one is a member, is an addict, is in recovery, for it to be so. And here, despite the benefits individuals may gain through the "re-socialization" offered in recovery, is where we run up against the movement's limitations. Thinking and feeling replace action as the mark of reality and truth here, as they do not in classic AA. This is the root of the social problem of recovery-as-social-religion. It *is* a religion, after all, and one without a social crusade, beyond the marginal one of keeping people up and functioning, one more day at a time.

Michel de Certeau (1984) has suggested that in the breakdown of traditional belief systems, "membership" in a political or religious organization becomes "more reverential than identifying . . . marked only by what is called a *voice*" (p. 177). "All that is required," he says, is that one *says* one belongs to such groups, one believes in the party line. One need not, as in traditional times, however, do anything; and so it is "inertia," not action, that marks the believer. "Our society has become a recited society," he says, "defined by *stories* . . . by *citations* of stories . . . and by the interminable *recitation* of stories (p. 186). Such, surely, is the brave new world of recovery, as it is experienced and practiced by members. In the next chapter, we will look at the sources for these stories, the best-selling "self-help" books–now numbering in the thousands upon thousands of titles, the millions upon millions of copies–which provide the informing terms and narratives upon which the foundations and building blocks of the recovery movement stand.

✦

CHAPTER FIVE

Women Who Read Too Much:
Getting a Life at Barnes & Noble

Where do the stories that hold together the widely, even eccentrically, diverse recovery movement come from? Where, indeed, do the slogans and catch phrases that now form so regular and familiar a part of our daily TV fare originate and take their fullest form and shape? Although the media hype about the recovery movement itself leads one to think otherwise, it is probably not the 12 Step groups. True, if one is a hard-core drunk, one will almost certainly—freely or by legal compulsion—come to recovery and its master narratives through the groups. But for most women "believers," those whose issues and pains are less acutely life-threatening or socially dangerous, the road to recovery will more than likely start more casually, in hearing about—from Oprah, or Geraldo, or Phil, or Sally, or a friend who heard it on one of these shows—and then reading one of the mass market self-help paperbacks which have been flooding the market since the mid-1980s.[1] It is true, of course, that America, in general, learns about recovery and its discourse from television talk shows and docudrama—the main outlets for the movement's ideas because of television's pervasiveness and power. But it is self-help books, whose authors are the star "experts" and consultants on these shows and whose ideas inform them, that provide the shows with their material. And these books, with their thorough sets of rules and plans for changing one's life, are where the truly troubled and suffering—as opposed to the more general audience of interested but casual TV viewers—are most likely to turn for personal aid. Self-help books are also the source of help to which TV itself most often sends those of its viewers who are most personally troubled and in need of immediate aid. TV is the major conduit of general ideology. But it is books that provide the "advanced classes" sought by would-be "practitioners" of recovery.

When I started writing this book, my local chain bookstore allotted four floor-to-ceiling, six-foot-wide shelves to Recovery and another six to Psychology and Self-Help. By the time I finished, the entire back of the store had become a mini-mart of self-help guides, workbooks, and pocket-size "Inspirational Day Books" offering a line a day, for the 365 days of the year, to specialized audiences suffering every possible sub-category of addictive disorder.

It seems to me highly unlikely that most of the newer self-help groups, especially those dominated by women, such as ACOA and CODA, would even exist without the impetus of certain blockbuster books—Melody Beattie's *Codependent No More* (1987), Robin Norwood's *Women Who Love Too Much* (1985), John Bradshaw's many books, especially Bradshaw's *The Family* (1988) and a few others. It is these books that laid the theoretical groundwork for the movement and that—with the help of media publicity—were the key agents of propaganda for the fledgling groups which formed, during the early and mid-1980s, in their wake. Indeed, these newer groups—based as they are on such concepts as "codependence," family "dysfunction," "adult children," and "addictive" relationships—could not possibly have developed, or become official branches of the Anonymous movement, without the books which originally coined these terms, many of which now figure in Anonymous group titles (the Women Who Love Too Much, WWLTM, network is the most obvious example). And it is still the books, far more than the often confusing and incoherent utterances heard at many meetings, that provide the "master narratives"—slightly altered versions of which are repeated in one book after another—that have come to be adopted by so many as theoretical/autobiographical blueprints by which to explain, communicate, and share our common experiences.

The newer, more female-oriented "fellowships" tend more and more to rely on subtly different terminology from that of classic AA and other more traditionally organized groups like SA. Words like "disease" and even "addiction" are still heard, of course, but other words—"dysfunctional," "codependent," "love hunger"—terms popularized in the self-help literature and referring to vaguer emotional states directly related to family and relationship patterns—are far more often invoked, since the actual issues, and what is supposed to be done about them, have shifted, more and more, to such matters in these groups. Even "addiction," when it is used, refers to a different kind of phenomenon than dependency on alcohol or drugs.

There is also a major difference between the way the older and newer groups seem to function. In classic AA–in those "good" groups which do in fact keep many members mostly sober at any rate–members learn the rules and dogma through meeting ritual. In OA, ACOA, and CODA, on the other hand, members usually come into the meetings having learned whatever they know of recovery theory from books sought in stores or borrowed from friends. Indeed, if one doesn't already know the intellectual ropes–and one can't get these details on TV–one is probably going to be in trouble since there is little effort these days to indoctrinate or incorporate new members in most meetings. Sponsors, even friendly, welcoming social conversation, are not typical in these often cliquish groups, nor can one even be sure that basic materials–the Xeroxed handouts and books for sale–will be available every time. In my experience, in many cases, the person responsible for bringing and selling official literature simply failed to show up or remember her charge, an oversight to which little attention was paid by regulars. If one does not know the ropes already–as I found out quickly–one is therefore generally left to scramble up the slope unassisted. And the ropes come from literature, not group process.[2]

My own interest in the subject of recovery, before I began this book–and before the era of talk TV–came from books. I would never have dreamed of attending a 12 Step meeting on my own, before my friend invited me. But I had been a casual reader of self-help books, about women's issues and problems, all my life. I began the self-help habit in my teen years, when psychological best-sellers were very popular among young women trying to figure out the mysteries of forbidden sex. We turned to Freudian-influenced guidebooks, which taught us to mistrust our own feelings and desires and fit ourselves to the needs of men. My friends and I devoured these books, puzzling and giggling over them far into the night at sleep-over parties.

Endless articles and advice columns in women's magazines helped me navigate the treacherous terrain of conventional marriage and motherhood, and then having gotten "cured" of this habit by reading Doris Lessing and Simone de Beauvoir and joining the women's movement, I continued to pore over other kinds of manuals more suited to my new "lifestyle." "Knowing" that sixties-era sex manuals like Alex Comfort's *The Joy of Sex: A Gourmet Guide to Love-Making* (1972) and Masters and Johnson's *Human Sexual Response* (1966) were ideologically loaded with masculinist assumptions didn't stop me from sneaking looks at them in bookstores, just to see what other people, in their nonfeminist versions of sexual liberation, were up to that I might be missing.

My interest in actually writing a book about recovery began with an article I wrote in 1994 for a national magazine reviewing a series of best-sellers about women's love addictions, including books by Beattie and Norwood. In that article lay the seeds of this book, the idea that love addiction books did, indeed, say many things I, as a feminist, knew to be true about the lingering problem of sexism in relationships, despite the gains of feminism. In all of these phases of self-help reading, I have found much to hold my interest and much—and here the findings of my research are in accord with my own experience—of use in sorting through personal issues too embarrassing or even "politically incorrect" to risk sharing with others.

The TV shows which have entered the recovery game in the last decades, of course, now play the strongest role in disseminating the news of recovery and purveying its language and thought. But female viewers who are taken with the message on a personal level but who do not want to attend group meetings are most likely to turn to books as ever available reminders and elaborators of the truths and comforting words which Oprah and Sally offer regularly but more fleetingly. Even women who try groups after watching TV may understandably turn to books when their experiences of meetings are less than agreeable.

Moreover, the very problems which make the groups so disappointing and unsatisfying to so many who try them out after reading about them do not exist in the books. It is in the nature of the book, as object, especially in an age of corporate, consumerist mass-production, to offer the kind of certainty only the most cultlike versions of the Anonymous programs offer. They are written and edited to be consistent, clear, and adapted to the needs of a clearly researched market segment seeking a very clearly understood set of analyses and guidelines for a specific set of problems. Unwelcome intruders cannot jump into the middle of one of these books and yell things like "Me! Me! Me!" to no purpose, as does indeed happen regularly in groups like CODA. An author cannot jump off the track of a story in order to tell a juicy tidbit about her mother that does not relate specifically to the matter at hand, the matter promised in the book's title, as also happens in female-dominated groups.

The highly rationalized and disciplined corporate workforce and publication process are not insignificant factors in explaining the greater reliability of books over meetings in delivering what they promise. Books have a clear market to reach and a bottom line to consider; groups have none of this disciplinary structure. This is why only the most desperate and committed group member can make the program work.

Moreover, books are more "addict-friendly" than most groups. A book cannot make the reader feel ignored, alienated, frightened, or self-conscious. Books speak only to the reader and are at her disposal and her whim. They aim to please and do not criticize. Also, the act of reading is itself a process which one has the ability to regulate in certain ways which are not true of group interaction. As those who study audience responses to the reading of texts have demonstrated, readers do indeed exercise a certain amount of control over the reading process and can pick and choose among passages, underline or ignore sections, and even, over time, find passages they at first skipped to be suddenly of new interest. Readers can even con-structively "misread" anecdotes to their own purposes, substituting their own particular career, sexual orientation, and other characteristics for the not-quite-right-for-me examples offered in a way which is far harder to do with live speakers (Radway 1984, Fiske 1987).

Books have other reassuring qualities. They speak with an authority that even therapists, in one-on-one physical proximity, do not necessarily com-mand. As French textual theorist Roland Barthes has said in explaining the power of books, "The text is a moral object . . . it subjects us and demands that we observe and respect it" (1975, p. 32) in a way that other human be-ings have a harder time doing. In the case of self-help books, especially, we are reading the words of those who have indeed been helped, who know whereof they speak, and of those who, by virtue of the celebrity best-selling authors now achieve, have social authority of a kind not equaled by most therapists and group members.

I am not suggesting that the group network wholly lacks this quality of authority. On the contrary, the recovery movement as a whole works to in-still confidence and belief because it is, indeed, an arm of the larger institu-tional world in which we live. And of course, in the real "working" groups like AA, the authority of those who testify to having been where you now are and who are getting better is one of the therapeutic mainstays of the pro-gram. I am simply suggesting that it is not group activity–which is hard to maintain and predict–that is *most* responsible for the power of the move-ment in society at large (as opposed to its affect on individual participants of course). That power rests on the mediated circulation of the recovery ideas and stories in books and on TV that are most culturally compelling–that most powerfully and broadly affect women.

There is another reason why the recovery movement, insofar as it has be-come a mass social movement held together by a set of ideas and beliefs about social and personal life, is more dependent upon discourse–upon books, TV programs, conferences, and seminars–than upon actual group or individual activity to determine membership and identity. We live in a world in which feelings, more and more, have come to seem more "real" and significant than actions, as I have argued earlier. It is a world in which, increasingly, people feel powerless, politically, and have little faith in the power of organized activity of any kind to affect social and even personal change. That is of course the appeal of groups like AA, which promise tools for actual change. But this failure of faith is also AA's, and far more relevantly, the newer groups' biggest problem in keeping members: it is so very difficult– absent the dictates of traditional institutional authority, backed up by the threat of legal and other sanctions–to keep people actually obeying the rules, as opposed to merely "believing in" the ideas.

Michel de Certeau's suggestion that, because of the crisis of authority in our political and religious institutions, we now live largely in a "recited" society, held together by stories and repetitions of stories, rather than laws and rituals to which all subscribe and participate, is an idea that helps to explain the current evolution of 12 Step programs away from strict behavioral disciplines into groups loosely unified by shared experiences and stories. Even in AA, after all, only the most desperate manage to stick with the program. And in the looser groups, there is very little effort made to require people do anything at all *except* tell and believe in stories and their morals. In our postmodern world, de Certeau asserts, belief becomes a function of *saying* one believes, rather than proving one's belief through actions (1984, pp. 177– 79). Given this historic and social context, it is not surprising that books and television–forms of myth and storytelling–have become the dominant means by which the recovery movement's ideas are spread. The movement's great power is in its ability to make us think and feel differently, not in its far less remarkable record (the limits and fallacies of which are all too apparent) in actually helping people change. And it is in books, not behavior-changing groups, that a woman finds the most direct access to the foundational stories which help her construct her identity as an "addict" in the process of "recovery."

To be sure, books do promote change in many cases, but that is not their main appeal. According to Wendy Simonds in her study *Women and Self-Help Culture* (1992), "inspiration," "comfort," "explanation," and "validation of how [they] already felt" (p. 7) were the primary reasons the women Simonds interviewed gave for reading self-help books. These books offer complete, powerful models of the universe, so to speak, in which all current problems make sense. Every self-help book on the recovery shelves has a common format and style. Each one repeats the common dogma, tells a set of predictably upbeat stories of cure, and sets out a predictable set of exercises and tests in an effort to provide readers inspiration, comfort, explanation, and validation—to do with as they will (or won't).

Glancing at the table of contents of the three books which happen to be at the top of the pile here on my desk, for example—John and Linda Friel's *Adult Children: The Secrets of Dysfunctional Families* (1988), Helen Larimore's *Older Women in Recovery* (1992), and Minich, Meier, Hemfelt, Sneed, and Hawkins's *Love-Hunger: Recovery from Food Addiction* (1990)—I can readily predict what I will find. The first begins with a unit on identifying oneself as an adult child of an alcoholic, including chapters called "Who Are We? What are our Symptoms?" and "Two Stories." Other units describe typical "Family Systems," including chapters on "The Traps that Get Set" and "When Families Get Off Course." The final unit, all too predictably, is called "Recovering: What Do I Do Now?" and includes chapters on "Uncovering and Admitting," "Working a Program," and "A Word about Healing and Spirituality."

The second book, *Older Women in Recovery*, varies this standard format only slightly. It begins with the obligatory "Who We Are" which lists the most typical problems of aging women with "addictive" patterns and goes on to "Recovery Defined," chapters listing particular "Pitfalls" for older women, including some good advice about money problems, mother/daughter conflicts, and loneliness. Finally, there is "Spirituality, Good Spirits, and Affirmations."

And the final book, understandably a bit longer on Steps and regimens and shorter on common sense homilies since it is dealing with eating rather than aging, nonetheless follows the model of all self-help books. It begins with definitions, goes on to tell exemplary stories, lists programmatic steps to recovery, and warns of pitfalls. And even though it is written by medical doctors, not therapists, it includes a lengthy chapter called "Joining a Footpath Society," which turns out to be another name for the 12 Step groups. Included here are the ubiquitous Steps and other stories and words of wisdom about the miracles of AA, ACOA, and OA.

What these books offer is often sensible, on a purely personal level. The stories reassure, the Steps are clear and bolstered by concrete suggestions for succeeding, and the voice of the author is always warm, personal, and authoritative. These authors have all been there themselves and, as their smiling, well-groomed pictures indicate, they have all gone from "bottom" to tip-top shape. But most important, each book is consistent with every other book you have ever read on the subject. The lists, recipes, and tips may differ a bit, but the overall plan is the same. Slip off one wagon; jump back on another. A new book is a new day and a new chance to get it right. Like Bible reading, self-help reading is a way of reconstituting one's sense of identity and belief and reaffirming one's faith and determination to be saved.

SELF-HELP AND POSTFEMINISM: A CORPORATE MARKETER'S DREAM

Books in the "recovery" and "self-help" sections of my local bookstore have proliferated along with 12 Step groups. Among the inspirational companions specifically for alcoholics, for example, were those addressed to young mothers; working women; women survivors of general sexual abuse, incest, and domestic violence; women in menopause, women grieving, women with a variety of cross-addictions as well as alcoholism; women in bad marriages; women just leaving bad marriages; women who do too much—and on and on. There was even a special book of *Daily Meditations on Healing through Humor*, written by Ann Wilson Schaef (1990), for those women who had, understandably, overdosed on the cloying spiritual solemnity of most of these volumes. Unlike the other books, which tended toward such sobering reminders as "I humbly recognize my right relationship to this earth, other beings, and my creator" (Maureen Brady, *Daybreak: Meditations for Women Survivors of Sexual Abuse*, 1991), the Schaef volume contains such upbeat thoughts as "Recovery is not so bad. It's kinda like walking backward through molasses up to your crotch with your legs tied together" (July 24).

Virtually every major form of addiction has a good supply of such little print companions devised to suit every sensibility and to guide readers through the next several years without their ever having to read the same thought twice. Specialized guidebooks, workbooks, and inspirational "quick fix" books for every conceivable sub-branch of a specific kind of addict, written to serve every conceivable kind of activity, issue, and even mood swing that women fitting each subcategory might find themselves in, apparently sell briskly.

In fact the glory of self-help is also the glory of consumer capitalism and its driving force, mass production. The explosion of these books at such cheap prices is a function of the logic of mass production that drives all other forms of mass consumption, from cereal to movies to frozen dinners (Davis 1984, pp. 270–73). Like Kellogg's cereals, Silhouette romances, and Sylvester Stallone's "poor boy makes good" movies, these books have become a marketing miracle of corporate consumerist America. They expand and diversify to fit an infinitely divisible and fragmentable view of Americans as markets to be tapped and tapped again with the same infinitely unnecessary and repetitive commodity.

The trick of the 12 Step–based addiction books, and the secret of their longevity–their ability to proliferate more widely than other women-oriented self-help books about relationship management–is, according to the editors and authors interviewed by Wendy Simonds, their canny knack of fitting personal family conflicts into books which combine the insights of addiction therapy with the worldview they call "New Age philosophy" (1992, pp. 116–17). Where other such books tell "how to" do daily life, addiction books put this advice in a spiritual package that is especially appealing to those in trouble.

That these books use feminist-tinged ideas as well is easily explained by experts too. It is not just that women buy more self-help books, they tell us. It is that "women buy and read more books than men as a whole" (Simonds 1992, p. 114). But where earlier mini-trends–the spate of *Smart Women Foolish Choices* (Cowan and Kinder 1985) books which professed to teach women to choose men more wisely and then manipulate the kinks out of them, for example–tend to peak and die, these books just go on and on. The reason? Once one reads *Smart Women, Foolish Choices* and follows its advice–which either works or doesn't (usually the latter)–one drops its idea and goes on to something new. There is a finite set of tips and truisms these authors can offer. They tell you they can guarantee you will meet and marry a good man, for example, but they can no more guarantee such results than the authors of Chinese fortune cookie messages or tarot card readers. And once you give up on their systems, they have no hold on you. You will not reread a book whose advice only further depressed you with the hopelessness of your plight. Recovery books however do not "fail to work" in the same way. If you fail to achieve your goal with them, the failure is not so easily attributed to *their* weaknesses but rather, inevitably, to *your* failure to work your program. Try, try again.

The recovery books have, willy nilly, through trial and error marketing come up with a fail-safe formula. Advice is always in demand. The addiction angle adds a bit of science to the most common, troubling issues of our day. And once you add the spiritual angle, you have hit all the bases: relevance, method, and totalizing, spiritually informed worldview. It is this all-inclusive combination, found in every book, that provides what I am calling a "master narrative," by which all aspects of a reader's experience can be fitted and explained–the key to the success of the self-help genre.

The list of topics and titles above touches only the surface of what one finds in bookstore retreats for the troubled. There are so many categories and approaches to addiction these days, and they change and grow so rapidly that there would be no point in my listing the major ones at any given moment.

Within the constant flux and change, however, two things remain the same. The first is the 12 Step programmatic structure. And the second is the gender balance of the titles. Where the 12 Step groups have significant segments devoted to men and male-style problems—AA, SA, Gamblers Anonymous—the book market is still primarily a women's space. A good 85 percent of these books, by my calculations, are written exclusively or primarily for women. To the extent that men ingest the material of the books, it is, as readers and editors all attest, largely through the "teachings" of the women with whom they are involved (Simonds 1992, p. 113). It is after all, still women's job in life to analyze, negotiate, and mend failing relationships in the family and elsewhere.[3]

What interested me most during my periodic check-ins at my local bookstore was what the changing trends in recovery categories told me about the intersections of feminism and corporate marketing that have developed over the last few years. Keeping up with the recovery shelves is a good way to track the serpentine ways in which corporate interests continuously try to redefine the ongoing struggles of women for gender equity, and to gain a sense of how the recovery movement has proved so effective a structure within which to resolve such contradictions.

When I first looked into the topic of this book, for example, I found no books whatsoever addressing women sex addicts. The standard "relationship" problem for women as invariably love, or romance addiction. Sex addiction—which, as my group experiences corroborated, affected men primarily—was not, at first, deemed a good bet for the largely female book market. By the end of my work, however, a mere six years later, the market had changed. Suddenly, women sex addicts had emerged from their closets to reveal themselves as another category of women addicts, and recovery books were available for them.

The most interesting of these books, Charlotte Kasl's *Women, Sex, and Addiction* (1989) indicates at least one of the complex reasons for this sudden emergence of books about what can only be called sexually predatory, as opposed to passively victimized, relationship "addicts." Women, Kasl claims (see pp. 54–90), are now more likely to look to relationships to fulfill their desires for power, just like men.

But while some of this new market share is no doubt due to the social changes wrought by feminism and their impact on women's sexual behavior—women are in fact becoming sexually more aggressive—that is only a partial explanation for the rise of this new category of "addiction." There are still relatively few such female, self-identified "sex addicts," if my experiences in SA are any indication. The common female complaint about men and sex, surely, is still, overwhelmingly, the classic garden-variety "love addiction" which involves a compulsive desire for romance and emotional security, more than erotic pleasure.

The new subset of women "addicts" targeted by publishers cannot be assumed necessarily to represent a whole new female population segment. It may more importantly represent the workings of the marketing mechanisms of the publishing world, always working to define and construct new markets. As *films noirs* of the 1940s tells us, after all, the femme fatale as sexual predator is not unheard of in American cultural history. Not at all. It is far more likely that such women—previously left out of the "addiction" loop because their behavior did not seem like an addiction but rather a form of atypical sexual behavior—have only recently been roped into the ever-widening net to fit the needs of the movement, and the publishers whose needs so nicely merge with it.

But let's assume that both explanations are true—as I'm sure they are—and return to the first: the idea that sexual aggressiveness among "liberated" women is indeed on the rise; that women are more and more "acting like men" in their bad relationships, seeking to dominate and use their sexual partners. The growing number of recovery titles geared to women in positions of personal and social power these days, and suffering from "addictions" to abusive uses of power, stress symptoms, and so on, indicates quite clearly that at least some new addictive disorders are responses to real progress in women's quests for social equity and power. Feminism, in this reading of the trend, does indeed get credit for effecting real changes in women's lives.

But even here we meet with contradictions. That recovery books about power *and* victimization in relationships are almost entirely addressed to women indicates something much less encouraging. It is still after all women, always women, who worry about abusive sexual behavior, who perceive it as unhealthy and even immoral, who seek help in changing themselves so they can do better with men—and men who stay the same unexamined, unrecovered "Others." Guilt-free power trips, the kind men socialized to power and insensitivity seem to go on, are sadly different from the "new" female kind, which seem to involve typically "female" bouts of self-doubt and remorse, and a "compulsive" desire to make things better by reading self-help books.

Here we have a depressing situation. Women–apparently–are indeed being sexually assertive, even aggressive, in ways they would not so easily have been before feminism. But they are being led to see this new behavior too as a "disease." And they are being led into "recovery" as a way of assuaging the pain they feel as newly independent women in a world out of sync with feminism, instead of handling their discomfort by making the sexist world accommodate them. Sex addiction may indeed be as emotionally problematic as love addiction. But to simply say this much–to label it an addiction and leave it at that–is to fail to acknowledge the ways in which feminism, even in an age of "backlash," is at work in changing the nature of our problems and our ways of constructing our identities.

Returning to the classic relationship problem addressed in these books, love addiction, we find yet another telling sign of the contradictory effects of feminism on women's lives today. Many of Wendy Simonds's (1992) young women informants are quoted as saying that they turn to self-help books largely because of a peculiar situation they find themselves in today. In spite of the many positive changes in their lives, as a result of second wave feminism, they still find themselves suffering emotionally from relationship problems and they are very critical of themselves quite often. "I think it's harder to be a woman," says one typical young woman whose sentiments are echoed throughout this book and, indeed, by women I casually chatted with in the stacks I came to haunt.

> I think that our roles right now are very complex . . . it's kind of embarrassing almost, to talk about it. Especially, I have a hard time because all the women I work with are older than I am, and their experiences are different. I mean, they even had a harder time being women. And yet, they had an easier time, because . . . they came at the height of the women's movement when it was good to be a feminist and we're kind of at the tail end . . . where it's "What are you bellyaching about? Everything's wonderful now." . . . My impression of the sixties and early seventies is that it was much easier to network. And now, because we're supposed to be assimilated already, I think it's much harder. (p. 42)

For many of the women cited by Simonds, the habit of reading self-help books was a kind of postfeminist substitute for what the women's movement had provided to their elders. And indeed, the same was true for the women I spoke to who had been a part of second wave feminism and now read the books because, like the woman quoted, they felt embarrassed and frustrated by the fact that their man problems had not gotten better but had, often, gotten worse. They were down on themselves for this "failure" to maintain non-sexist, gratifying relationships such as their mothers would never have thought of seeking. And their self-contempt was fueled—not allayed—by their feminist consciousness.

A generation or two ago, women believed their relationship norms were in fact healthy and that if they could not adapt well to them, they were "abnormal." Today we have learned from feminism that the old rules themselves were perverse and that we have a right to something better. But we are not—a lot of us—finding something better. We are not, in many cases, even seeking something better. We are, as the sale of the many self-help books shows, trapped in the very patterns our mothers acted out; only this time around it is not because we are "abnormal," not "real women." It is because we are "failed feminists." Thus the need to deal with this problem secretly and alone, through books which we hide in laundry baskets just as I once hid *The Golden Notebook*, but for oddly different reasons.

All of this is in keeping with my understanding of the relationship between feminism and the recovery movement. A revolution was begun and then thwarted, or at least stalled in its ability to deliver the goods we optimistically anticipated in the sixties. And in the wake of the confusion, the social chaos and upheaval, and the still insistent demands of women and girls for changes in their social and personal conditions, a movement—based at best on feminist truth and at worst on spiritually-informed ways of redirecting these demands away from social change—has grown up to "sell" (and that is the operative word) a 12 Step "cure" for problems that are far more complicated than addiction discourse allows.

For those who are not falling apart and breaking down, but who are merely in typically female stages of pain and confusion and embarrassment over "retrograde" aspects of their lives, recovery books offer a lot of sensible advice and support. Feminism plus Higher Power equals a solution to all your problems. And, as the sex addiction example shows, the spiritual framework allows for inclusion of every possible new twist and turn in gender experience and relationship that social and historic shifts may turn up. If "love addiction" gives way to "sex addiction," a feminist analysis would insist that the problem had changed. Not so a spiritual analysis, in which all un-

healthy acts are reduced to a common cause: one has stopped working one's
program, lost touch with one's Higher Power, and so become prey to some
kind of problematic behavior which God and self-help can cure.

THE NEW MASTER NARRATIVES:
FROM LIBERATION TO SALVATION

One of the most satisfying aspects of my study of the 12 Step phenomenon
has been the extent to which my hunch about the ideological roots of the
current phase of the movement in 1960s feminism and New Left thinking
proved to be true. The bulk of the market for self-help books, in fact, is made
up of variations on a common set of themes which can be traced back to the
key set of books I listed earlier–Bradshaw, Beattie, Norwood–plus one or
two others, all of which echo, in interesting ways, key ideas of the 1960s.
These books repeat, again and again, the core "story" of the American family
in modern life and the gender in generational dynamics it tends to foster as
1960s feminists first told it, and offer help in escaping from this historic briar
patch by jumping into the godhead, directly or otherwise. They "narrati-
vize" our common experiences and feelings in a way which points blame in
certain directions and not others, and leads to cures in a similarly circum-
scribed way.

The idea of narrative, of the act of "narrativizing" one's life, or any series
of events, as the key way in which human beings construct their own sense
of who they are and of how their actions and experiences come to signify, to
have meaning, is now widely understood to be a central aspect of the way in
which identities and cultures cohere. Barthes and de Certeau, whose works
I've quoted, base their theories upon this insight and so, increasingly, do a
great number of psychologists who deal, on a daily basis, with the materials
of autobiographical narrative.

Jerome Bruner, for example, in his fascinating book *Acts of Meaning*
(1990), explains how, as a society, we come to *learn* the stories of our lives
and our families, our communities, our nations, our religions. "Children,"
he says, "come to recognize early on . . . that what they have done or plan to
do will be interpreted not only by the act itself but by how they tell about it"
(p. 77). In this way, they learn what the rules and values of their family are
and how to behave and speak in ways which will be greeted with predictable
responses. And, he explains further on, common cultures develop collective
narratives which become "canonical," official versions of what was done and
how we judge it (pp. 76–81).

Such canonical readings of events tend, invisibly, to omit things that don't suit the larger meanings and emphasize things that best do. Indeed, such social constructivist views have recently entered the realm of psychoanalytic theory, and theorists such as Donald Spence (1982) and Roy Schafer (1981) have written extensively on the process by which patients and analysts actually "construct" together a common narrative of the client's past, a "story" that will "work in helping the two find ways to help the client change her attitudes and behaviors."[4]

My experiences in the recovery movement brought home to me how important such theories are. Women who had gone through the women's movement—two of whom I had known during that period—told their stories to me, now, in very different terms than would possibly have occurred to them back them. Husbands' and boyfriends' behavior, previously called "sexist" was now called "damaged," and so forth. Wounded inner children were now seen to lurk in the hearts of these oppressive males, radically shifting the interpretation of what their behaviors meant, and how the women should respond to them.[5]

Moreover, the sequence of events in these women's stories was radically altered in their newly constituted memories, as shaped by the dominant narratives of recovery theory. What came first in the old days—learning about the sexual double standard and retreating to marriage and monogamy, for example—now disappeared from the story completely, to be replaced by different—suddenly important—events. In one woman's memory of her first retreat from a dangerously uncontrolled sexual encounter, for example, it was the *aftermath* of the sexual experience—she gorged on pistachio ice cream—which was suddenly elevated to prominence, in the current retelling. Her feelings of guilt over unfamiliar sexual desires—which in the days of "sexual liberation" were so emphasized by feminists—were omitted. Food addiction became the point rather than sexual repression of women, the symptom thus replacing the political disease, so to speak.[6]

I heard many stories, indeed, in which experiences with sex, work, and especially drugs like marijuana and LSD were suddenly given entirely new meanings from the ones I used to hear in the old "Flower Child" days. And there was no doubt in my mind that the speakers were reconstructing *actual memories* which, in the context of countercultural euphoria, had *felt* exciting, but which now, as recalled through the prism of antidrug hysteria, seemed dangerous and scary. To achieve this transformation of collective emotional memory, details were added and dropped to fit the norms of the new worldview, and narratives of hope and optimism gave way to self-critical stories of weakness and addictive excess.

One woman, for example, vividly recalled a drug experience which pre-ceded a missed exam and subsequent withdrawal from college. In fact, as I probed deeper, I "led" her to recall many other details which would give very different meaning to her "decision" to let her studies go and live on a com-mune, some of them, not surprisingly, political reasons. She had, it turned out, been helping to run a women's center at the time.[7] But in her initial tell-ing of her "born-again" tale of jumping off the fast track for a few years, it was now drugs that stood out in her mind as the salient "cause" of her "downfall" and "failure" to succeed in middle-class society. That drugs were here singled out and demonized as having enormous powers of evil, even when used sparingly, was not the most disturbing aspect of this story. That the woman, now a successful executive, blamed her use of drugs for leading her down the "obviously" crazy path of social rebellion and political activ-ism was more disturbing.

Hearing these re-narrativized versions of a common past, I felt old and somewhat deranged, as though my own experiences were being taken from me and replaced by some other person's life story. And indeed this is very much what was going on. To stay in these meetings as a true participant, to continue to "share" with these women, would have put me in a position in which I would have felt increasing pressure to "come to believe" their ver-sion of what actually happened to me as a young woman or fake it, in order to fit in. (This was not much different from many women's prefeminist days of "faking" such things as orgasms, I might add; nor were the reasons any different. One does want to fit in, to be "normal" no matter what the current standards are.)

It was not that the addictive behaviors these women now exhibited were not problematic; it was the ordering of issues and causes and cures, and the foregrounding of the *addiction* itself as the major issue that was disturbing to me. I heard so many stories of self-contempt and weakness around mat-ters of food, love, and sex. I heard almost no expressions of outrage—as I used to—at the limits placed on women's experiences. And all these stories reflected the way in which new narratives, privileging one set of events over another and suggesting one course of action over another, had, through recovery-thought, come to reorient us in our understanding of who we are as women and who we have a right and desire to become.

ANOTHER TALE TO TELL:
THE ENDLESS STORY OF YOUR LIFE AND MINE

During my weeks of attending meetings and interviewing members, I hap-pened, in preparation for a course I was teaching, to be rereading a sampling of women's autobiographical writings, including Kitty Dukakis's *Now You Know* (1990) and *This Bridge Called My Back*, a collection of *Radical Writings by Women of Color* edited by Cherríe Moraga and Gloria Anzaldua (1981). I was struck by the ways in which these two books in particular seemed to reflect the very insights about "narrativizing" and the construction of identity and memory I was becoming aware of in my readings, interviews, and meetings about addiction. The case of Kitty Dukakis, the wife of 1988 presidential hopeful Michael Dukakis is a glaring example of the way in which typical, even traditional problems suffered by women in postfeminist, postindustrial society, are being interpreted and reinterpreted in ways which fit the standard terms of addiction-thought and close out other options (Rapping 1994, pp. 227–34). It is considered "understood" by everyone in America, I daresay, that Dukakis is an "addict." Her story was told and retold so many times and ways by the media and in her own autobiography, *Now You Know*, during and after her husband's campaign for the presidency, that its meaning has been inscribed in our culture as obvious.

By her own admission, in her best-selling book, Dukakis's addiction to diet pills, far from being "progressive," was for twenty-six years held stably at one pill a day. During those twenty-six years Dukakis was a social drinker of moderate indulgence. A drink or two at dinner was her limit. Then, suddenly, under the enormous stress of a grueling and unsuccessful campaign in which her husband lost the election, she became depressed and anxious. She was quickly diagnosed as a "drug addict" because of her diet pill dependency and hospitalized. Later, she "relapsed" and developed "a drinking problem." At this point–when she decided she was "an alcoholic"–she was still drinking one or two cocktails at dinner. After several hospitalizations and much publicity about her "addictions," she suffered what was undoubtedly a nervous breakdown.

In her book, Dukakis identifies herself as "an alcoholic, drug abuser" and a few other things. But what is really mysterious is that, while her condition worsened and all attempts at treatment–including several stays at the very best treatment centers in the country–failed, she became convinced, more and more, that her problem was "addiction" and that the recovery movement was her salvation!

In fact, a feminist would "read" her story and its issues very differently. Had she gone to a consciousness-raising group instead of a 12 Step treatment center she would have been encouraged to see that the cause of her distress was that she was a perfect "good girl" and "good wife" to a man who rarely communicated with her about her feelings or problems, as she went on for decades automatically playing the role of perfect helpmeet to a public figure. It was only when the contradictions and stresses of this position worsened, under the grim realities of Dukakis's publicly exhausting and humiliating efforts to become president, that his wife's "disease" seemed to "progress." But nowhere in her book, or apparently in her treatments, was it ever suggested that she might indeed be leading a life almost totally devoid of emotional or personal gratification. Nothing she did was for herself. She exhausted herself trying to look and act as her husband's role and ambition required her to. She did not allow herself to even consider that this life, this marriage, was exacting a toll she could not any longer afford to pay, for her very health and state of mind were in jeopardy.

From a feminist perspective, what Kitty Dukakis needed in her moment of disillusionment with her role and increased level of stress and despair was not "treatment" for a one pill, one or two drink "cross-addiction," but self-determination and independence. Her helpmeet job took everything she had and, at this last instance, seemed to be giving nothing back. She was symbiotically tied to a man who gave little emotionally and whose public power, the lure for so many unhappy wives, was fading.

This feminist reading of her plight is right there in her narrative, a glaringly vivid subtext to anyone coming upon it with a politicized, feminist perspective. In fact, the torturous route Dukakis takes to make her story fit the addiction/recovery mythology is transparently inadequate. Nonetheless, in today's world, when public discourse so fully embraces this way of thinking, it seems to have occurred to no other reviewers that in this particular case at least the recovery dogma makes no sense. Everyone from Barbara Walters to Gloria Steinem has accepted Dukakis's self-portrayal as a tragically disintegrating "progressive addict" not yet "ready" for real recovery.

Dukakis's "crisis" was so obviously situational and so obviously (to me) connected to gender and patriarchy more than addiction, that her convoluted effort to force her story into the mold of "recovery" narrative was among the most absurd I heard during all my meeting going. What interests me here, however, is the way in which–once Dukakis determined to fit her life into the master narrative of addiction–her very choices of words and incidents to "recall" and relate became preordained. In the beginning, for example, she recalls her mother's influence as a female role model in a way which stresses something she was not even aware of at the time–that her mother "never cooked a meal . . . without a glass of vermouth sitting on the counter next to her." "I'm not saying my mother was an alcoholic," she remarks, "truthfully I can recall only one incident in which she had too much to drink. I am saying, however, based on *what I've experienced and learned* [my emphasis], my mother was dependent on diet pills and may have been dependent on alcohol as well" (p. 65).

Throughout the narrative, Dukakis seems to search for the smallest detail of her past experience which would fit into her preordained thematic focus: how she became "a drug addict and an alcoholic." Although until the actual failed presidential campaign, she had lived her entire adult life with a single pattern: one diet pill a day and a cocktail perhaps, with dinner! At the end, for example, she notes a typically trivial incident, the occurrence of "negative thoughts about myself" as important to mention because, schooled as she has been on literature and therapy from the Hazelden center, she has "come to learn these feelings [are] the precursors of my illness" (p. 121).

Nowhere in the book does Dukakis openly criticize her husband or complain of her extremely difficult, ungratifying, and lonely life as the ever-on-view wife of an emotionally distant, ambitious, failing public figure. But when she realizes she is "an alcoholic," her explanation includes the idea that this state was "progressive" and excludes all mention of social context. "The day after the election," she recounts, "my staff had a party for everyone who had worked for me during the campaign. The day after the party I became a binge drinker," she asserts with confidence, exactly then, and exactly for that reason. For, she continues, "an alcoholic can contain himself for only so long. When a crisis hits, the restraints snap" (p. 243).

This is an incredible piece of writing for a woman who had never drunk more than a single drink or two at a time in all her fifty-odd years of life until this incipient, humiliating "crisis." But the idea that alcoholism is "progressive" is so embedded in her mind that she can only see this path toward explaining—and dealing with—her obvious misery in her chosen married life.

Looking now at a brief piece by Cherrie Moraga called "La Guera," one finds a life story grounded in far more dramatically negative experiences than any Dukakis recalls, and—more important—a far more potentially discouraging example of female experience in the figure of her mother. The "daughter of a woman who, by the standards of this country would be considered illiterate," Moraga—because her point is to explain her development as a Chicana lesbian/feminist activist—recalls for the reader all the ways in which her mother, through her "stories" of a painful past, instilled in her daughter a belief that "my life would be easier than hers" (p. 27). It would make more sense, perhaps, to assume that these terrible stories would lead Moraga to a sense of her own inevitable failure to overcome her heritage. But instead she seeks out only those elements of hope and encouragement—

wherever they occurred—as signs of retrospect, of what must have driven her so optimistically to prevail.

Throughout this brief narrative, Moraga recalls moments which might, for a failed, "addicted" woman be used as indicators—as Dukakis uses her mother's fondness for vermouth—of her impending tragic fate. "These stories my mother told me crept under my *guera* skin. I had no choice but to enter the life of my mother," she writes (p. 31). But somehow, because her narrative structure and terminology has been determined by the need to explain how she *became* what she is today, someone so very different from her mother, she is forced to recall and retell the feelings which spurred her on rather than those which (and there were surely some of these) left her feeling hopeless and doomed.

It is Moraga's tone and language that feels most familiar to me, as a veteran of early feminism, because hers is the kind of story I was used to hearing, the kind of story I learned to tell as a way of believing in my own ability to transcend the limits of my own mother's and sister's lives. The racism, sexism, and homophobia which Moraga encountered and overcame, through her experiences as an activist, are recalled by her as what they were— obstacles to her realization of her own potential. Dukakis, on the other hand, cannot even recognize the obvious garden-variety sexism that plagues her marriage as an obstacle to *her* self-realization. Instead, she searches for and manages to find signs of her "illness," her "disease," her "genetic predisposition" inside her waiting to erupt and bring her to ruin.

Not only are the terms these two women use to sort out the whys and wherefores of their life paths dramatically different here. Their choices lead to very different paths, both in their narratives and in their actual lives. Words like "illness," "dependent," "binge," "alcoholic," and so on lead inevitably to a failure on Dukakis's part to look—at all—at the role of society in her unhappiness. She cannot even see her own mother's (apparently mild) use of alcohol while cooking and diet pills to maintain her weight as a sign of any kind of possible distress in *her* life. Looking everywhere for signs of why she became "ill," she finds any hint of genetic causality significant. The fact that she and her mother led similarly repressed lives is ignored in favor of a fatalistic, quasi-"genetic" explanation.

The differences between Dukakis's story and Moraga's came to my mind often as I listened to many women tell their stories of 1960s experiences in terms of 1990s constructs. The more extensive narratives did not often occur in group meetings where, as we've seen, "shares"—certainly in the more female-populated groups like CODA and OA—tend to be less traditionally autobiographical and even less narrative in structure. I heard the long, detailed stories of overeaters and codependents, for the most part, in private interviews over coffee after meetings. Here, given the chance to tell her "life story," my companion would invariably tell me some version of events, the patterns and highlights of which soon came to be predictable, in a narrative surprisingly similar to the anecdotes found in the self-help books. Gradually, I came to recognize that a certain few authors, and their kinds of examples, were always present in my informant's ways of telling their stories, whether or not they realized it. Bradshaw, Norwood, Beattie, and to a lesser extent, the works of Ann Wilson Schaef, especially *When Society Becomes an Addict* (1986) in which larger social issues are examined, pretty much sum up the totality of recovery theory as a social narrative and blueprint for personal change. Almost every story told by the women I met in recovery groups seemed to fit, like magic, into the formats and terminologies of these works (or the derivative works of followers and clones).

These key documents of the recovery movement offer a wonderful example of how collective, canonical stories come to be revised in keeping with new values and beliefs. In fact, as I suspected, all the works of Bradshaw, Norwood, Beattie, and Schaef are all rooted in feminist/New Left theories about "dysfunctional" (to use the jargon) social and gender arrangements which are caused—in the original versions—by patriarchy and capitalism, but now are attributed to disease and Godlessness.

These books, like much of the writing of early feminists, draw the reader into their world by telling personal anecdotes of family and work life that illustrate universally experienced tensions and sufferings in contemporary life. Just as the stories told in consciousness-raising groups moved women to say "Yes! That happened to me too," so do stories told in the recovery movement. Many among the generation most likely to be reading these books and entering these groups grew up in a family in which the father was either authoritarian and brutal, or so humiliated by his inability to fit that macho model that he retreated to some very common compensatory behavior—drinking, passive aggressiveness, sexual failings, child abuse, whatever. The point is that men living under a system of patriarchal capitalism are raised to fit into a socially constructed world which, increasingly, is disappearing, or at least changing dramatically. And those for whom it may still exist, in any event, are not necessarily happy or fulfilled by it.

The great power of John Bradshaw's *The Family: A Revolutionary Way of*

Self-Discovery (1988) is its way of taking what is in effect a Left/feminist analysis of family life, one developed by feminists and counterculturalists in the Sixties, and applying it to a religious/addictive model. What remains intact, however, what really makes sense, is Bradshaw's insight into the role of history. He offers a master narrative of how patriarchal family structures became unnecessary and destructive to human growth in an age of corporate capitalism, and his narrative is mostly on target.

His "story" makes clear why traditional male behavior, suited to the agrarian way of life in which families were materially productive units of survival, working the land in very hard circumstances, no longer work. We no longer need such strict, authoritarian male figures in the family because, for one thing, (although Bradshaw doesn't say so) the corporate structure—as employer and purveyor of commodities—has replaced the individual family as the source of ideological sovereignty and the disciplinary agent for workers (who are now, in a real sense "employed" as corporate consumers and services, like women, rather than producers).

In the 1960s, for feminists, this insight into the anachronistic nature of the patriarchal family led to a demand that gender roles and power relations be redefined through a process of social transformation of all sexist institutions. The family was the most obvious target, but the government and corporations, which now foster the same patriarchal values the family used to promote so "naturally" were also obviously seen as in need of transformation.[8]

Anyone who wants a taste of the utopian idealism that so inspired feminists in the late sixties and early seventies should check out Marge Piercy's wonderful 1976 science fiction/utopian novel *Woman on the Edge of Time*, as idealistic and thorough a version of what the Left and feminists actually envisioned in those heady days, when words like "democratic socialism" and "cultural revolution" tripped from the tongue as easily as "groovy" and "far out." Her book is as inspirational in its own way as Bradshaw's. But where Bradshaw's ends with a promise of "bliss" through "personal love and oneness with God," Piercy's ends with a similarly ideal feminist heaven on earth achieved through political struggle and the restructuring of economic and social institutions and reallocation of resources.

Such social radicalism—the idea that "bliss" might not be possible without a transformation of material life—of course, is where the recovery movement parts ways with early utopian feminism. Bradshaw's introductory pages, nonetheless, are indebted to the insights and values that fuel Piercy's fantasies.

In explaining how mad men came to dictate the terms of our emotional lives, for example, Bradshaw retells the major political atrocities of the century–the Holocaust most notably–which he explains as signs that "the old worldview [had] definitively ended" with the world wars. "Mankind had been basking in the illusion of inevitable progress. Rationalism and technological advances had assured everyone that progress was inevitable . . ." (1988a, p. 17), he writes, in explaining the great disappointments of the later century and the desperate turn to such monster/prophets as Adolph Hitler– abused children of dysfunctional fathers themselves, quite often–who promised to make the modernist myths of progress through patriarchal power and wisdom come true, against all odds.

Bradshaw does a nice job of tying up a lot of the loose ends of a declining civilization–the Puritan ethic, Nazi Germany, and other patriarchal horrors. He also explains, convincingly, how the roots of addiction can be found in efforts of families to live by the old, mad patriarchal rules and why that is no longer necessary in a world in which daily life does not require the same kind of authoritarian discipline and hardship. (That hardship of a very different kind is all too common among families who don't fit the white middle-class model Bradshaw presents as universal is another story entirely. The hard-core addictions, of course, are most troubling in poor communities. But the recovery movement's homilies have little to offer these sufferers of postmodern social madness. Their target audience is white and middle class, the kinds of paying customers that have made the recovery movement so big.)

Up to this point, page 22 of *The Family* to be exact, Bradshaw is impressive. Anyone reading him can see why the family is such a mess for so many people. But this kind of analysis–based as it is on the assumption that major political change, rather than a mere change of thinking, will be necessary to solve our problems–does not sell millions of copies (unfortunately). And so Bradshaw leaves this terrain and jumps quickly to the more commercial stuff. The bulk of the book, like all the recovery books, offers a series of universally applicable stories and examples of what has happened to us in this anachronistic family structure, stories in which everyone–with the possible exception of Wally Cleaver–will certainly recognize his or her own family experience.

Bradshaw paints a quick picture of several classic styles of dysfunctional family and offers a few classic examples of how they operate to cause neuroses and addictive tendencies in everyone. The "Blue Family" is chemically addicted. The "Orange Family" is addicted to food, the "Purple Family" to

religion and so on. Every emotional trauma caused by gender and generational inequality is mentioned and explained in terms–often rightly–of the
male-dominated family. The father who cannot express emotion, the
mother who cannot tell the secret that defies the sexual rules of patriarchy,
the kids who twist and turn in their efforts to achieve or refuse the rigid sex
and generational imperatives foisted upon them by the family's particular
dogma of "success," "love," and so on.

Each verbal snapshot includes moments of typical horror–incest, domestic violence, impoverishment due to drink, the shaming of children for
failing to be "good" boys and girls. The "work addicted" "White Family,"
for example, suffers "denial stress." "Mickey is a severe work addict and
Mathilda enables him by continually defending him" (1988a, p. 101), says
the author. And one knows exactly what that means and how it feels. One
also recognizes the specific ploys which such a family will use to avoid
healthy communication, the insistence that "nothing is wrong," the sexual
dysfunction and betrayal, and so on.

All of this makes sense. How could it not? And it is a relief to this dysfunction described as common to everyone, almost, and a greater relief to be presented with rules and exercises and little sayings to remember as ways of
escaping from its traps. "In relationships you bounce back and forth between being a victim and being an offender," is one of the guidelines for testing your own kind of dysfunction and the possible addictive tendencies that
accompany it. "Well, sure, I can relate to that," you think. And the cure?
There are any number of rules to follow involving the protecting of one's
boundaries, deep breaths, repeated affirmations, and especially, invariably,
"surrender and recovery" through the 12 Step programs.

Some of these tricks really do work, if you use them conscientiously. And
some of these books, Bradshaw's for example, are very useful indeed in helping one sort out one's feelings and rethink one's behavior patterns. But they
are not going to change the structure of the family in American society because that structure serves a social function which goes far beyond its admitted role of offering comfort, security, and love to its members.

The family is the basic unit of socialization in this society, the place where
we are groomed for our social roles and functions. And until and unless the
rules of the economic and political sphere change, there is little one can do
to alter the terms of *social* identity and status upon which family norms are
based. In fact, to the extent that these books, and the recovery movement
generally, do help us fix our families, they give us a full-time, uphill job as
husbands, wives, and parents which leaves little room for any social con-

cerns beyond the family. For, as we saw as far back as early AA, the stresses of modern economic life are so severe that they put increasing pressure on family life, and depend more and more on women, especially, to deal with that worsening situation. That, in a nutshell, is the biggest problem with Bradshaw's prescription for healing the modern family.

Bradshaw does indeed understand these large social matters. His historic analysis shows that. He even includes sections with headings like "Codependent Traits of Society" in which stories about gambling addictions are linked to capitalist values. *The Family* ends with a chapter called "How to Discover Your True Self," however, not "How to Discover–and Build–a New Society in which Gambling Would Make No Sense."

IT'S A GIRL THING: CODEPENDENCE AND LOVE ADDICTION

I started with Bradshaw because he lays out so clearly the social and structural analysis in which the recovery movement is rooted and makes dramatically clear the debt these authors and gurus owe to feminism and other 1960s ideas. But before Bradshaw, with his seminars and cruises and toys for wounded inner children, there was Robin Norwood, whose *Women Who Love Too Much* (1985) provided the primary model for analyzing women's relationship problems with men as "addictions." Norwood had been working as a counselor to people with drug and alcohol problems for several years when, she says, "I made a surprising discovery. Sometimes my clients came from troubled families and sometimes they did not. But their partners [always addicts] nearly always came from severely troubled families. . . . By struggling to cope with their addictive partners (known in the alcohol treatment field as 'coalcoholics') they [the women] were unconsciously recreating and reliving significant aspects of their childhood" (p. xiv).

In seeking to explain why these women, from nonalcoholic families, nonetheless exhibited addictive habits in their intimate relations, Norwood turns–and here she provides the recovery movement with its key trick–to biology. "Due to an interplay of cultural and biological factors," she goes on, "they try to protect themselves and avoid pain through" a variety of compulsive activities the most common of which is a relationship with "a damaged and distant man" (p. 27). Addiction, with a single word, "biology," is suddenly an explanation for destructive sexual attractions.

Voilà! Men in damaging families become drunks; women become coalcoholics to these drunks, and the addiction industry, of which Norwood is a part, hits pay dirt. Millions of women in bad relationships with all sorts of damaged men, women who had not been raised by addicts, and whose

mates were not addicts either, found their own stories in this book and began to form groups to support each other in their "addictions." The
WWLTM groups still exist. But far more successful and important was Norwood's idea of relationship addiction, in which "damaged men" and their
"codependent" others are viewed from the angle of addiction therapy, and
in which addictive families produce addictive children. Today, of course, one
need not have been in an alcoholic family to be "codependent." The movement, through groups like CODA, ACOA, and Love and Romance Anonymous (LRA), welcomes anyone whose current or childhood family and
relationships are "toxic" or "dysfunctional" which, they say, includes 96 percent of us. But the metaphor of biological addiction, and of "damaged men"
who are not sexist but addictive remains, and in dominating the discourse, it
ensures that the women's efforts to free themselves from unhealthy relationships with men will remain personal and spiritual, never political.

As in Bradshaw's work, Norwood bolsters her originating narrative of
toxic families and poisoned relationships with endless anecdotes of typically
messed up male-female relationships in which emotional control and emotional and sexual withholding, victimization, and power games, and patriarchal assumptions about men's rules and women's subservient position
dominate. Women tell stories of marrying because "finally, here was someone saying *he* loved *me*" which is what they had heard marriage was about.
"You see," they say in one way or another, "I had no idea how I felt about anything. . . . It all seems so crazy now, doesn't it?"

Norwood doesn't fail entirely to grasp the cultural roots of her patients'
traumas. She explains these feelings and their sources, many times, in terms
of sexist culture perpetuated by mass media. "The society in which we live
and the ever-present media," she writes, "confuse the two kinds of love [eros
and agape] constantly" and keep us from seeking "a partnership in which
two caring people are deeply committed" because "they share basic values,
interests, and goals" and "tolerate good-naturedly each other's differences"
(pp. 44–45), she says at one point in her analysis. But she seems not to want
to address the fact that the media, as a source of these false romantic models,
is fostering *sexism* not alcoholism. It is sexism, after all, that leads to the
"toxic" patterns in families she describes and that teaches us not to seek the
kind of egalitarian partnerships, based on honesty and mutual support,
which she describes as ideal.

Like Bradshaw, Norwood insists upon 12 Step homilies and rules which
apply to physical addictions rather than looking to the wider causes of the
dysfunctional family and the sexist relationships it fosters. The women read-

ing her book, who formed groups, wrote her letters, and often left their partners, were not all in relationships with alcoholics. But if the behavior of
many male alcoholics seemed to mirror the behavior of so many more men
damaged in other ways, it was surely not because emotional habits are genetic, or catching, but because alcoholism is one of many ways in which men
(typically) try to cope with the demands of masculinist ideals.

The guidelines offered by Norwood at the end of her book, like the many
stories of female suffering she cites, are models for the lengthy readings I was
given in my CODA and ACOA meetings. They are short on "Steppism"–actual demands for "abstinence," for example, which would probably mean
leaving the guy–and long on ways of coping with a bad relationship by cur-
ing what's "wrong" with you, not him. In this way they reveal quite clearly
how the Anonymous traditions of discipline and denial came gradually to
incorporate a set of problems whose cures lay in *thinking differently* rather
than *living differently.*"

Of course, these groups and Norwood's book recommend change. But
not the kind of radical change alcoholics are forced to make. Women who
"love too much" are given rules for "taking care of yourself" and "being
selfish" as a way of altering the terms of the relationship to make it more
bearable. But they are not instructed to leave the marriages. There are never
any final chapters in which hopeless situations are described and termina-
tion recommended.

Moreover, in the process of figuring out how to "take care of" oneself inside a bad marriage, as Norwood describes it, early feminist ideas about demanding justice, equality, and social reform, within the marriage as well as
in the larger world, give way to talk of illness and victimization in which
everyone is sick and needs to heal herself or himself with God's help.

That Norwood's book, like virtually every other of the hundred or so
books I read, drew its analysis of female experience and behavior from feminism seems to me so obvious as to make it rather amazing that none of the
authors credit this intellectual source. But then, as I have been arguing, feminist ideas today–at least some kind of mild version of them–are so widely
assimilated into mainstream thought that some authors may not even be
aware that they are using *political* ideas. This is especially true of the most recent books, the second generation (if a mere few years can be called a generation, even in today's postmodern world) in which Norwood, Bradshaw, and
Beattie serve as foundational thinkers whose ideas are considered original
and never questioned.

Among the leading recovery thought writers, Norwood is perhaps the most obviously indebted to feminist thinking in her "sudden" awareness of so dramatic a pattern of female victimization in the relationships of women in therapy. Melody Beattie, however, is the writer most responsible for popularizing the idea of female addiction to unhealthy relationships with the wider nonfemale world at large. Norwood's book was read by women and had an enormous influence on female culture. But in taking Janet Woititz's term "codependency"[9] as a general term to describe relationships which, nonetheless, primarily victimized women, Beattie was able to spread Norwood's ideas about male-female dynamics to a mainstream general audience which appealed to and included men as well.

Beattie's codependents tend mostly to be women who need to control, to please, to help, to rescue because that is the role they learned as girls. But one need not be a woman to have these habits, and that is the appeal of her work. It avoids even the twinge of feminist identification Norwood's book clearly had by being geared only to women, and appears to be an equal opportunity cure-all. Rid of the taint of the F-word, it can go on to provide a narrative of family and relationship life in which women, as caretakers as well as lovers, act out all kinds of self-destructive behavior in relation to the men they bond with—fathers, husbands, lovers, sons—in a far more inclusive way than Norwood could, while yet denying the gendered nature of her analysis.

It is an easy few steps from Norwood's love addiction, to Beattie's "relationship" addiction, to Bradshaw's toxic family system. But in each version we recognize a male-dominated structural context (although this is left unsaid) in which men and women tend to act out certain roles in an unfulfilling quest for gratification and self-esteem. The failures to achieve these goals, of course, are built into the larger society. But the tricks and games we all learn to work in our efforts to thwart that system do indeed lead to addictive habits. And the habits are often different for men than women in ways which the addiction industry, in its frantic quest to convert women, understands all too well.

Among the rules and examples Beattie (like all the authors) provides, are many which speak directly to the social roots of codependency and its fit with the needs of a highly disciplined economic structure. And here is where we return, against the grain of Beattie's own insistence on spiritual analysis, to the larger social vision which implicitly informs all these books (and which they are at such pains to ignore).

"Rescuing," for example, in Beattie's lexicon, is a term which means that one rushes to help out a child or partner when they should be taking care of themselves. It is a typically female habit, which is why Beattie's examples of it, as of most of her ideas, present women as sufferers and (usually) men as the objects of their quests for relief. Women want to be useful, needed, and "good," and so they compulsively rescue men. But it is interesting to note that the very attributes which, in heterosexual relations, define "female" behavior, in the public sphere are less clearly gendered and more generally signs of all power relations.

Among the behaviors Beattie offers as tests to see if you are a "rescuer" are these: "Doing something we really don't want to do" and "Saying yes when we mean no." These traits are common to women and lead, too often, to sexual and emotional and economic exploitation—in a word, to sexism—in personal life. But—and this leads me to my "master narrative," Ann Wilson Schaef's *When Society Becomes an Addict* (1986)—these "rescuer" traits also lead to an equally problematic set of behaviors by workers, of both sexes, in oppressive workplaces. It is not only women, of course, who get treated badly in unequal institutions and relationships. In the corporate world that has replaced the patriarchal family farm and business, most men have, to some extent, become "feminized," stripped of their macho traditions and gratifications and powers and made to obey and pander to bosses to whom they feel no real loyalty or respect.

In a postindustrial world, like ours, even middle-class professional male workers are finding themselves, as I've suggested, more and more often in positions in which they are powerless and forced to please and perform for their superiors. It is no wonder then that Beattie's books, which use female examples but do not by definition exclude men from the codependency model, would have greater success even than Norwood's, in the long run. The growth of the men's movement, along with the influx of men, certain kinds of men at least, into the more feminized addiction groups, points to the ways in which men, in these gender-confused times, are finding themselves experiencing many typically female emotional problems in personal and work relationships.

Schaef, who has authored countless addiction/recovery books, mostly aimed at women but more recently more general in appeal, is a prominent consultant to many businesses on matters of worker/management relations. It is her theory that the old-style male behavior patterns which Bradshaw diagnosed as obsolete in postagrarian and postindustrial society are the cause of the misfunctioning of all our social and political systems, which she terms "Addictive Systems." The system is fraught with disease, she says, but "the good news is that the System, like the alcoholic/addict, can recover" by means—you guessed it—of 12 Step principles. So welcome has her message to management been that she has become almost as wealthy and influential as Bradshaw.

Going Bradshaw one better, Schaef doesn't simply present a historic narrative and then drop it like a hot potato; she actually converts that very narrative of social and economic history into a grand master narrative of collective, progressive addiction. America, the nation, is diseased, she preaches. It has very nearly "hit bottom" in fact. And because of this crisis, she feels, "it may now be ready for the ideas discussed here" (1986, p. 5). These ideas—and they have indeed been taken up by many men and women who are alarmed at the distress and alienation in the corporate work force and political system—are, like all the other books, based on stories of "bad family" dynamics in the public sphere which lots of people recognize. And having spelled them out, Schaef, like her peers, includes systematic suggestions for "Whole-System Recovery" aimed, apparently, at our business and government leaders. She assumes, apparently, that the most powerful men in our nation, once they have read her book, will rush frantically to her seminars and workshops (or to the many very similar groups that constitute the so-called men's liberation movement) and put themselves into recovery from "power and success addiction."

That this is absolutely silly as a political idea is not the point. What is distressing to me is that so many men and women, like the ones I met in CODA, who used to be actively progressive and liberal, and who still consider themselves such, have turned from social and political activity of the sort that aims to change social reality and are now reading self-help books and practicing "self-love exercises" in a misguided belief that such self-healing will somehow change the political system.

For one thing, this belief is based on a myth about who actually has power in this society—even among men—and about who is actually suffering—even among men. It is not people like Ross Perot and Donald Trump, or even Bill Clinton and Al Gore (although these two opportunistically use the language at times, for certain audiences), who are running to the men's movement to free themselves of their "power addictions." No, these guys seem to be pretty happy and comfortable in the world they manipulate so readily. The men who are rushing to Schaef, and her male counterparts, to learn how to smell the roses and stop craving money and power are the middle-level professional types who are indeed increasingly powerless and even unemployed as a result of the madness of postindustrial corporate life.

The men I met in the ACOA and CODA groups were not power brokers or military honchos. They were men in increasingly feminized careers, in marriages to women who were increasingly successful, and in positions in which their skills were undervalued and the fruits of their work were–contrary to the hype they had gotten in business and professional schools–out of their control. They are the kind of men Barbara Ehrenreich describes in *Fear of Falling: The Inner Life of the Middle Class* (1990). These men are scared and insecure precisely because *they do not have the power* they were raised to expect, and they do not, any longer, believe in the myths their fathers told them about progress, Horatio Alger, and the American Dream. These sad figures are seeking, in the recovery movement, a way of rethinking their priorities and lifestyles that might help them adjust to the great disappointments of their adult life in which neither family nor work life seems to fit their expectations any longer.

In the 1960s, these very men, or others of their generation and class, were youthful activists, molders of a vision of society–deeply informed, I do not lose a chance to repeat, by feminism–in which the unhealthy conditions of corporate industrial life were clearly analyzed. They built strategies–dumb, youthful, overly idealistic and optimistic strategies, often–for destroying the old system and replacing it with a brave new world of utopian bliss. But the political documents of those days, written by people in the student and women's movements, and the New Left, were not. To look back at the most ambitious of these documents is to see–one last dramatic time–how fully the recovery movement, in its theoretically seminal documents, steals from those feminist and feminist-influenced movements and distorts their goals.

To see how these theories have worked their way into the more elaborately developed versions of recovery theory, we might look briefly at some rather amazing, now forgotten documents which came out of the idealistic, ultra-democratic student movements of the sixties. Here, we can see–in ways which may seem astonishing in their optimism and grandiosity–the very best and most inspiring efforts of those years and that generation, many of which are still with us.

In those days–although it was hard for me to remember this until I dug around in some of my old books and papers–it was quite usual to hear people talk convincingly about a new brand of "democratic socialism"– with no links whatever to the troubles of the Eastern bloc–which was about to be realized through an incipient revolution of some kind. After all, in the wake of Vietnam and Watergate, the feeling that the system was indeed in collapse was not hard to understand. We faced down a near-Constitutional crisis in those days, following a humiliating, disillusioning military defeat in a small impoverished nation. And so unexpected and unthinkable did these events seem that there was much concern, even on the Right, about the stability of the current system. Revolution, at this moment, did not seem impossible, especially to the idealistic young. Nor did the possibility of a utopian democratic alternative to the one which obviously (and this belief is still with us of course) was wearing down and not awfully likable even when it was working.

What the new American utopia would look like, according to New Left and feminist visionaries, was not very far from the imaginary futurist society of Marge Piercy's *Woman on the Edge of Time* and–emotionally at least– from Bradshaw's descriptions of eternal "bliss." Its dimensions and logic were actually spelled out in a fascinating document, written by an unlikely author, in 1970. Michael Lerner, currently editor of the progressive Jewish magazine *Tikkun* (who has been known to visit the White House to converse with President and Mrs. Clinton about bringing a "politics of meaning" back to American life), wrote a book in that year, when he was still in his twenties, called *The New Socialist Revolution* (New York: Dell, 1970) which was published as a Dell paperback. In it he laid out an incredibly detailed schema for transforming society along lines which–except for the economic and political analysis and blueprints–is based on ideas very much like those of Schaef and Bradshaw.

Speaking of the modern world, in historical terms much like Bradshaw's, Lerner explained how scarcity and hardship produced the necessary evils of patriarchy and the nuclear family it fostered. "Control over women and children," in agrarian societies, he wrote,

> was certainly functional for the physically tougher men, who would use women and children to do needed work and could then hand on the accumulated material surplus to the children. In short the same dynamic that led men to fight against and enslave one another was the dynamic that led them to enslave women: material scarcity. (p. 99)

He went on to present a full feminist critique of the family, much like Bradshaw's except for the terms and political commentary, and to suggest ways of changing these dynamics which, again, were not too different from the guidelines offered by recovery gurus, except for Lerner's ideas about building new institutions.

Speaking of other evils produced by contemporary, dysfunctional settings, Lerner suggested, as do Bradshaw and Schaef, that addictive habits (not his term) of acquisitiveness and control are systemic in our world. "The good life," he wrote, "seems to be defined in terms of having more than the next person" which leads to an obsession with consumerism and a workplace driven by competition and alienation.

"When one's attention is focused on consumption, when work is considered a wasteful distraction from what life is really supposed to be about" (p. 37), he argued, people turn to personal life for fulfillment. But, as Bradshaw and Schaef also realize, the private sphere is every bit as contaminated by these false, stress-producing values as the public.

Quite remarkably (as I found, when I flipped through this old book after decades in which it had slipped from my memory) Lerner had the audacity to claim that his version of socialism would guarantee an end to such evils as crime itself. "Most of the crimes that we know today would simply disappear under a socialist society," he stated. "Why steal when there is abundance for all? And when a society has been constructed in which every person has a stake and in which each is allowed to develop those parts that seek fuller realization, antisocial behavior becomes minimal" (p. 313). Lerner did caution that certain transitions to this dreamworld might be a bit rocky, but he offered actual blueprints for getting through the hard parts in a chapter called "After the Revolution."

It is easy to laugh at these youthful fantasies from another, cheerier time, written by a member of a generation and class that did not know the anxiety over material survival which young people live with today and certainly did not understand the many complications of American social life and culture which today make the idea of socialist revolution so hard to believe in. Not only do we lack belief in our own ability to create such change, most people, even on the Left, have had their faith in the idea of socialism itself, certainly as traditionally understood, shaken by recent events.

But if one laughs at Lerner's "socialist-feminist" visions, one must feel at least as uncertain of the recovery movement's promise of "bliss." After all, they are suggesting that total peace of mind, human fulfillment, harmonious gender and generation dynamics within families, and even social institutions will all be easily accomplished without even touching, or thinking about, the power relations and material inequalities in the economic and political and military institutions Lerner so thoroughly analyzes and plans to overhaul. "Once we begin the journey inward," promises Bradshaw, "a new kind of peace and calm comes over us . . . the intuitive faculty . . . [which is] the power of immediately experiencing God . . . becomes more and more available . . . and we come to experience bliss" (1988a, 235). Quite a promise, I would say.

Nor are Lerner's insights about the fit between emotional well-being and social and economic justice outdated or wrong, no matter how naive his idealistic stating of them, or how farfetched his schemes to eradicate them. Indeed, they are the very values which most progressive thinkers and activists adhere to still–although with far less grandiose and ambitious claims and overtones.

Stanton Peele, whose seminal work with Archie Brodskey, *Love and Addiction*, was published in 1976, before the recovery movement began to transform our understanding of human suffering from political to religious terms, uses many of the same social examples as Lerner in describing the ways in which addictions to things other than chemicals are produced through unhealthy social relations and values. "The real cure for addiction," he wrote, "lies in a social change which reorients our major institutions and types of experiences people have within them. . . . We cannot begin to cure [addiction] in the absence of a more universal access to our society's resources and to its political power" (pp. 223–24). It is interesting to note, however, that his book has been out of print for many years and is never mentioned in any of the best-sellers which are now so influential in the recovery movement although, like the utopian feminist ideas which similarly inform these works, his ideas are clearly incorporated into those best-sellers and are the source of much of their power.

As Barbara Ehrenreich and Deirdre English have written in their book on the medical establishment's treatment of women, *For Her Own Good* (1979): "The Woman Question in the end is not the question of *women*. . . . The Woman Question becomes the question of how shall we all–men, women, and children–organize our lives together. This is a question which has no answer in the marketplace or among the throngs of experts who sell their wares there" (p. 323).

This is a truth that all the recovery authors instinctively or consciously realize. That is why, instead of offering simple "self-help" rules about daily life, they have been forced to turn to the AA model, with its ultimate turn to a Higher Power and a spiritual substitute for social happiness to give their ideas theoretical and emotional power. But even with the AA model of disease and prayer, the recovery gurus could not have created the great social movement they have without feminism and its insights and instructions for leading a fairer, more rewarding personal life. And feminism's ultimately political impulse toward the creation of a better world exists most clearly–if most perilously perhaps–in the many new political movements which incorporate elements of both feminism and the 12 Steps. These movements will be our last stop in our wide-ranging tour of the contemporary recovery movement.

CHAPTER SIX

✦

The Diseasing of Politics:
Solipsism, Survival, and Self-Esteem

I have been arguing that feminism has had a profound and salutary effect upon the recovery movement, offering indispensable assistance in its smooth evolution from a 12 Step program to keep alcoholics from drinking, to a totalizing approach to social malfunction at its most pervasive. But what about the quid pro quo? What has recovery done for—or perhaps "to" is more apt—feminism? That is perhaps the most important question of all. For it leads me, finally, to my major concern, my primary reason for writing this book: that we may indeed, many of us, in so trustingly embracing the rhetoric of addiction and recovery, as we once embraced second wave feminism, be veering off in a politically dangerous direction.

The main problem with the politics of the recovery movement is its contradictions. The movement is at once the most political and the most apolitical of recent social developments. Determined, by its very nature and vision, to focus on the *self* as a spiritual and biological, but *not* a social, entity, and to offer guidance in personal, internal growth and transformation, in a political vacuum, it nonetheless borrows from and lends to the larger political culture in many ways.

Even when those involved have no conscious awareness of or concern with recovery-thought, I have felt its presence, its inflection, its ramifications, in political events and gatherings and writings, both feminist and not, which I encountered as I worked on this book. In fact, I became increasingly aware, as my own sensibility became attuned to the nuances of recovery culture, of how *both* feminist- and recovery-inspired attitudes and ideas have permeated the liberal-to-progressive political world in ways now so deeply intertwined as to make them hard to distinguish. It is not only ex-activists, now steeped in personal transformation issues, who are today spouting Bradshaw-isms and preaching self-healing. It is, increasingly, activists themselves who, with the best of intentions and many good reasons and arguments, have "come to believe" in these therapies as political panaceas.

This New Age-ish blurring of the boundaries between the political and the therapeutic or spiritual—a result of the merging of feminist and recovery thought—is visible and tangible everywhere. From the 1992 campaign rhetoric of Bill Clinton and Al Gore, to the widespread use of the serenity prayer ritual, to the increasing inclusion of 12 Step meetings in TV shows and movies, the signs of recovery's rise to prominence are evident.

I want to look, in this concluding chapter, at a few of the areas in which this trend is most disturbing because it works to distort and impede the development of feminism itself.[1] In certain parts of the women's movement of today—in the so-called men's movement, with its many organizations, rituals, therapies, and writings; in the fast-spreading movement of state-based Self Esteem Task Forces and other agencies, with their mandates for social and political change based on a variety of theories rooted in self-transformation; and in a variety of other less coherent and effective movements and campaigns for all sorts of personal and political ends—we find what are the most disturbing ramifications of the jumbling of politics and spiritual therapeutics which the merger of feminism and recovery has produced.

During the time I spent researching this book, I attended several "speak-outs" organized for women victims/survivors of abuse—self-abuse as well as abuse by others—modeled after the feminist speak-outs held in the heyday of the second wave, in which women broke their silence about such shame-filled secrets as illegal abortions, rapes, and physical abuse by husbands or boyfriends. But the new, 1990s versions of these speak-outs were different from their more politicized precursors in sometimes subtle ways.

In the 1960s and 1970s, feminist speak-outs had a dual purpose. On the one hand—and here the tradition is maintained—speak-outs allowed women to break our silence about things we had been forced to keep secret because they were socially condemned. In "speaking bitterness" about the truths of female victimization, women were able to transform those experiences from individual and private ones to collective and public ones. We were able to force ourselves, collectively, into invisibility as identified and named victims of political crimes of gender. We were able, also, to name our enemies—men and male-defined institutions endowed with the state-sanctioned power to legitimize such crimes—and hold them accountable.

I remember attending some of these events and feeling exhilarated and empowered by the experience. I remember also that they were politically enlightening in their inclusion of the experiences of diverse women. At a conference and speak-out on domestic violence, for example, I remember being awed at the testimony of women of color–black and native american and latina–whose own tales of abuse were at once the same and very, very different from the by then more familiar tales of white, middle-class sexism, because the conditions of their lives–their resources and their access to support and information and power–were so different.

In those politically optimistic days, such events always ended with some plan for organizing to end the troubles named and grieved over. To recognize oneself as member of a "class" (in legal parlance), capable of taking a "class action" to make a "structural change" in society–for these were the words we used so easily then–was an empowering experience because it transferred the problem from *us* to *them*. Of course, the very process of speaking out, in anger and grief, was personally transforming. But the personal transformation was not an end in itself. Rather it was one part of a process, the end result of which was aimed at changing *them, out there*; the ones with power to accost and maim us.

There was, to be sure, a tenuous balance to be maintained between the personal and political; and between sisterhood and difference. And it was not very long, as we saw, before the utopian moment–in which "feminism" seemed to be one simple, all-encompassing term; in which the phrase "the personal is political" seemed a simple truth to explain the troubles of the world–came to an end, as our differences led to conflicts and splinterings among and between us (Epstein 1990, 1991; Kauffman 1990). Nonetheless, the driving spirit and intent of those meetings were valid. For in trying to build, of our many private sufferings, a common strategy for social change, we were focusing outward, toward their sources.

I was reminded of these early speak-outs and the spirit–naive perhaps in some ways, but so important in others–which informed them, as I attended the updated versions held in the 1990s. One event in particular–a fundraiser for a women's center offering feminist counseling and therapy for women with eating disorders–seemed to sum up my mixed feelings about the recovery movement.

Unlike the 12 Step meetings I attended, OA for example, this event did indeed incorporate a sophisticated feminist analysis into its proceedings–or it tried to. The organizers, themselves veterans of the second wave, were committed to an agenda which refused the label of "victim" and stressed "empowerment" and "self-esteem" as the road to freedom from compulsive eating. There were statements made in the opening presentations which charged social institutions–the media, the fashion industry, and so on– with fostering female self-hatred and self-abuse. And there was even a healthy dose of old-fashioned collective feminist rage hurled at appropriate institutional targets.

Nonetheless, when the actual speak-out began, the spirit of the opening session was subtly subverted. The reason was simple: the point of the meeting, the goal of the women who used the services of the center, was much narrower than the earlier speak-outs I had attended in which "the personal" was explicitly linked to "the political." The goal of these women, on this day, was not to change society but simply to change themselves. They wanted to like their bodies and to stop allowing food to control their lives. They did not seek, at least in this context, to change the *external* sources of their pain and self-loathing.

As one woman after another rose to "speak bitterness" about her personal, humiliating experiences with food and sexual abuse–which turned out, as in most OA meetings I attended, to be a common experience for women with eating disorders–the mood of the room shifted from empowering and angry to sorrowful and defeated. And if there was any suggestion for ending this sorrow, it was in the form of therapy for the *eating problem*, not in tactics to end the abuse. In fact, what was most disturbing to me here, as it was in OA, was the way in which the sexual abuse somehow became secondary to the behavioral effects it produced. The women spoke of abuse but their goal was to heal *themselves* of the damage it produced; not to put an end to the abuse and in this way solve the eating disorder problem at its root.

The therapeutic message of this event–self-esteem as the road to overcome compulsive behavior–was often lost in the thundering wave of horror stories which came tumbling out of the previously silent sufferers. As the afternoon proceeded–and this again was similar to OA meetings–there were more stories of relapse and pain than of victory. One woman after another stood and sobbed as she related her private anguish and shame and defeat to the sympathetic murmurs of the rest of us. Yes, most attendees had known such moments. Most women probably have at some time been plagued and shamed by their bodies and appearances. But there was no political or social solution offered to what, as the opening statements all agreed, was at least in part a political matter.

The answer that *was* offered at this event was therapy, the same answer women are offered by television. Most daytime talk shows devoted to women's problems offer 12 Step rather than feminist *methods*, even though many works by feminist therapists on compulsive behaviors and relationship issues are available.[2] On occasion, an audience member may manage to express a feminist therapy insight. Such moments are heartening, of course, as is the existence of feminist therapy itself. I do not–and this needs to be emphasized–discount the importance of therapy, especially politically informed feminist therapy which should be supported and encouraged in every way. It is one of the most important by-products of second wave feminism, and it has saved and reshaped lives in ways which goals of the recovery movement do not predict nor encourage.

But therapy, even feminist therapy, has a limited, if crucial, place in our lives as feminists. It needs to take place in a broader context of struggle for social change. For by itself, therapy can only do so much in a world in which material conditions and differences do indeed have an impact on consciousness and emotional experience. One can "get one's life in order" as best one can, through therapy, self-help, and so on. But that life will still be lived in a context of social reality which therapy, alone, does not address, except–and this is not insignificant of course–indirectly. More, and different, activities are needed.

The need to acknowledge social and material reality became dramatically clear to me at one particularly tense moment at the women's center speak-out, when an extremely obese woman rose from the floor to ask what others felt about the fact that every woman on the stage–prominent writers and therapists all–was "thin and gorgeous" (in her words) while most of those in the audience were not. The woman's observation–shocking, disturbing, embarrassing–stopped the proceedings cold for a moment, since it pointed to a real contradiction in the day's message: that therapy aimed at changing one's self-image would, by itself, solve the problems of women in this society.

Issues of class and race privilege, and–as the speaker pointed out–sheer luck in the draw from the gene pool, in a world in which women are still judged and rewarded for their looks, had clearly made profound differences in the lives of the very women gathered that day, helping to put some of us onstage as intellectual and social leaders, while others had suffered their days in shame, invisibility, and emotional and material want. Of course, even the "stars" suffered the pains of sexism. But there were differences. Those on stage (the featured speakers included Gloria Steinem and Naomi Wolf among others) were indeed in many ways blessed as most women are not. And as much as we ourselves may deplore the results of these unequally distributed blessings, they had to be acknowledged and addressed as more than a matter of "self-image."

The real issues here, it was obvious to me, were ones which self-help and even therapy cannot finally address, unless it admits that we are *not* all alike, any more than Mariette Hartley is just like the prostitutes and welfare mothers and junkies that precede and follower her onto the daytime talk shows she appears on. Some of us are born poor, and dark-skinned, and in shapes and aspects which cause others to reject and hurt us, to deny us respect and housing and income and love and physical safety. And others of us have managed to live our lives without suffering nearly as much–in some cases actually very little–and so have more easily developed what is now called "self-esteem"; and the material rewards which seem to accompany it.

Political equality is not a subjective thing. How we feel about ourselves is not entirely a matter of psychological or spiritual health. It is to a great extent socially determined. And to only address an inner child's wounds–from family or society–without addressing the conditions that produced those institutions, is not to be straight about what causes our suffering.

There was no question that this gathering was explicitly feminist. The speakers shared the political values of the second wave, and, most important, they were aggressively and explicitly opposed to 12 Step groups, like OA, which advise giving up one's life to a Higher Power. Keynote speakers, as well as those who "shared" experiences in the speak-out, made copious references to the evils of media- and male-mandated images of beauty and used words like "sisterhood" regularly. A film was shown about the relationship between media images of beauty and eating disorders such as bulimia and anorexia. And the sponsors of the event, who identified themselves as feminist therapists, distinguished their own theories of weight control from the addiction theories which are now so popular. Unlike events and meetings I will discuss next, and unlike many other feminist trends and groups which *are* explicitly linked to the recovery movement, this gathering–and this was my main reason for attending–sought to present an alternative to the 12 Step therapy endorsed by OA.

Nonetheless, even here, in this fastidiously "political" gathering, it was impossible to escape certain dangerous tendencies found in the recovery movement, not because of stated ideology, but because of what was unstated: that there was no goal beyond a personal "cure" for what–no matter what it was called–was addressed as a personal problem.

I was troubled about the decision to have this kind of speak-out–modeled as it is on a very different kind of political event–because it pointed up to me how far even we feminists have moved from our original gutsy visions of what we could and should do for ourselves. The desire to heal ourselves, as an end in itself, is limited. The use of the words "survivor" and "empowerment" are at least a bit euphemistic. In fact, rape and incest "survivors" are rape and incest "victims" in a profoundly important political sense which I am loathe to forget. We may have survived the act, as Holocaust survivors survived *their* atrocities. And that is certainly a positive, even empowering thing, in a personal sense. But unless we name and attack the perpetrators of our abuse and put them out of business, so to speak, we have not fully dealt with our status as victims or overcome it.

In the speak-outs I attended, I heard numbers, shocking numbers, marking the extent of incest and other child abuse in this nation. And the idea was always the same: we must heal ourselves and so end the cycle of violence. But this "cycle" of violence and abuse assumes a very truncated view of society and history. The only institution addressed and acknowledged is the immediate family. And the only time span addressed is two generations long—from parent to child.

This, it seems to me, is pure Bradshaw. It assumes that all we need to do is be good to ourselves and our own children and the world will heal. It assumes that "empowerment" need reach no further than our own arm span, our own ability to reach inward, to our own souls, and outward, to our own kin.

I do not dispute these recovery terms, in their limited senses, or dispute the positive effects which some may receive from using them. But I do dispute their adequacy to the problems they address. I prefer the old-fashioned sixties idea that if one woman is still a victim we all are victims because I believe that notion addresses a social and material reality which still exists, and that losing sight of its impact on all of us leads to the kind of political blindness and spiritual miasma that has brought so many women to the recovery movement in the vain hope that it will heal them of the wounds of sexist society.

IRON JOHN BENDS THE POLITICAL AXES OF POWER

The speak-outs I have just described, which felt to me like New Age versions of feminist events, were a lot closer to the feeling of 12 Step meetings than to consciousness-raising. Nonetheless, there was no question that they were feminist; that they addressed issues in which women were victims and men and male institutions were responsible for their pain. No matter what course the actual proceedings took, there was always a clear understanding that women were less powerful than men, even if nothing was suggested to alter the situation and – as was sadly apparent – many women left feeling less empowered and more alone than when they came.

But the odd mix of feminism and recovery thought that permeates so many other liberal and progressive political developments these days is not always so carefully balanced or respectful of feminist political truths. In fact, in my wanderings through the meetings and books and documents of other social trends, I have been more and more amazed at how feminist ideas have been twisted and incorporated into agendas in which issues of power imbalance – or power at all – have virtually disappeared.

In the teachings of what has come to be called the "men's movement," or even the "men's liberation movement" – another political trend which leans heavily upon recovery-thought – the idea that women are at the weaker end of the power axes upon which gender struggles turn is not only not acknowledged; it is blatantly denied. While an important strand of this movement certainly does grow out of and espouse feminist ideas and goals,[3] the most prominent and culturally influential strands of the men's movement have been notoriously hostile to feminists and women generally, even as they have been at pains to link themselves ideologically, if only for contrast, to our ideas.

"Feminists say black; we say white," is often the little boyish "nyah, nyah, nyah" attitude with which male liberationists address the issue of gender relations. The movement would not exist, of course, if not for feminism (just as the New Right would not exist without the New Left). But far from acknowledging that they represent a backlash, these men – Robert Bly, Sam Keen, Warren Farrell, Shepherd Bliss, to name a few – insist that feminism itself has nothing to do with their mission to improve what they see as the degrading and unfair position of men in Western societies, which, they insist, has always been far weaker and less honored than the position of women. Women, they argue, have had everything their own way throughout history and yet have continued to whine and complain and demand more from their beleaguered, helpless mates.

In the many books and seminars and conferences which now proliferate and enrich, *à la* Bradshaw and Schaef, the male liberation gurus, the ideas of feminists are invoked, turned on their heads, and used against women. And it is the ideas and methods of the recovery movement that have made it possible for the men's movement to accomplish this political sleight of hand. Many of the leaders of the movement began as feminists in the 1960s, as a matter of fact. (Thus their almost scholarly expertise in the ideas of gender and power which feminism developed.) But it was when they discovered that their wounds were more deep and bloody than ours that they found their true mission in life: to free themselves from women, especially feminists.

But how to get from patriarchy to an inverse vision in which *women* rule? The teachings of the recovery movement, especially the writings of Bradshaw and his followers, held the key. For while the explicit antifeminism which so virulently fuels the chants and tracts of the men's movement is not present in the writings of Bradshaw and the others, their very refusal to deal with political concepts makes them easy to co-opt for sexist purposes. For if family systems are *not* fueled by the needs of masculinist economic and social structures—if, as Bradshaw suggests, they function as autonomous engines of abuse and addiction production, cut off from their original economic moorings—then it is all too easy to read them as female-dominated, since mothers do indeed play so central a role in family management. (The irony of all this must not be lost on feminists.)

It is especially easy to see how the men's movement manages to blame women for the family's ills when you consider that recovery starts from the perspective of the wounded, abused child. And the wounds of childhood, as remembered by the child himself, are indeed most often administered by the seemingly all-powerful mother, who was given the role of domestic top sergeant, so to speak, and left at home to play it out while the father either left home or passively looked on.

Robert Bly was the originator of much of this rhetoric. He publicly and lucratively mourns the "lost warrior spirit" and blames feminism for knocking it out of the modern male. His own "missing contact with men and his overexposure to strong angry women" (quoted in Faludi 1991, p. 306) as a child, he asserts, were the cause of his own, archetypically repressed masculine development. And if his all-powerful mother didn't do enough damage, the feminists of the sixties, as he is fond of recalling, finished off the job of destroying his male ego with their "hurt feelings" and "promises that we will sleep with you if you are not too aggressive and macho" (ibid., p. 308). Dan Quayle echoed Bly's most famous idea, that the problems of the world can be blamed on the fact that too many women are "raising boys with no man in the house" (as though that were always a choice made by women).

Hard as it may seem, for anyone with any sense of history or social theory, to follow this line of thinking, it is indeed what passes for argument and moral assertion in these circles, in which wounded males howl out their rage at women for ruining their lives. Warren Farrell, who like Bly started out as a feminist but has since regretted his youthful ways, is the best recent source for this kind of ahistoric logic. He too is enraged because feminists have "blamed men" when it is men who are the real "victims" of sexual inequality. According to his much read and cited *The Myth of Male Power: Why Men Are the Disposable Sex* (1993), and the interviews he has given since its publication, there is no truth to the claim that women are paid less for equal work in today's world. On the contrary, "there's *no* difference in pay between the sexes" he insists, once you "control for variables like the number of hours worked outside the home and men's willingness to commute, work inconvenient hours, relocate to undesirable places and take on danger" (Stone 1993, p. 145). Nor is it true, according to Farrell, that men have not traditionally been nurturing, as women so often complain. ("Complaining," according to Farrell is the most important thing "men can learn from women" since it is the source of all the sympathy, attention, and unfair demands women get and make on male society!) In fact, says this guru of "men's equality," "financial support is a form of nurturing" (ibid.) which men have always provided.

In this kind of logic, we see the end of all political sense and meaning. Alice herself could not have stumbled into a more topsy-turvy Wonderland than this world of men's movement politics, in which weakness is power, money is love, privilege is oppression, and men are the wretched of the earth. Nor are Bly and Farrell alone in this reasoning. Terry Kellogg, another men's movement therapist and guru, carries doublespeak to even greater heights with his particular take on the codependency issue. In talking about sexual violence, for example – and I mean here the men who beat and abuse their daughters and wives and others, sexually and brutally – he explains that while feminists were right to focus on power as a political issue, they "missed the fact that . . . the victim and the offender are in the same line and that they have the same issues . . . a basic victimization." "Power," Kellogg explains, "is an illusion," since "women's codependency is their power through powerlessness. . . . Men's codependency is their powerlessness through power" (1991, pp. 100–101).

The idea that money is not power but slavery, or nurturance, or whatever slogan is popular in Wonderland today, while power itself is weakness, could only grow out of a worldview – the recovery worldview – in which material conditions of existence have no bearing whatever on the pains and sorrows of our lives; in which institutions other than the family – which seems to exist in a social vacuum – do not even exist as factors in our experience. All is reduced to the very limited and distorted view of life as a small boy in a dysfunctional nuclear family. And even more troubling is that this nuclear family is one in which the real power of the father is invisible or lied about— as is so common, especially from a child's perspective—while the apparently dominant role played by mothers is made to seem larger than life, and definitive, since the larger male world which has actually positioned her and given her this role is masked from view.

The men's movement rhetoric is filled with talk of "wounded inner children," "abused little boys" whose mothers inflicted "inappropriate dependence" on them and somehow or other sent their "lost fathers" running—to alcohol, adultery, or points unknown. It is also filled with talk of empowerment, liberation, and other terms borrowed from feminist and other sixties social movements. Only this time the victims in need of empowerment are the "lost fathers" and their sons, who are reclaiming their mythic roles as heads and heir apparents of the household, demanding—suddenly—custody rights, and other traditionally female responsibilities, as though these obligations were sources of power previously denied to men by a female-run, indeed a feminist-run, state.

The intricacies and elaborations of this thought system are intriguing. By shifting the concept of "abuse" or "oppression" to a realm in which *only* childhood, family-based experiences have any power over our development, and in which these childhood wounds are the *only* causes for current sufferings, virtually every male action, in the quest for wealth and power, becomes a sign of victimization, addiction, disease.

Thus, for example, the "disease" of "workaholism" is said by men's movement theorist Mike Lew to be a result of childhood abuse in the family. The incentives for workaholism in men would seem to be multiple: increasing costs of food, housing, medical care, and education for one's family in today's economy; competition for limited promotions within an industry; mistaken notions of what is considered "manly"; and rewards for some in board and country club memberships. How then can workaholism be a disease caused by women? Simple. It is a response to the pain still felt at being abused and emasculated. The more deep the pain, the more work becomes a "narcotic" to mask it. "Workaholics . . . get affirmation from numbing strategies that focus attention away from the abuse," says Lew. "And no one gets to see the isolated, frightened child hiding behind the bulging biceps or the BMW and the three-piece suit" (1991, p. 145). The problem here is not that these men are considered sufferers or that the source of their suffering is in part the traditional family. Of course these things are true, as feminists have long been saying. The problem is Lew's distorted analysis of the family as the only powerful institution in society, and the woman-bashing this analysis endorses.

I chose the workaholism example randomly from a wide variety of men's movement books and articles, in virtually all of which the same kinds of ideas and explanations turn up again and again. The American involvement in Vietnam, for example, a very different kind of political issue, is interpreted by Kellogg not in terms of political concepts but of addiction discourse. The war, for him, "was the tolerance break of a codependent culture. It was acting out. It was the arrogance" (1991, p. 111) of a small child in a powerless family situation, in which healthy masculinity was stunted and shamed.

The Gulf War inspires a similarly trivializing analysis. "Yeah it's about oil and prices, but even without the oil issue" we still wouldn't be able to get out, Kellogg opines, because, as "codependents in a family we set up the dynamics and then we can't win" (1991, p. 112). We and the Arabs, he would have us believe, are in a dysfunctional family dynamic in which we have set ourselves up as codependents. Simple as that. But, what, we might insist upon asking, *about* the oil and oil prices? What about the engines of progress and global power which do indeed *depend* upon these fossil fuels? This, of course, is a minor issue. Let the world ride horses to work, live in caves, and howl into the urban winds. The only issue, in this critique of male excess and mayhem, is our need to free the American male from the feminized family. That done, there will be no more Vietnams, no more Gulf Wars, no more Cold Wars.

These ideas make any sense at all only in relation to a very privileged class of white professional men. Their influence is nonetheless felt more broadly through the products of the mass media. The culture industries–especially the movies, which are, after all, produced and marketed almost entirely by upscale white men–have been very much interested in the ideas of the men's movement recently.

We have discussed earlier how recovery-thought offers TV movies and talk shows about social issues a way to acknowledge and address important gender problems without actually dealing with feminist demands for social change. The movie industry, however, does not have the same incentive to acknowledge women's valid claims and feelings since the movie industry is far less beholden to female dollars and loyalties. (This is not primarily because male moviegoers outnumber female, but rather, because most moviegoers today are dating or married couples, the male member of which, even in the 1990s, is more likely to choose the movie and pay for the tickets than the female, according to marketing researchers). Movies about sensitive men acting as *both* father and mother to their sons while the hapless women of the house are either invisible, incompetent, or downright criminally neglectful, filled the screens—especially the summer "family oriented" screens of the mall cineplexes—during the late 1980s and early 1990s, from white yuppie tearjerkers like *Sleepless in Seattle* to otherwise exemplary films about blacks in the inner cities like *Boyz in the Hood.* And in most of these films the ideas of the new men's movement—in which the sexual power imbalance is somehow seen to have been at *men's* expense, since *they* were deprived of the *right* to be parents, have feelings, and stay home and do housework—are blithely assumed or explicitly stated. But the men in these movies do not—as Farrell insists they are dying to do—give up their positions in the economic and public worlds to achieve their new roles as nurturers. On the contrary, women simply disappear, for all serious purposes, while men take on the Superman role of being all things to all people, privately and publicly. And do it with ease and grace to boot, by some mysterious means to which real women have not been granted access.

Movie househusbands and single Dads—since the days of Dustin Hoffman in *Kramer vs. Kramer*—seem effortlessly to handle the double day and its many stresses in a way that denies, as does the recovery movement itself, the material realities of most people's lives—certainly those of single mothers. But that's Hollywood, where people have always been able to dance upside down on ceilings, and otherwise defy the laws of nature, gravity, and the market economy.

I don't wish to give the men's movement undue importance, since its actual political impact is negligible. In fact, if one looks closely at the make-up of the groups and seminars and weekends and conferences at which the followers of these gurus gather, one finds a very narrow social and racial demographic slice. Indeed, the male membership of this movement overlaps greatly with that of the recovery movement itself (Lenfest 1991; Farmer 1991; Farrell 1993). Men's liberationists, like the followers of Ann Wilson Schaef, with whom they intermix, are mostly white, middle-class professional men who are taking the greatest blows from the downward mobility that has hit the educated professional middle classes in recent decades (Ehrenreich 1990, pp. 196–227).

Their rage, while understandable, is misdirected, however, since the real source of their disempowerment is not women but the corporate power structure. They are overtrained and under-needed in today's economy, and—like the white working-class men who feel a similar rage at the black workers who, *they* think, are responsible for taking *their* jobs and incomes—

their rage at women, who are doing even worse economically and professionally, is misplaced. Women, like blacks, are a safer, easier target than the actual culprits, in this "Kick the dog" drama of pecking orders gone wild.

Given the demographics of the movement, it is no surprise that men's liberationists tend to be oblivious to the greater class and race injustices from which most American men suffer. As in the speak-outs on eating disorders and sexual abuse, men's gatherings tend to exaggerate the importance of middle-class injuries and addictions but fail to make important distinctions between the *kinds* of addictions which plague different social groups. Street drugs—the scourge of poor male populations—are not mentioned. Absent white middle-class fathers may be relatively functional alcoholics, but most are not hard-core drug users in ghettoes or prisons. And workaholics and failed warriors, who loom very large indeed in the minds of these men, are hardly likely to represent vast numbers of American men, given the recessionary epidemics of unemployment and underemployment plaguing most working-class communities and families.

Narrow though its constituency may be, the ideas, if not the activities, of this movement *are* important because these are the men who write and speak to the media and who take time to organize the campaigns—for father's rights and so on—which do receive so much attention. They are also the men who have time to write and speak and very often organize around broader social and political agendas, many of which are setting the agendas for liberal and progressive movements which address far more important matters than freeing oneself from the Big Bad Mommy in one's head. And their impact is being felt in wider political circles these days.

SELF-ESTEEM: A "SOCIAL VACCINE" AGAINST CLEAR THINKING

Feminist speak-outs and men's movement seminars are events of relatively marginal political impact, of course. But there is another arena in which recovery movement ideas and spokespersons are having a much more central impact on American politics by directly reaching the seats of government: the growing, very successful movement to establish "Self-Esteem Task Forces" as parts of state legislatures. In the many states where they have already been established, these task forces are empowered to set up agencies and programs and projects meant to solve actual social problems such as unemployment, street crime, and poverty—the kind of projects the recovery movement itself, much less the men's movement, does not even refer to—through the teaching of "self-esteem" to those who are indeed society's victims. The idea is that if the poor, the criminal, the addicted, can be taught to feel good about themselves they will clean up their acts and start treating themselves and others with love, respect, and responsibility. This, in turn, it is assumed, will lead, automatically, to progressive social change.

Spearheaded by a 1990 publication called *Toward a State of Self-Esteem* published by the California Task Force to Promote Self-Esteem and Personal and Social Responsibility, this movement has managed to get a National Council for Self-Esteem established, of which, at this writing, there are sixty-six chapters in twenty-nine states (Herman 1988, p. 55). Peopled by liberals and progressives in the California legislature, social services, universities, and elsewhere, the Task Force is dedicated to "a pioneering effort to address the causes and cures of many of the major social ills that plague us all today" through "an historic and hopeful search for a 'social vaccine'"–self-esteem (p. xii).

"In the 1960s," writes California Assemblyman John Vasconcellos, author of the enabling legislation, in the preface to *Toward a State of Self-Esteem*, scientists "unlocked the secrets of gravity and empowered us humans to enter outer space." But "in the 1990s," he continues, "we human beings have the opportunity to enter our own inner space . . . unlock the secrets of healthy human development" and "point the way toward a successful effort to truly improve our human condition" (p. x). What is this great new secret uncovered by modern thinkers? And how will it bring about such revolutionary transformations in human existence? The secret is "self-esteem," of course. And its miracle-working powers will be unleashed, the document asserts, by simply setting up–with amazingly small costs to taxpayers–programs in schools, jails, community centers, and hospitals where those suffering from social and family deprivation can be saved from tragic lives through the bolstering of their sagging egos.

The document is filled with advice and guidelines for "Nurturing Self-Esteem and Personal and Social Responsibility" based on ideas straight out of the recovery movement. It recounts the now familiar litany of ills caused by family dysfunction and addictive disorders and blames them for the growing ranks of convicts, rapists, drug dealers, prostitutes, welfare mothers, and even disgruntled workers. (Advice is offered to corporate managers, for example, on how to present "Managerial Decisions" in ways which "nurture self-esteem and personal and social responsibility" (p. 130). The slogan "You are terrific; you can do anything you put your mind to" is the motto of this movement, and its ace in the hole for every social evil it encounters.

Reading this effusively optimistic document, one is struck by the profound imbalance in the California program, as laid out, between the gargantuan efforts aimed at improving psychological ills, and the negligible to nonexistent remedies proposed for political and economic disadvantages. This imbalance clearly explains why the costs are so low. Self-reliance (rather than aid, in the form of money or services) is assumed to be as all-powerful here as it was in Emerson's famous essays of that name, in which the great American spirit of individualism and personal freedom was said to make all things possible to those who lived and thought correctly, no matter the circumstances of their existences.

This is not of course what the founders of the Self-Esteem movement actually say or even believe. They are liberals, committed to *helping* others and engendering "social responsibility" (as they endlessly repeat) and a sense of collective identity and concern. Nonetheless, given the institutional and economic limits of their programs, self-reliance is unfortunately left to do most of the work.

Money does not change hands in this utopian world of ego bolstering and spiritual healing. No one suggests—at least in this program blueprint—that drug addicts be given job training, decent housing, and child care, and sent off to work for wages approaching those of their newly nurturing supervisors. No one suggests that teen pregnancy be addressed in terms of free, accessible, legal reproductive rights and services, much less job training and opportunities for young women from poor and minority backgrounds.

Nowhere in *Toward a State of Self-Esteem* is much of anything in the way of structural or institutional change suggested. Even the sections on education do not address matters of cultural deprivation or curriculum reform, much less funding to pay for better, happier teachers, new books, computers, media equipment, and so on. And no one suggests that medical care be provided, even to infants who surely have no self-esteem problem yet, but quickly will acquire one as their mental and physical development are impaired through poverty. It is not even suggested, anywhere in the document, that the authors realize the importance of such things, as necessary prerequisites to the efficacy of all other programs. It is implied, rather, that self-esteem development is all that is needed, and that such development is indeed possible, no matter what the other circumstances of one's life. The only thing approaching a structural change in the recommendations for "Education Reform," for example, is that "parents need to become involved in their children's education," and "teachers and administrators need to include parents in their ongoing plans" (p. 72), a recommendation which, given the material conditions of failing families, is at best circular, and at worst downright ludicrous.

How could a group of intelligent, liberal policy makers come to such con-clusions? To spell out the thinking here in more detail, the idea–based on the teachings and methods of the recovery movement–is that once we learn to stop abusing ourselves and feel good about our ability to function and be productive citizens, we will automatically begin to treat others–no matter what their racial, sexual, cultural, and behavioral differences–as respectfully and lovingly as we treat ourselves. Thus, the ills of the world, all seen to result from self-hatred projected onto others, will gradually abate and disappear.

Of course there is much common-sense truth here. One need not be a therapist or even a recovering drug addict to see that. But there is also a slew of logical slippages and blindspots in this blithe assumption that all social ills stem from psychological wounds inflicted upon us as children. Most serious among them is the circular, politically skewed idea that evil originates with those who have been damaged by previous mistreatment, while the original evils of the primary forces are somehow forgotten. It is as if we are all now on a level playing field of damaged souls, striking out at each other randomly, with no greater goal than inflicting pain in revenge for our own wounds.

What is missing is the original feminist idea about power relations in a materially unequal world. The idea that the weaker among us–*women* (and by extension other disenfranchised groups)–suffered blows to our egos and bodies and purses through the institutionalized, economically and politi-cally enforced sexist attitudes and practices of our fathers, bosses, and legis-lators has somehow been transformed into the idea–at least partly true of course–that *everyone* in America has suffered such blows to the ego and re-quires this kind of emotional affirmative action to get him or her moving and shaking. Thus, every perpetrator, as we saw in the men's movement rhetoric, is himself a victim of the entire, "dysfunctional" system, and his sins will be absolved and rectified through his own self-transformation.

This logic is not as easy to debunk as I am making it sound perhaps. Like the thinking of the men's movement, and the recovery movement generally, it rests to some extent upon truths discovered and spoken by feminists. The idea that everyone suffers in a world of injustice and irrationality is a true one, which comes from the early thinking of Left/feminist utopianism. It was indeed feminists who said, back in those heady days, that if only sexism and other policies of oppression and bigotry were ended, everyone would be happier and more fulfilled.

But we also said, very loudly, that these magic feats of social transforma-tion would not come about without some bloody struggles over power and money, in which those now empowered by the system–no matter how spiritually suffering—would be loathe to give up their luxurious forms of suffering; would, indeed, have to be dragged kicking and screaming away from the many privileges they would be forced to share with us.

We did not assume that our enemies would gladly change. Nor did we assume that our own efforts at self-transformation, at self-"empowerment" in our personal relations, would automatically "empower" us politically, as the Self-Esteem movement believes. Far less did we assume—since we had experience here—that our boyfriends and lovers and husbands would sit still for all this shifting of power relations, would happily see how much better they felt when they were nice guys, and gladly move over and make space for us, lend a hand to ease our burdens, out of "benevolent self-interest," the rewards of which would be warm, fuzzy feelings.

So why do so many of us seem willing to believe it now? Why are we willing to retreat from the hard-nosed political truths and strategies we understood so well in the sixties, into a fantasy landscape in which good feelings will achieve what aggressive action did not—at least to the extent that we expected. The answer is right there, of course, in the disillusionment and exhaustion of our present situation. We have lost faith in our ambitious ideas and plans because—just at the moment—they are hard to believe in.

There are few contexts in which such ambitious endeavors make sense, and so many disappointments to make us blame ourselves for not having accomplished what we promised. And so we have even so prominent a feminist leader and thinker as Gloria Steinem joining the cheerleading forces for the new Self-Esteem movement for reasons that point very clearly to the links between 1960s feminism and 1990s recovery, and their troubling, if understandable, ramifications.

In her massive treatise on self-esteem, *Revolution from Within: A Book of Self-Esteem* (1992), Steinem lauds the California effort, among many other recovery-based examples of New Age politics, for their strides in moving us toward what she calls a "meta-democracy" based not on "patriarchy, racism, class systems, and other hierarchies that ration self-esteem" but on more ancient ideas which assume "a oneness with all living things and with the universe itself" (p. 32). In this worldview, distinctions and differences among sufferers are less important than the welfare of the universal system in which we all play a role. And so, the focus on conflicts between and among us is replaced by one in which harmony and good will lead to progress (p. 32).

Steinem is no fool, nor has she ceased to be a feminist. On the contrary, she is careful throughout her often moving book to make clear connections between her espousal of self-healing and the mission of activists to change the world. Indeed many of her chapters tell stories in which individual activists, inspired by the spiritual teachings of the recovery movement, have successfully waged impressive campaigns for social change. She is most certainly still a major voice and actor in the struggle for women's equality, and her book, to the extent that it keeps all this in mind, is among the most valuable and helpful of the many treatises on women and recovery I have looked at.

But in shifting from a traditional political concern with power hierarchies like patriarchy, to what she calls a "circular, universal" worldview, she has indeed moved away from a clear sense of what the social problems are for us and why they have proved so hard to eradicate. And the reason she has done this is that she–like most of the women I talked to who have moved from feminism to recovery–has taken to looking inward and blaming herself for the limits and road blocks which have stalled feminist progress, more than is appropriate or reasonable.

In her "Personal Preface" Steinem writes of how she suffered what we would call "burnout" in her years of selfless activism, of trying to heal the world, because she was not addressing her own needs. In her compulsive activism, she tells us, she now sees that she "was more aware of other people's feelings than [her] own; that [she] had been repeating the patterns of [her abused] childhood without recognizing them" and that she was "codependent on the world" because she lacked self-esteem (p. 7).

From there–from the idea that one's inner wounds are the fuel for one's actions–even one's *political* actions (unless of course one is in recovery as she now is)–it is easy enough to drift to the next intellectual revision: that men and women alike suffer this *same* solipsistic malady in which actions reflect inner, not outer, issues and realities. "The more I talked to men as well as women, the more it seemed that inner feelings of incompleteness, emptiness, self-doubt, and self-hatred were the same no matter who experienced them," she writes. And, being careful "not to gloss over the difficulties of equalizing power," she nonetheless insists that it is more important to recognize that people, all people, "seemed to stop punishing others or themselves only when they gained some faith in their own unique, intrinsic worth" (p. 5).

So far does she ride on this train of thought, in which self-esteem and the lack of it are all-determining, that she ventures to psychoanalyze Ronald Reagan, George Bush, Saddam Hussein, and President Ceausescu of Romania all as victims of childhood abuse within dysfunctional families and attributes their acts and policies to this simple causal factor, with no regard for politics, economics, history, or even more complex psychological factors. She sees these four figures of extreme, far-reaching, and damaging power as victims, blindly acting out, in their adult years, the rage and fear and shame they experienced as helpless little boys. Hussein and Bush, Steinem explains, were beaten by authoritarian fathers; Reagan and Ceausescu, respectively, "learned endless denial" and "sadism" from alcoholic fathers of two different classic types; and so—as the men's movement leaders also teach—their political actions are rooted in their family systems. If only we can change our childhood socialization institutions, especially the family, she argues, we will go far toward ending such atrocities in the future. And if we don't do this, she also argues, we have absolutely no hope of social progress.

I have heard all of these arguments before from friends and acquaintances in recovery who accuse me of being in denial and warn me that "we cannot change the world until we change ourselves." But there is a problem in this logic. It assumes what is not the case: that inner experience and attitude are actual predictors of political belief and behavior; and that, even more to the point, all people who experience similar childhood abuses turn out the same. This is way off base, as even the most cursory look at heroes and tyrants of different times will show. There are just too many wonderful people who have survived abusive families and too many terrible ones who seem to have come from relatively loving and caring families. Indeed, sometimes the very families that produce one sort of child also produce the other. Nor do people stay good or bad, progressive or reactionary, kind or brutal, in all situations and time periods.

This is because more than family dynamics are at work in creating a human being and setting him up in a situation in which he thinks and acts in ways which are good or evil. George Bush, after all, was not formed only by his violent father. He was formed by a life of privilege in which he was cut off from the experiences and realities of most of those he sought to govern, for one thing, and mixed only with those who thought as he did. He went to elite, ruling class schools, moreover, in which he was taught to believe *ideas*— well thought out classic ideas very often—about race, class, and gender inequalities which do indeed support elitist policies in the name of God, reason, and social welfare.

It is after all not only abused children who believe women and blacks and Arabs are inferior and evil. Very often, in my own classrooms, I look down at the smiling white suburban faces of very nice, decent students who tell me that they *know* that homeless people are lazy; that homosexuality is "gross";

that blacks are less intelligent than whites; and give "evidence" and examples to prove it. And the source of their attitudes and the behavior it justifies is a lot more complicated than bad parenting.

One of the most disturbing aspects of the recovery and Self-Esteem movements, actually, is their implicit anti-intellectualism, their insistence on reducing all experience to a simple belief in psychological causation, against the grain of all evidence that human behavior is complex and that history, class, nationality, and many more factors–including reason and debate and persuasion–play roles in our lives and thoughts and feelings.

Self-esteem, after all, is itself a socially determined concept, as even the California study inadvertently attests to. Some studies, the authors admit, were actually found to "assert increases in self-esteem due to substance abuse" (p. 49), amazingly. And some poor unwed teenage girls actually claimed to have gained in self-esteem through motherhood (ibid.). In fact, motherhood is one of the few meaningful states many young women can imagine for themselves in a world in which other opportunities for growth and service are not available.

Of course there are methodological and linguistic explanations and corrections in the document which explain away these aberrant findings. Nor, to be fair, are they the most typical ones. But the fact remains that it is not so easy to be sure that what one person finds gratifying and empowering will be the same for everyone. Too much depends on the specific circumstances in which the good feelings are encouraged. And in a context, in which moral and social values are not spelled out, but are rather assumed to grow automatically from good feelings, we will surely get some results that the liberal Task Force members will not be happy with.

In a book about and for women by Judith Briles called *The Confidence Factor: How Self-Esteem Can Change Your Life* (1990), for example, we learn that women–in the context of current social mores and values–who rate highest on the "self-esteem indicator scale," tend to be those who use make-up, moisturizer, have professional manicures, and color their hair professionally (pp. 84–93). And why shouldn't they? They probably earn more money and get more reinforcement from others. After all, we live in a world in which appearance, for females–and too often violence and machismo for males–are the markers of social status and power. This reality was clearly a complicating factor in the women's center speak-out I described, when the issue of the "thin and gorgeous" speakers and experts, so different, physically, from the majority of audience members, came up. There, as in the self-esteem literature, matters of difference and privilege and inherited social status were dismissed far too easily as negligible or easily overcome through therapeutic efforts to change one's self-image.

The problem with assuming that self-esteem cures all social ills, and that it can be safely and predictably produced by the methods suggested by the California Task Force, is actually under scrutiny these days by more and more experts, as the programs set up by these task forces in other states are put in place and observed. In an Op-Ed piece in the *New York Times,* in July of 1993, Lillian G. Katz, a professor of education, takes the Self-Esteem movement to task for encouraging what she calls "narcissism"–an overvaluation of one's value and importance in relation to others–which leads to laziness and passivity, among other things.

By failing to encourage actual educational goals like curiosity and mastery of skills, lest they make children overly aware of their actual inadequacies and weaknesses in relation to more talented and skilled others, she argues, these plans often lapse into mindless self-congratulation for simply being alive and a thwarting of the curiosity and creativity and mastery that education should further. She cites a case in which children who visited a dairy farm, for example, were praised for such responses as "I liked the cows." But no effort was made to encourage or praise children for such responses as "What I want to know more about is . . ." or "What I found interesting was . . ." In this way, she argues, self-satisfaction is encouraged inappropriately while real educational goals are forgotten.

Rooted in just this kind of excessive, uncritical concern for hurt feelings and discouraging messages, the Self-Esteem movement offers homilies about training case workers to treat welfare recipients "with dignity" and offering inmates "opportunities for self-esteem education." And of course no one could argue with this sort of thing on the surface. But looking beneath the surface, it becomes clearer that this method not only tends to downplay the economic and political; it also leads indirectly to some questionable political biases. The California study, *Toward a State of Self-Esteem,* concludes that "self-esteem is central to most of the personal and social problems that plague human life in today's world" and since "the family has always been the primary environment that shapes a person's . . . self-esteem," the authors find "the conclusion . . . inescapable: the family must be the first and fundamental focus of our attention" (p. 45).

This family focus is in fact the very agenda traditionally associated with the Right, not the Left, because it insists that *private* efforts and funds and personnel should take on most of the burden of socialization and security and care of children, the elderly, the ill, and other dependents, while government should keep out of such matters. In so strongly invoking the family, the Self-Esteem movement drifts, ironically, far too close to the cold-blooded indifference that, in the Reagan/Bush years, managed to unfairly and cruelly overburden private citizens with more responsibility than they were equipped, economically or emotionally, to handle.

The fact is that – Reagan and the recovery movement to the contrary – we live in a world in which most things happen not because families decide on them or clumsily cause them, but because economic and political forces insist on them. Nor will the teachings of therapists or spiritual leaders do much to help families hold their own in such a world, unless these figures are aligned with other leaders and organizations committed to addressing the social and economic issues which *must* be tackled for the poor embattled family to survive, much less cure itself of "dysfunctions."

But it is, alas, families and spiritual leaders and therapists and self-help programs that this movement naively looks to, as it suggests plans and behaviors which the Right actually welcomes and agrees with, but for far less humanistic reasons. In fact, it is an irony of this movement that it has liberals and progressives asking the wealthy and powerful for the most piddling amount of material help, as it seeks to make the victims of power *even more* unfairly responsible for the circumstances which they – no matter what their "diseases" and "dysfunctions" – did not create for themselves. But this is indeed the logic of the recovery movement which, as I have been arguing, has from the start managed to take the best ideas and impulses of feminists and democratic leftists and twist them in ways which offer a certain amount of support and help while leaving untouched, and increasingly invisible, the root causes of our troubles.

In my travels through the Land of Recovery I felt at times like Dorothy in the Land of Oz. Everywhere I went I met people like the Cowardly Lion, the paralyzed Tin Man, the Scarecrow who thought he had no brains, walking down the Yellow Brick Road to find the Wizard who would give them what they thought they needed. Like these characters, and Dorothy herself, the addicts seeking recovery learn, when they actually reach their goals, that the answers they seek, the powers they need, are within, and that home and family life are the only true sources of happiness.

But while I love this story and think that it is indeed empowering – especially for little girls, just learning that it is possible to separate, have their own adventures, and still be welcomed home – it is as limited as the recovery movement itself. For it asks us to believe that the glorious Emerald City – a land more wonderful and bright than any we have yet known–is a mirage, and that the search for such utopian vistas, such urban communities of difference and wonder, is a useless fantasy which will only disappoint us.

The truth is that our original political vision of a better world was not a fantasy or a false promise. Nor is it true that–as Steinem and the many other Dorothys I encountered and interviewed, who were burned out and disillusioned with politics and wanted only to go home, to find shelter from the postfeminist storm, seemed to believe–we have done so badly in our struggles to achieve it. The very fact that the recovery movement is so dependent upon feminist ideas and has felt the need to use them to make the old religious and family and work ethics seem relevant in today's world, is a sign of our power and our success. For feminists have indeed changed the world of family and public life in ways which make the old ideas meaningless.

For all its limits and problems, the literature of CODA and OA and ACOA and SA prove that we have changed the world for the better. They are a big advance over classic AA's concern with men as workers in their attention to women's issues and relationship dynamics. Just as the books of Bradshaw and Norwood and Schaef and Beattie are a big advance over the copies of *Good Housekeeping* and *Ladies Home Journal* my mother kept on the family coffee table. And the docudramas and talks shows of Oprah and Sally and Jane, about codependency and bulimia, are a big advance over the *Leave it to Beaver* and *I Love Lucy* episodes I grew up with.

But it is not only in the recovery movement that we see signs of feminist success and power, of the ways in which we changed the political and cultural maps of our world. The world of women at work, at home, and in the public sphere has indeed changed in the years since the second wave began its crusades for gender equity. The changes are uneven; the slipbacks and backlashes are real; the work we have to do and the difficulty of doing it appear ever more formidable as we learn more and more about the deep and insidious ways we have indeed been injured, and "discover," politicize, and become more and more outraged over ever more kinds of sexual abuse and prejudice. Incest, lesbian bashing, sexual harassment, date rape–these all existed long before 1975 or 1985 or 1995. But it was only when feminists named and politicized these acts, brought them into the open, that they came to loom so large in our lives. Because only then did more and more of us begin to recognize, report, publicize, and seek redress for them; to realize in fact that they were the causes of our suffering. And while this surge in awareness of gender crimes may seem discouraging and even overwhelming, it is also, more important, a necessary stage in the struggle of feminists for gender justice.

We can expect more and more issues of oppression and abuse to surface even as our influence and power over public consciousness increases. And we can expect more and more women to turn to recovery groups and teachings as they feel more and more overwhelmed by the realizations of what feminism actually means and what feminism actually brings into our line of vision and awareness. Nor is this inappropriate or to be condemned.

The fact is–and the recovery movement is the most real, if confusing, sign of this–that we are *in the midst* of an ongoing, but far from finished, revolution in gender politics. The revolution was begun, and is to this day being carried on with vigor and success, by the second wave feminist movement. There are any number of setbacks and pitfalls which the movement itself, as well as each of us involved–in whatever ways–in furthering it, will suffer. No massive change of the kind begun by feminists is going to come easily or quickly, or without huge complications and contradictions.

The recovery movement is important in this regard because it is perhaps the most contradictory, confusing, and impressive development to arise out of the ongoing movement toward gender justice. It is at once our most exciting and most depressing "accomplishment" depending on how you look at it. The latter judgment will prevail and be proven true, of course, if we allow ourselves to accept its intermediate position as a foregone, permanent conclusion. It is no such thing. The very great changes the recovery movement exhibits in the way in which even reactionaries must address matters of gender and private life are tributes to feminism. They will remain *ours* as long as we keep sight of the larger–and longer–struggle in which they represent a particularly difficult stopping point. But the unfinished revolution women began thirty years ago will not be stalled for long.

I did not write this book to attack the recovery movement. I am more concerned with building and defending feminism, not simply as an organized movement, for it is more than that, but more broadly as a way of seeing our lives and envisioning our futures, as we live and plan for them. But to achieve our goals in today's cultural climate, it is necessary to look critically at the uses to which feminism has been put by the recovery movement and to reclaim and reaffirm its original, more inspiring uses. For it is not some Higher Power that will bring us the delivery we rightly seek. Nor is it mere shelter from the storm of modern life that we need to be seeking, at least as our ultimate goal. It is the storm itself after all that is doing the damage. And staying dry, while important for survival, is not really our ultimate goal.

Notes

Introduction

1. Wendy Kaminer's much-discussed *I'm Dysfunctional, You're Dysfunctional* (Reading, Mass.: Addison-Wesley, 1992) is the most well known. In many ways Kaminer's critique of the recovery movement is insightful and useful. My own view of the movement, however, after lengthy and in-depth study, is that it is far more contradictory and complex than the easy dismissals by such critics acknowledge or perhaps grasp.

1. Oprah, Geraldo, and the Movie of the Week

1. Although there are numerous theoretical works on the power and role of home television in constructing and negotiating the flow of public thought and discourse, Raymond Williams's early and brief but infinitely suggestive *Television: Technology and Cultural Form* (New York: Schocken, 1975) is the work which most impressively maps out television's rise to a position of cultural and social dominance in post–World War II democracies and explains the implications of that rise as I am discussing it. Williams's work was an informing force in the development of the British Cultural Studies tradition. The contemporary thought of those working in that tradition is presented in many anthologies. A good overview of theoretical approaches to television studies rooted in social and cultural models of media, which also provides a good introductory essay on the importance of television and television studies generally, is Robert C. Allen, ed., *Channels of Discourse, Reassembled: Television and Contemporary Criticism*, second edition (Chapel Hill: University of North Carolina Press, 1992). See also Robert Avery and David Eason, *Critical Perspectives on Media and Society* (New York: Guilford Press, 1991).

Two excellent works on the relationship between television's rise and the role and representation of women and families in the media are Lynn Spigel, *Make Room for TV: Television and the Family Ideal in Postwar America* (Chicago: University of Chicago Press, 1992) and Ella Taylor, *Primetime Families: Television Culture in Postwar America* (Berkeley: University of California Press, 1989).

My own writing on the subject includes *The Looking Glass World of Nonfiction TV*

(Boston: South End Press, 1987), *Media-tions: Forays into the Culture and Gender Wars* (Boston: South End Press, 1994), and *The Movie of the Week: Private Stories/ Public Events* (Minneapolis: University of Minnesota Press, 1992).

For two interesting studies of the power of news media, specifically, to mold and engender public thought, see Daniel Dayan and Elihu Katz, *Media Events: The Live Broadcasting of History* (Cambridge: Harvard University Press, 1992) and Daniel Hallin, *We Keep America on Top of the World: Television Journalism and the Public Sphere* (New York: Routledge Press, 1994).

2. While the term "docudrama" technically refers to a "based-on-fact" movie produced for television, as opposed to the more generic "TV movie," or "made-for-TV movie," which refers to any movie produced for television, throughout the book, for reasons of economy, and because the term is more and more used in this generic sense in common parlance, I use the term docudrama to refer to any made-for-TV movie.

3. For an interesting study of therapeutic discourse in a wider variety of TV genres, see Mimi White, *Tele-Advising: Therapeutic Discourse in American Television* (Chapel Hill: University of North Carolina Press, 1992).

4. There are any number of theoretical and historical works on the coming of industrialism and its effects on daily life and work patterns in America, as well as on our more general spiritual and emotional life. For our purposes, Stuart Ewen's *Captains of Consciousness: Advertising and the Social Roots of Consumer Culture* (New York: McGraw-Hill, 1976) and Stuart and Elizabeth Ewen's *Channels of Discourse: Mass Images and the Shaping of American Consciousness* (New York: McGraw-Hill, 1982) give an especially concrete picture of the way in which these changes molded cultural experience. Harry Braverman's *Labor and Monopoly Capital: The Degradation of Work in the Twentieth Century* (New York: Monthly Review Press, 1974) is a classic work on the changes in work processes due to the coming of the machine and the factory. And Herbert Marcuse's *One-Dimensional Man: Studies in the Ideology of Advanced Industrial Society* (Boston: Beacon Press, 1968) is another classic work on the spiritual implications of these changes.

5. It is worth commenting briefly, at this point, on my own differences with a very prominent school of academic and popular critical thought on this matter most widely associated perhaps with the work of Neil Postman, especially in *Amusing Ourselves to Death: Public Discourse in the Age of Show Business* (New York: Penguin Books, 1986). Although Postman's basic idea—that television is responsible for a serious decline in rational, socially healthy thought and discourse in American life—is widely held and accepted, at times it seems, almost as a truism, in this chapter, and in my work on media generally, I implicitly take issue with this view by approaching television as a socially constructed force which is contradictory, dynamically changeable, and especially reflective of the various forces, some progressive, most not, which play a role in producing its content. In this model, TV

talk shows and docudramas are particularly open to progressive, feminist influence for a variety of reasons which I discuss in the works cited throughout the chapter.

6. For a good anthology, accompanied by a solid introduction, on the classic woman's film see Christine Gledhill, ed., *Home Is Where the Heart Is: Studies in Melodrama and the Woman's Film* (London: British Film Institute, 1987).

7. It is important to note, at this point, that the talk shows to which I refer in this book are *not* the more recent, highly publicized and sensational variety in which guests are allowed to yell, scream, even physically attack each other, and little in the way of a coherent point is ever discernible. This trend, understandably given much media attention, was brought to prominence by the success of *The Ricki Lake Show* in about 1994, and has since spawned a long list of clones, most short-lived, such as *The Jenny Jones Show, Montel Williams, Richard Bey,* and others. In the mad scramble to compete for ratings, the original talk shows—*Phil Donohue, Sally Jessy Raphael, Geraldo*—have often followed suit, offering a significant peppering of bombastic and chaotic shows, along with their more usual formats. Oprah Winfrey, in refusing to follow suit, has seen her own ratings slip. Nonetheless, the number of more traditional talk show segments dealing with addiction issues –the ones discussed here– has not decreased nor has their audience declined. It is only that the newer, more tasteless and pointless entries have temporarily garnered a huge amount of media attention.

8. Much interesting work has been done on the different ways in which women viewers watch and "read" television and talk about it to each other. Two good works which shed light on areas tangentially dealt with here are Andrea Press, *Women Watching Television: Gender, Class and Generation in the American Television Experience* (Philadelphia: University of Pennsylvania Press, 1991) and Ellen Seiter *et al.,* eds., *Remote Control: Television, Audiences and Cultural Power* (New York: Routledge Press, 1989).

9. See also Sonia Livingstone and Peter Lunt, *Talk on Television: Audience Participation and Public Debate* (New York: Routledge Press, 1994).

2. Personal Politics

1. Two recent books in particular, Brett Harvey, *The Fifties: A Women's Oral History* (New York: HarperCollins, 1993) and Wini Breines, *Young, White, and Miserable: Growing Up Female in the Fifties* (Boston: Beacon Press, 1992) present an overview of what life was like for women in the years preceding the second wave. Marty Jezer, *The Dark Ages: Life in the United States, 1945–1960* (Boston: South End Press, 1982) is a cultural history of those years from a political perspective. A classic collection of documents from the early years of the second wave itself is Robin Morgan, *Sisterhood is Powerful: An Anthology of Writings from the Women's Liberation Movement* (New York: Vintage, 1970).

2. In what follows I generalize quite a bit about political ideas and strategies,

about various versions and structures of "feminism" and feminist organizing. The sixties was an extremely heady and confusing time, a time in which thousands upon thousands of women – mostly young, idealistic, and new to political thinking – found themselves launched into a round of activity which did indeed transform their lives and assumptions about everything. Women previously docile and passive suddenly found themselves speaking, marching, writing, and living lives radically different from what they had been raised to know and do. And in this time period, understandably, ideas and groupings and alliances and theories formed, fell apart, and were reformed. Much of what was done and said in these times was historic and world shattering. Some of it was a bit mad and off the mark in ways too numerous to count. How could it have been otherwise? I am not going to map out all of the meetings, the infightings and splits and takeovers, and the excesses of passion and logic, but rather I will draw upon the best and most important features to sketch out key ideas and processes which did indeed survive – in very different forms and combinations very often – and find their way into recovery circles and thoughts.

3. See Alice Echols, *Daring to Be Bad: Radical Feminism in America 1967–75* (Minneapolis: University of Minnesota Press, 1989) for a far more thorough rendering of the nature of this movement.

4. Throughout this book I use the term "recovery movement" to refer not to AA and other early fellowships, such as Narcotics Anonymous whose sole goal was to stop members from chemical abuse, and whose membership – by edict and custom – was largely if not exclusively male. I refer, rather, to the new and vast network of Anonymous/12 Step groups founded in the 1980s and 1990s which deal with emotional/relational issues, attract largely if not exclusively female memberships, and significantly, often dramatically, alter the original 12 Steps and 12 Traditions and the other underlying assumptions and customs of AA to fit a new crop of personal, but not chemically related, compulsive behaviors, feelings, and even thought processes. It is in these groups, not in AA (as chapters 3 and 4 will elucidate), that the ideas and processes of consciousness-raising to which I here refer are dramatically visible and felt. Unlike the classic AA meetings I visited, in which any mention of issues beyond physical drinking and its immediate ramifications was discouraged, even disallowed, these newer groups – the ones I am calling "recovery movement groups" – institutionalized a way of talking about and dealing with so-called "addictive disorders" which was based largely upon insights and ideas borrowed – often explicitly – from feminist discourse and analysis. Here almost all discussion of addiction, as it were, involved – indeed required – a fairly elaborate form of personal narrative, very different from traditional AA's "sharing," in which family and other relationship dynamics were introduced and generalized about, as they had been in CR. Indeed, the idea of addiction, for most of these groups, makes absolutely no sense at all without such feminist-inspired elaborations of the social and emotional context in which the stigmatized behavior – continuous involvement in an abusive relationship for example – occurs. And while many newer chemical-addiction groups now also

use such methods and ideas, and thus fall into the network of "recovery" I am charting, those groups which still adhere to classic 12 Step procedures, set forth by AA in the 1930s and 1940s, are not included in my definition of "recovery" although the term itself, of course, originates there.

5. For background material on the social movements of the period and historic overviews of it, see Todd Gitlin, *The Sixties: Years of Hope, Days of Rage* (New York: Bantam Books, 1987) and Judith Clavir Albert and Stewart Edward Albert, eds., *The Sixties Papers* (New York: Praeger, 1989).

6. Anita Shreve, *Women Together, Women Alone: The Legacy of the Consciousness-Raising Movement* (New York: Viking, 1989) is an excellent overview of what the CR movement, as it affected more mainstream women, was like and, in particular, what happened to the women who participated in it in the years following.

3. Recovery, Inc.

1. My primary source for AA's history is Nan Robertson, *Getting Better: Inside Alcoholics Anonymous* (New York: Fawcett, 1988). I chose Robertson's version because it is written by a member who is also a feminist writer and who was given access to and permission to quote from official sources. The official texts of the movement are *Alcoholics Anonymous* (the "Big Book") (New York: A.A. World Services, Inc., 1939) and *Twelve Steps and Twelve Traditions* ("the 12 and 12") (New York: A.A. World Services, Inc., 1953). *Living Sober* (New York: A.A. World Services, Inc., 1975) and *Came to Believe . . .* (New York: A.A. World Services, Inc., 1973) are two classic texts on AA's methods and principles. *Dr. Bob and the Good Old-timers* (New York: A.A. World Services, Inc., 1980) is the official biography of cofounder Dr. Robert Smith, and *Alcoholics Anonymous Comes of Age* (New York: A.A. World Services, Inc., 1957) is Bill Wilson's brief history of the organization.

2. The 12 Steps are (from Robertson's *Getting Better*, 1988, p. 56):
   1. We admitted that we were powerless over alcohol – that our lives had become unmanageable.
   2. Came to believe that a Power greater than ourselves could restore us to sanity.
   3. Made a decision to turn our will and our lives over to the care and direction of God *as we understood Him.*
   4. Made a searching and fearless moral inventory of ourselves.
   5. Admitted to God, to ourselves, and to another human being the exact nature of our wrongs.
   6. Were entirely ready to have God remove all these defects of character.
   7. Humbly asked Him to remove our shortcomings.
   8. Made a list of all persons we had harmed, and became willing to make amends to them all.

9. Made direct amends to such people wherever possible, except when to do so would injure them or others.

10. Continued to take personal inventory and when we were wrong promptly admitted it.

11. Sought through prayer and meditation to improve our conscious contact with God *as we understood Him,* praying only for knowledge of His will for us and the power to carry that out.

12. Having had a spiritual awakening as the result of these steps, we tried to carry this message to alcoholics, and to practice these principles in all our affairs.

The complete text of the Traditions and other basic teachings are available in the sources referenced above.

3. *Professional Counsellor* magazine, an organ of the treatment industry, regularly runs editorials and articles alerting its readers to the dangers of moves to strike down laws in various states which make treatment and AA visits mandatory.

4. The work of Stanton Peele, *Diseasing of America: Addiction Treatment Out of Control* (Lexington, Mass.: Lexington Books, 1989) and, with Archie Brodskey, *Love and Addiction* (New York: New American Library, 1976) are especially lucid discussions of the way in which the disease theory of addiction becomes a social philosophy with serious, often dangerous political implications.

5. Obviously the idea that alcoholism is a disease is widely accepted as gospel. I am arguing against this idea, although I am making a distinction between addictions to chemical substances, which I do believe (I am not an expert obviously) are physically addictive in some cases for some people, and the many new kinds of "addictions" to things like gambling and eating and shopping. Three excellent sources for the theories and evidence disputing the "disease theory" are Peele, *Diseasing of America,* Nadelmann 1992a, and Thomas Szasz, "The Fatal Temptation: Drug Prohibition and the Fear of Autonomy," *Daedalus* 121, pp. 161–64. Peele in particular marshals massive evidence to show that AA is indeed no better at stopping people from drinking than other methods, including, he insists, no treatment at all. What AA and the other groups do achieve, then, in my own reading of this evidence, is related to their social aspects and has little to do with either "diseases" or, necessarily, "Higher Powers."

6. I am not suggesting that the recovery movement learned these specific procedural techniques from feminism. That is obviously not the case since the principles of AA, founded in 1935, were long in place when CR began. But, as we shall see in chapter 4, the original AA meetings (and most of the current AA meetings as well) adopt a narrower, more instrumental practice of these rules to insure that a particular physical behavior – the ingestion of a forbidden substance – is stopped, one day at a time. The more wide-ranging meetings of today's recovery movement, especially those groups dealing with problems that primarily affect women, like overeating and

codependency, use – and expand upon – the methods in ways which resemble CR more than classic AA in important ways.

7. I have become aware, in my continuing viewing of Court TV's *Lock and Key* programs, for example, which present live coverage of parole hearings, that it is almost universally assumed that a convict must be in need of recovery of one kind or another and that regular attendance at meetings has become, at the very least, a prerequisite for parole of most prisoners, even when, to my way of thinking, evidence of addiction has not in any way been demonstrated. It is this kind of social enforcement of 12 Step thinking that serves as a kind of control mechanism, keeping people who are likely to break the rules – any rules – attending a group meeting in which socially coercive and (presumably) beneficial behavior is continuously prescribed and reinforced through confession and fellowship rituals.

4. In the Rooms

1. Before reporting on my ethnographic observations of this cultural grouping (for that is after all what it is) I need to say a few words about my personal position and attitude toward the meetings I attended and the people I observed and will now be describing and quoting. There are ethical questions, it seems to me, in doing this kind of research and, perhaps more importantly, there are substantive issues to address about my obvious "judgments" of what I saw.

First of all, attending so many meetings in so condensed a time span was at the start a bit like traveling to Lilliput or Mars. My response to being thrown into this world was extreme. One does not easily respond to so much passion, faith, and propaganda with indifference. If one's initial stance is, as mine obviously was, critical and investigative – a spy in the house of God really – there is obvious confusion and ambivalence. I was there under false pretenses, after all, in a space in which honesty and self-exposure are basic requirements. At first I tried lying about my purposes, pretending to be a suffering alcoholic, codependent, or whatever. Very soon, I found this impossible to do. The sincerity and obvious pain of so many I observed made me feel increasingly sleazy. Finally, I decided to meet any questions that arose (there were very few) by saying that I was writing a book about women and addiction. Naturally, and to my discomfort and moral anguish, everyone assumed I was "on their side" and greeted my mission with gratitude. I was reminded constantly of Joan Didion's observation that "writers are always selling someone out."

Being a far less cynical writer than Didion, I had never identified with that statement before. There were moments, however, in these rooms, when I very much did. Many stories were heartbreaking; many recoveries were heroic. Most important, I identified with a great deal of what I heard and saw in the rooms. Most amazingly, especially in groups in which the most anguish and despair was expressed, I found myself caught in a state of mixed, contradictory consciousness. On the one hand, I was hearing things which verged, at times, on near incoherence, on behavior so far beyond the pale of functional, much less "normal," as to be frightening. And yet, in the words and cries of these most lost of souls, especially, I felt a shock of recognition. I *knew* what they were talking about, what they were feeling; I understood what had been done to them. After all, I too was a woman born into family and social madness and misogyny.

Later, I will discuss this aspect of the groups more fully–their opening up of space in which the unthinkable can be uttered and validated by others. For now I want only to suggest my stance in writing this chapter: I am highly critical of much that I saw; I am deeply concerned about the political implications of all of it. And, to be honest, the posturing, the manipulation, the self-indulgence and narcissism, the sheer fakery I observed outweighed the number of truly moving and impressive exchanges I observed.

Nonetheless, I feel empathy and sympathy for the people, no matter how misguided, I encountered in their searches for peace of mind and a "cure" for our common diseases; nor do I discount the very real, often life-saving gains they made in recovery. Not since I attended my first consciousness-raising meetings have I felt so profoundly the sense of being with people who had felt things I had felt and never spoken of. And I learned from and was inspired by many of them, by their honesty and courage and survival.

Nonetheless, I never doubted the "morality" of what I was doing there, spying on and judging these proceedings. I relate my reactions not in the spirit of self-disclosure or confession but rather to give a sense of the power of the movement and the roots of that power in real, true insight and experience. The recovery movement speaks to common pain as early feminism did; that is its power. That this power is ultimately twisted and abused in the interests of a profoundly conservatizing agenda and worldview is a problem I am more concerned about than ever, having so immersed myself in it.

2. Marc Galanter's *Cults: Faith, Healing, and Coercion* (New York: Oxford University Press, 1989) analyzes cult behavior generally, from a psychiatric perspective, and includes AA in his analysis. Arthur Deikman's *The Wrong Way Home: Uncovering the Patterns of Cult Behavior in American Society* (Boston: Beacon Press, 1990) does not mention AA, but his analysis of the functioning of cults and their social implications is in keeping with much that I observed in AA, as is Robert J. Lifton's earlier *Thought Reform and the Psychology of Totalism* (New York: Norton, 1961).

3. Laing's most well-known work, in this regard, is *The Politics of Experience* (New York: Ballantine, 1967). Another example of the "countercultural," radical social approach to issues of madness, one which includes discussions of religious cults and of others, like the Manson family, is Flo Conway and Jim Siegelman, *Snapping: America's Epidemic of Sudden Personality Change* (New York: Delta, 1978).

4. I am of course basing these remarks on my own necessarily limited experiences. I chose to visit regularly these two groups specifically because they did represent the extremes of the movement as I observed it. Nonetheless, what I saw and

heard were only variations on a range of behaviors, forming a continuum of various degrees of behavior within the limits of these two extremes.

5. *The Fall of the Public Man* (New York: Norton, 1974). See also Anthony Giddens, *Modernity and Self-Identity: Self and Society in the Late Modern Age* (Stanford: Stanford University Press, 1991).

6. Sources which praise the 12 Step programs are extensively quoted and analyzed in chap. 5. As informative as they are, however, they give no hint of the wildly diverse experiential qualities of the various groups, meetings, and fellowships. These sources serve to provide, far more rigorously and dogmatically than actual meetings, the very ideological and practical uniformity which is so often missing from actual group process. It is clear that the real ideological core of the movement, the source of its educational power, is to be found in its mass-mediated outlets rather than in its actual interpersonal exchanges.

As for the movement's critics, they too lead the reader to assume that the movement is more homogeneous than it is in practice because, often for good reason, they are critiquing its more overriding, socially dangerous aspects. The best of these works are Katherine Van Wormer, "Co-dependency: Implications for Women and Therapy," *Women and Therapy* 8 (1989), pp. 51–63, and her "Hi, I'm Jane; I'm a Compulsive Overeater" in P. Fallon, M. Katzman, and S. Woolley, eds., *Feminist Perspectives on Eating Disorders* (New York: Guilford Press, 1994); Ellen Herman, "The Twelve-Step Program: Cure or Cover?" *Utne Reader*, November/December 1988, pp. 52–63.

Wendy Kaminer's much-cited and praised *I'm Dysfunctional, You're Dysfunctional* (Reading, Mass.: Addison-Wesley, 1992) is the one negative book which does indeed purport to present an overview of actual meetings, as well as various other recovery events such as seminars, conferences, and even talk show discussions. It is, I discovered as I delved into my own "field work," a disappointingly superficial and limited treatment of what is in fact a far richer, more suggestive, and multi-faceted social phenomenon than Kaminer's single-minded attack upon the movement would have one believe. And while many of her criticisms are valid, as my own work makes clear, many of them are lacking in subtlety, thoroughness of research, analysis and comprehensiveness and, I would add, understanding and compassion for the socially engendered sufferings of Americans today which drives so many to the movement.

5. *Women Who Read Too Much*

1. That self-help books based on 12 Step models are read by legions of Americans—and that the bulk of these readers are female—is documented in Wendy Simonds's *Women and Self-Help Culture* (New Brunswick, N.J.: Rutgers University Press, 1992). Much of the documentation for this chapter comes from Simonds's work.

2. Again, I want to repeat that my observations are not scientifically founded but are based on extensive, varied, personal observation over a period of several months. My views were also corroborated by many people I interviewed and, increasingly, by concerned articles in the many publications aimed at addiction professionals.

3. Obviously, the list of men's movement publications and other books for male addicts influenced by these ideas is growing. However, I do not consider this growth particularly significant. For one thing, the men's movement is in its own way a sub-category of feminist culture. Most important, however, is that its significance, marketwise, is really marginal. Month after month, the addition of men's addiction books is much less significant than the addition of the far greater number of women's titles.

4. The philosophical and clinical problems raised by this methodology are beyond the scope of this study. Issues of "repressed memory" and the validity of other therapeutic "truths" constructed in the process of treatment are now being raised increasingly in high-profile cases involving childhood sex abuse. AA itself has come into the courtroom recently, when the claim of confidentiality among AA members was denied in the case of an AA member who had confessed to a murder at AA meetings and whose confessors were subpoenaed to testify against him (*New York Times,* June 25, 1994, p. A18). While the outcomes of these cases are often politically and therapeutically unfortunate and do indeed put a chill into the entire context of therapeutic exchange and process, the theoretical issue of "constructed" biographical narratives is nonetheless an important matter which can work both ways. Biographies are indeed constructed and some narrative models – feminist for example – are indeed more progressive and "truthful," in a social sense, than others, particularly those constructed by dominant groups in the interest, conscious or not, of preserving their hegemony.

5. As we shall see in chap. 6, the men's movement has very cleverly reorganized the narrative elements of feminist narrative models to fit a newly masculinized master narrative in which power relations between genders and within families are now stripped of all sense of power politics and are seen to be mutually abusive relationships among, apparently, political equals, or even, worse yet, political relationships in which women dominate!

6. I am not implying that eating disorders, this one and all others, are "caused" by sexual repression. I am not diagnosing the syndrome at all, as a syndrome. I am simply suggesting that in this particular case – a common enough story women tell when talking about food disorders – discomfort over sexual feelings was indeed assuaged through food.

7. Again, let me comment upon the relationship between my arguments here and the current controversies surrounding "repressed memories." What I am saying may be seen to give credence to those who would deny the validity of claims about sexual abuse of children, especially incest, in its support of ideas about the "social

construction" of memories. While I do indeed believe such therapeutic abuses take place at times, I do not believe that most survivors "dream up" these memories, nor would I wish to support reactionary efforts to discredit therapists dealing with abuse. Sexual victims have enough trouble being heard and attended to without this red herring which would set back feminist efforts to force society to take responsibility for male sexual crimes. Nonetheless, the manipulation of memories and stories is a serious issue which must be addressed, especially since its practitioners—as I am arguing—are far more likely to be enemies than friends of women.

8. See Karen Hansen and Ilene Philipson, eds., *Women, Class, and the Feminist Imagination: A Socialist-Feminist Reader* (Philadelphia: Temple University Press, 1990) for some classic readings in feminist analysis of family power relations under patriarchy and capitalism; and Rosine Perelberg and Ann C. Miller, eds., *Gender and Power in Families* (New York: Routledge Press, 1990) for a collection of essays, by feminist family therapists, about the issue as seen in concrete therapeutic practice.

9. Janet Geringer Woititz's *Co-dependency: An Emerging Issue* (Deerfield Beach, Fla.: Health Communications, Inc., 1984) is the classic, originating text which put the term "codependent" into common therapeutic use as a description of the kinds of oppressive, "dysfunctional" relationships which came to be called "addictive" because of their tendency to involve compulsive, habitual patterns of unhealthy symbiosis from which those in close relationships found it difficult or impossible to extricate themselves. Melody Beattie, five years later, made the term a household word with her best-selling book *Codependent No More* (1989).

6. The Diseasing of Politics

1. Throughout the book, but most obviously in this concluding chapter, I touch implicitly upon issues currently hotly debated (too often unfortunately in politically distorted form in the mainstream press) among feminists and antifeminists of various stripes. I have avoided getting into these theoretical and strategic debates about the state and direction of feminism because they would distract from my own main purpose which is to focus on the relationship between early feminism and the recovery movement from an historical and cultural perspective. To the extent that these issues are relevant here, I address them, within the limits of my own concerns and perspective. But, generally, the work of this book does not fit easily or fully into any one "camp" of feminist thought (as they have been categorized largely by media pundits, it should be noted) any more than it fits easily into either the "pro" or "con" camps in the dominant debates about the recovery movement itself.

My own contribution, specifically, to the debates about "victim" vs. "power" feminism can be found in Nan Maglin and Donna Perry, eds., *Good Girls/Bad Girls: Women, Sex, Violence, and Power in the Nineties* (New Brunswick, N.J.: Rutgers University Press, 1995).

2. Some of the many works of feminist therapists on eating disorders and rela-

tionship issues which present invaluable analyses and self-help guidelines and re-source information, much of which I am indebted to in my own thinking as a feminist and in the writing of this book, are: Claudia Bepko and Jo-Ann Krestan, "Codependency: The Social Reconstruction of Female Experience," in Claudia Bepko, ed., *Feminism and Addiction* (New York: Haworth Press, 1991); Susie Orbach, *Fat Is a Feminist Issue: A Self-Help Guide for Compulsive Eaters* (New York: Berkley Publishing Group, 1979) and *Fat Is a Feminist Issue II: A Program to Conquer Compulsive Eating* (New York: Berkley Publishing Group, 1982); Harriet Goldhor Lerner, "Problems for Profit," *Women's Review of Books* (April 1990), pp. 15–17, and *Women in Therapy* (New York: Harper and Row, 1988); Kim Chernin, *The Obsession: Reflections on the Tyranny of Slenderness* (New York: Harper Colophon, 1981).

3. It is important to cite here some of the most important works of feminist men who are writing about gender politics and participating in the men's movement, especially those who perspective, like mine, is cultural and based on social constructionist views of gender. An excellent anthology of writings is Harry Brod, ed., *The Making of Masculinities: The New Men's Studies* (Boston: Allen and Unwin, 1987). See also Victor J. Seidler, ed., *Men, Sex, and Relationships: Writings from Achilles Heel* (New York: Routledge Press, 1992), R. W. Connell, *Gender and Power* (Stanford: Stanford University Press, 1987), and Arthur Brittan, *Masculinity and Power* (New York: Basil Blackwell, Inc., 1987).

References

Albert, Judith Clavir, and Stewart Edward Albert, eds. 1989. *The Sixties Papers.* New York: Praeger.

Alcoff, Linda, and Laura Gray. 1993. "Survivor Discourse: Transgression or Recuperation," *Signs* 18 (2), pp. 260–90.

Alcoholics Anonymous. 1939. New York: A.A. World Services, Inc.

Alcoholics Anonymous Comes of Age. 1957. New York: A.A. World Services (written by Bill Wilson).

Allen, Robert C., ed. 1992. *Channels of Discourse, Reassembled. Television and Contemporary Criticism.* 2d ed. Chapel Hill: University of North Carolina Press.

Avery, Robert, and David Eason. 1991. *Critical Perspectives on Media and Society.* New York: Guilford Press.

Barnouw, Erik. 1978. *The Sponsor.* New York: Oxford University Press.

Barnouw, Erik. 1975. *Tube of Plenty.* New York: Oxford University Press.

Barthes, Roland. 1975. *Mythologies.* New York: Hill and Wang.

Bauer, Jan. 1982. *Women and Alcohol.* Toronto: Inner City Books.

Beattie, Melody. 1989. *Beyond Codependency and Getting Better All the Time.* San Francisco: Harper and Row.

Beattie, Melody. 1987. *Codependent No More.* San Francisco: Harper and Row.

Bellah, Robert, Richard Madsen, William Sullivan, Ann Swidler, and Steven Tipton. 1985. *Habits of the Heart: Individualism and Commitment in American Life.* New York: Harper and Row.

Bepko, Claudia, ed. 1991. *Feminism and Addiction.* New York: Haworth Press.

Bepko, Claudia, and Jo-Ann Krestan. 1991. "Codependency: The Social Reconstruction of Female Experience." Pp. 137–39 in *Feminism and Addiction.* Edited by Claudia Bepko. New York: Haworth Press.

Berenson, David. 1991. "Powerlessness—Liberation or Enslaving? Responding to the

Feminist Critique of the Twelve Steps." Pp. 67–80 in *Feminism and Addiction*. Edited by Claudia Bepko. New York: Haworth Press.

Blume, E. Sue. 1990. *Secret Survivors: Uncovering Incest and Its Aftereffects in Women.* New York: Ballantine Books.

Bradshaw, John. 1988a. *The Family: A Revolutionary Way of Self-Discovery.* Deerfield Beach, Fla.: Health Communications, Inc.

Bradshaw, John. 1998b. *Healing the Shame that Binds You.* Deerfield Beach, Fla.: Health Communications, Inc.

Brady, Maureen. 1991. *Daybreak: Meditations for Women Survivors of Sexual Abuse.* New York: HarperCollins.

Braverman, Harry. 1974. *Labor and Monopoly Capital: The Degradation of Work in the Twentieth Century.* New York: Monthly Review Press.

Breines, Wini. 1992. *Young, White, and Miserable: Growing Up Female in the Fifties.* Boston: Beacon Press.

Briles, Judith. 1990. *The Confidence Factor: How Self-Esteem Can Change Your Life.* New York: MasterMediaLimited.

Brittan, Arthur. *Masculinity and Power.* 1989. New York: Basil Blackwell, Inc.

Brod, Harry, ed. 1987. *The Making of Masculinities: The New Men's Studies.* Boston: Allen and Unwin.

Bruner, Jerome. 1990. *Acts of Meaning.* Cambridge: Harvard University Press.

Came to Believe . . . . 1973. New York: A.A. World Services, Inc.

Carey, James. 1989. *Communication as Culture: Essays on Media and Society.* Boston: Unwin Hyman.

Chatham, Lois. 1990. "Understanding the Issues: An Overview." Pp. 15–40 in *Women: Alcohol and Other Drugs.* Edited by Ruth Engs. Dubuque, Iowa: Kendall/Hunt Publishing.

Chernin, Kim. 1981. *The Obsession: Reflections on the Tyranny of Slenderness.* New York: Harper Colophon.

Clark, A., and S. Covington. 1986. "Women, Drinking, and the Workplace." *The Almacan.* September, pp. 10–11.

Comfort, Alex. 1972. *The Joy of Sex: A Gourmet Guide to Love-Making.* New York: Simon and Schuster.

Connell, R. W. 1987. *Gender and Power.* Stanford: Stanford University Press.

Conway, Flo, and Jim Siegelman. 1978. *Snapping: America's Epidemic of Sudden Personality Change.* New York: Delta.

Cowan, Connell, and Melvyn Kinder. 1985. *Smart Women, Foolish Choices: Finding the Right Men, Avoiding the Wrong Ones.* New York: Signet.

Davis, Flora. 1991. *Moving the Mountain: The Women's Movement in America since 1960*. New York: Simon and Schuster.

Davis, Kenneth. 1984. *Two-Bit Culture: The Paperbacking of America*. Boston: Houghton Mifflin.

Dayan, Daniel, and Elihu Katz. 1992. *Media Events: The Live Broadcasting of History*. Cambridge: Harvard University Press.

de Certeau, Michel. 1984. *The Practice of Everyday Life*. Berkeley: University of California Press.

Deikman, Arthur. 1990. *The Wrong Way Home: Uncovering the Patterns of Cult Behavior in American Society*. Boston: Beacon Press.

Denzin, Norman. 1984. *Hollywood Shot by Shot: Alcoholism in American Cinema*. New York: Aldine de Gruyter.

Dr. Bob and the Good Oldtimers. 1980. New York: A.A. World Services, Inc.

Dukakis, Kitty. 1990. *Now You Know*. New York: Simon and Schuster.

Echols, Alice. 1989. *Daring to Be Bad: Radical Feminism in America 1967–75*. Minneapolis: University of Minnesota Press.

Ehrenreich, Barbara. 1990. *Fear of Falling: The Inner Life of the Middle Class*. New York: HarperCollins.

Ehrenreich, Barbara, and Deirdre English. 1979. *For Her Own Good: 150 Years of the Experts' Advice to Women*. New York: HarperCollins.

Engs, Ruth, ed. 1990. *Women: Alcohol and Other Drugs*. Dubuque, Iowa: Kendall/Hunt Publishing.

Epstein, Barbara. 1991. "Political Correctness and Collective Powerlessness." *Socialist Review* 91, pp. 13–36.

Epstein, Barbara. 1990. "Rethinking Social Movement Theory." *Socialist Review* 90, pp. 35–66.

Evans, Sara. 1979. *Personal Politics: The Roots of Women's Liberation in the Civil Rights Movement and the New Left*. New York: Alfred A. Knopf, Inc.

Ewen, Stuart. 1976. *Captains of Consciousness: Advertising and the Social Roots of Consumer Culture*. New York: McGraw-Hill.

Ewen, Stuart, and Elizabeth Ewen. 1982. *Channels of Desire: Mass Images and the Shaping of American Consciousness*. New York: McGraw-Hill.

Faludi, Susan. 1991. *Backlash: The Undeclared War Against American Women*. New York: Crown Publishers.

Farmer, Steven. 1991. *The Wounded Male*. New York: Ballantine Books.

Farrell, Warren. 1993. *The Myth of Male Power: Why Men Are the Disposable Sex*. New York: S and S Trade.

Fingarette, H. 1988. *Heavy Drinking: The Myth of Alcoholism as Disease.* Berkeley: University of California Press.

Fiske, John. 1987. *Television Culture.* London: Methuen.

Forbes, David. 1994. *False Fixes.* Albany: SUNY Press.

Forth-Finegan, Jahn. 1991. "Sugar and Spice and Everything Nice: Gender, Socialization, and Women's Addiction." Pp. 19–36 in *Feminism and Addiction.* Edited by Claudia Bepko. New York: Haworth Press.

Foucault, Michel. 1990. *The History of Sexuality: An Introduction.* Vol. 1. New York: Random House.

Freudenheim, Milt. 1991. "The Squeeze on Psychiatric Chains." *New York Times* (October 26), p. L33.

Friel, John, and Linda Friel. 1988. *Adult Children: The Secrets of Dysfunctional Families.* Deerfield Beach, Fla.: Health Communications, Inc.

Galanter, Marc. 1989. *Cults: Faith, Healing, and Coercion.* New York: Oxford University Press.

Giddens, Anthony. 1991. *Modernity and Self-Identity: Self and Society in the Late Modern Age.* Stanford: Stanford University Press.

Gitlin, Todd. 1987. *The Sixties: Years of Hope, Days of Rage.* New York: Bantam Books.

Gitlin, Todd, ed. 1986. *Watching Television.* New York: Pantheon.

Gledhill, Christine, ed. 1987. *Home Is Where the Heart Is: Studies in Melodrama and the Woman's Film.* London: British Film Institute.

Goleman, Daniel. 1992a. "As Addiction Medicine Gains, Experts Debate What It Should Cover." *New York Times* (March 31), p. C3.

Goleman, Daniel. 1992b. "Study Ties Genes to Drinking in Women as Much as Men." *New York Times* (October 14), p. C14.

Goleman, Daniel. 1992c. " 'Wisdom' on Alcoholic's Child Called Stuff of Fortune Cookies." *New York Times* (February 19), p. C12.

Gomery, Douglas. 1983. "*Brian's Song*: Television, Hollywood and the Evolution of the Movie of the Week." Pp. 208–31 in *American History/American Television: Interpreting the Video Past.* Edited by John E. O'Connor. New York: Ungar.

Gordon, Barbara. 1979. *I'm Dancing as Fast as I Can.* New York: Harper and Row.

Greenleaf, Vicki. 1989. *Women and Cocaine: Personal Stories of Addiction and Recovery.* Los Angeles: Lowell House.

Hallin, Daniel. 1994. *We Keep America on Top of the World: Television Journalism and the Public Sphere.* New York: Routledge Press.

Hansen, Karen, and Ilene Philipson, eds. 1990. *Women, Class, and the Feminist Imagination: A Socialist-Feminist Reader.* Philadelphia: Temple University Press.

Harvey, Brett. 1993. *The Fifties: A Women's Oral History.* New York: HarperCollins.

Haskell, Molly. 1974. *From Reverence to Rape: The Treatment of Women in the Movies.* Baltimore: Penguin Press.

Heath, Dwight. 1992. "U.S. Drug Control Policy: A Cultural Perspective." *Daedalus* 121, pp. 269–92.

Herman, Ellen. 1988. "The Twelve-Step Program: Cure or Cover?" *Utne Reader* (November/December), pp. 52–63.

Jezer, Marty. 1982. *The Dark Ages: Life in the United States, 1945–60.* Boston: South End Press.

Kaminer, Wendy. 1992. *I'm Dysfunctional, You're Dysfunctional.* Reading, Mass.: Addison-Wesley.

Kaminer, Wendy. 1990. "Chances Are You're Codependent Too." *New York Times Book Review* (February 11), pp. 26–27.

Kasl, Charlotte Davis. 1992. *Many Roads, One Journey: Moving Beyond the 12 Steps.* New York: HarperCollins.

Kasl, Charlotte Davis. 1989. *Women, Sex, and Addiction.* New York: Harper and Row.

Katz, Jon. 1993. "Rock, Rap, and Movies Bring You the News." *Rolling Stone* (March 2), pp. 33–41.

Katz, Lillian. 1993. "Reading, Writing, Narcissism." *New York Times* (July 14), p. A25.

Kauffman, L. A. 1990. "The Anti-Politics of Identity." *Socialist Review* 90, pp. 67–80.

Kellogg, Terry. 1991. "Interview with Terry Kellogg." Pp. 95–124 in *Men Speak Out: In the Heart of the Men's Recovery Movement.* Edited by David Lenfest. Deerfield Beach, Fla.: Health Communications, Inc.

Kerr, Peter. 1991. "Chain of Mental Hospitals Faces Inquiry in 4 States." *New York Times* (October 22), pp. A1, D4.

Laidlaw, Toni Ann, Cheryl Malmo, and Associates. 1990. *Healing Voices: Feminist Approaches to Therapy with Women.* San Francisco: Jossey-Bass Publishers.

Laing, R. D. 1967. *The Politics of Experience.* New York: Ballantine Books.

Larimore, Helen. 1992. *Older Women in Recovery: Sharing Experience, Strength, and Hope.* Deerfield Beach, Fla.: Health Communications, Inc.

Lenfest, David. 1991. *Men Speak Out: In the Heart of the Men's Recovery Movement.* Deerfield Beach, Fla.: Health Communications, Inc.

Lerner, Harriet Goldhor. 1990. "Problems for Profit?" *Women's Review of Books* (April), pp. 15–17.

Lerner, Harriet Goldhor. 1988. *Women in Therapy.* New York: Harper and Row.

Lerner, Michael. 1970. *The New Socialist Revolution: An Introduction to Its Theory and Strategy.* New York: Dell.

Levine, H. G. 1978. "The Discovery of Addiction: Changing Conceptions of Habitual Drunkenness in American History." *Journal of Studies on Alcohol* 39, pp. 143–67.

Lew, Mike. 1991. "Interview with Mike Lew." Pp. 125–52 in *Men Speak Out: In the Heart of the Men's Recovery Movement.* Edited by David Lenfest. Deerfield Beach, Fla.: Health Communications, Inc.

Lifton, Robert J. 1961. *Thought Reform and the Psychology of Totalism.* New York: Norton.

Living Sober. 1975. New York: A.A. World Services, Inc.

Livingstone, Sonia, and Peter Lunt. 1994. *Talk on Television: Audience Participation and Public Debate.* New York: Routledge Press.

Lukina-Wiersma, Mary Ellen. 1990. "Employee Assistance Programs." Pp. 79–84 in *Women: Alcohol and Other Drugs.* Edited by Ruth Engs. Dubuque, Iowa: Kendall/ Hunt Publishing.

Maglin, Nan, and Donna Perry, eds. 1995. *Good Girls/Bad Girls: Women, Sex, Violence, and Power in the Nineties.* New Brunswick: Rutgers University Press.

Maine, Margo. 1991. *Father Hunger: Fathers, Daughters, and Food.* Carlsbad, Cal.: Gurze Books.

Marcuse, Herbert. 1968. *One-Dimensional Man: Studies in the Ideology of Advanced Industrial Society.* Boston: Beacon Press.

Marill, Alvin. 1987. *Movies Made for Television.* New York: Baseline.

Masciorotte, Gloria-Jean. 1991. "C'mon, Girl: Oprah Winfrey and the Discourse of Feminine Talk." *Genders* 11, pp. 111–26.

Masters, William, and Virginia Johnson. 1966. *Human Sexual Response.* New York: Bantam Books.

Meacham, Andrew. 1992. "History Shows Radical Swings in Drug Attitudes." *Changes* (October), pp. 26–27.

Meadows, Rosalyn, and Lillie Weiss. 1992. *Women's Conflicts about Eating and Sexuality: The Relationship Between Food and Sex.* New York: Haworth Press.

Miller, Mark Crispin. 1986. "Prime Time: Deride and Conquer." Pp. 183–228 in *Watching Television.* Edited by Todd Gitlin. New York: Pantheon Books.

Minich, Dr. Frank, Dr. Paul Meier, Dr. Robert Hemfelt, Dr. Sharon Sneed, and Don Hawkins. 1990. *Love Hunger: Recovery from Food Addiction.* New York: Fawcett-Columbine.

Moraga, Cherríe, and Gloria Anzaldua, eds. 1981. *This Bridge Called My Back: Writings of Radical Women of Color.* Watertown, Mass.: Persephone Press.

Morgan, Robin, ed. 1970. *Sisterhood Is Powerful: An Anthology of Writings from the Women's Liberation Movement.* New York: Vintage.

Munson, Wayne. 1993. *All Talk: The Talkshow in Media Culture.* Philadelphia: Temple University Press.

Musto, David. 1987. *The American Disease: Origins of Narcotic Control.* New York: Oxford University Press.

Nadelmann, Ethan. 1992a. "Historical Perspectives on Drug Prohibition and Its Alternatives." *American Heritage*, pp. 24–32.

Nadelmann, Ethan. 1992b. "Thinking Seriously about Alternatives to Drug Prohibition." *Daedalus* 121, pp. 85–132.

New York Times. 1993. "Spreading A.A. Message, One Broadcast at a Time" (March 5), p. B7.

Norwood, Robin. 1985. *Women Who Love Too Much.* New York: Pocket Books.

O'Malley, Pat, and Stephen Mugford. 1991. "Demand for Intoxicating Commodities." *Social Justice* 18, pp. 49–75.

Orbach, Susie. 1982. *Fat Is a Feminist Issue II: A Program to Conquer Compulsive Eating.* New York: Berkley Publishing Group.

Orbach, Susie. 1979. *Fat Is a Feminist Issue: A Self-Help Guide for Compulsive Eaters.* New York: Berkley Publishing Group.

Ouellette, Laurie. 1992. "Hyping the 'War on Drugs.'" *MediaCulture Review* 1, pp. 1–10.

Pape, Patricia. 1986. "Women and Alcohol: The Disgraceful Discrepancy." *EAP Digest* (October), pp. 49–53.

Peele, Stanton. 1989. *Diseasing of America: Addiction Treatment Out of Control.* Lexington, Mass.: Lexington Books.

Peele, Stanton, and Archie Brodskey. 1976. *Love and Addiction.* New York: New American Library.

Peluso, Emanuel, and Lucy Peluso. 1988. *Women and Drugs: Getting Hooked, Getting Clean.* Minneapolis: CompCare Publishers.

Perelberg, Rosine Jozef, and Ann C. Miller, eds. 1990. *Gender and Power in Families.* New York: Routledge Press.

Piercy, Marge. 1976. *Woman on the Edge of Time.* New York: Fawcett.

Postman, Neil. 1986. *Amusing Ourselves to Death: Public Discourse in the Age of Show Business.* New York: Penguin Books.

Press, Andrea. 1991. *Women Watching Television: Gender, Class, and Generation in the American Television Experience.* Philadelphia: University of Pennsylvania Press.

Radway, Janice. 1984. *Reading the Romance.* Chapel Hill: University of North Carolina Press.

Rapping, Elayne. 1994. *Media-tions: Forays into the Culture and Gender Wars.* Boston: South End Press.

Rapping, Elayne. 1992. *The Movie of the Week: Private Stories/Public Events.* Minneapolis: University of Minnesota Press.

Rapping, Elayne. 1987. *The Looking Glass World of Nonfiction TV.* Boston: South End Press.

Reinarman, Craig. 1988. "The Case of Mothers Against Drunk Drivers and Social Control in the 1980s." *Theory and Society* 17, pp. 91–120.

Robertson, Nan. 1988. *Getting Better: Inside Alcoholics Anonymous.* New York: Fawcett.

Room, R. G. W. 1990. "The Party Ends for the Wet Generation: Alcoholics Anonymous in U.S. Films, 1940–1965." *Journal of Studies on Alcohol* 50, pp. 1–50.

Room, R. G. W. 1983. "Sociological Aspects of the Disease Concept of Alcoholism." *Research Advances in Alcohol and Drug Problems* 7, pp. 47–91.

Room, R. G. W. 1980. "Treatment-Seeking Populations and Larger Realities." P. 212 in *Alcoholism Treatment in Transition.* Edited by G. Edwards and M. Grant. London: Croom Helm.

Room, R., and C. M. Weisner. 1984. "Financing and Ideology in Alcohol Treatment." *Social Problems* 32, pp. 167–84.

Sandmaier, Marian. 1992. *The Invisible Alcoholics: Women and Alcohol.* Blue Ridge Summit, Penn.: TAB Books.

Sanford, Linda T., and Mary Ellen Donovan. 1984. *Women and Self-Esteem: Understanding and Improving the Way We Feel about Ourselves.* New York: Penguin Books.

Schaef, Ann Wilson. 1990. *Laugh! I Thought I'd Die (If I Didn't): Daily Meditations on Healing Through Humor.* New York: Ballantine Books.

Schaef, Ann Wilson. 1986. *When Society Becomes an Addict.* New York: Harper and Row.

Schafer, Roy. 1981. "Narration in the Psychoanalytic Dialogue." Pp. 139–78 in *On Narrative.* Edited by W. J. T. Mitchell. Chicago: University of Chicago Press.

Schlesinger, Mark, and Robert Dorwart. 1992. "Falling Between the Cracks: Failing National Strategies for the Treatment of Substance Abuse." *Daedalus* 121, pp. 195–238.

Seidler, Victor J., ed. 1992. *Men, Sex, and Relationships: Writings from Achilles Heel.* New York: Routledge Press.

Seiter, Ellen, Hans Borchers, Gabrielle Kreutzner, and Eva-Maria Warth, eds. 1989. *Remote Control: Television, Audiences, and Cultural Power.* New York: Routledge Press.

Sennett, Richard. 1974. *The Fall of Public Man.* New York: Alfred A. Knopf, Inc.

Shreve, Anita. 1989. *Women Together, Women Alone: The Legacy of the Consciousness-Raising Movement.* New York: Viking.

Simonds, Wendy. 1992. *Women and Self-Help Culture: Reading Between the Lines.* New Brunswick: Rutgers University Press.

Spence, Donald. 1982. *Narrative Truth and Historical Truth: Meaning and Interpretation in Psychoanalysis.* New York: Norton.

Spigel, Lynn. 1992. *Make Room for TV: Television and the Family Ideal in Postwar America.* Chicago: University of Chicago Press.

Spigel, Lynn, and Denise Mann. 1992. *Private Screenings: Television and the Female Consumer.* Minneapolis: University of Minnesota Press.

Stacey, Judith. 1990. *Brave New Families.* New York: Basic Books.

Stammer, M. Ellen. 1991. *Women and Alcohol: The Journey Back.* New York: Gardner Press.

Steinem, Gloria. 1992. *Revolution from Within: A Book of Self-Esteem.* Boston: Little, Brown and Company.

Stone, Judith. 1993. "Male Power: Is It a Myth?" Interview with Warren Farrell. *Glamour* (August), p. 145.

Szasz, Thomas. 1992. "The Fatal Temptation: Drug Prohibition and the Fear of Autonomy." *Daedalus* 121, pp. 161–64.

Tannen, Deborah. 1990. *You Just Don't Understand: Women and Men in Conversation.* New York: Ballantine.

Tavris, Carol. 1992. *The Mismeasure of Woman.* New York: Touchstone.

Taylor, Ella. 1989. *Primetime Families: Television Culture in Postwar America.* Berkeley: University of California Press.

Teltsch, Kathleen. 1992. "Midwest Institute to Assist Addicts." *New York Times* (June 30), p. 44.

Toward a State of Esteem: The Final Report of the California Task Force to Promote Self-Esteem and Personal and Social Responsibility. 1990. Sacramento: California State Department of Education.

Treaster, Joseph. 1992a. "Four Years of Bush's Drug War: New Funds but an Old Strategy." *New York Times* (July 28), pp. A1, A11.

Treaster, Joseph. 1992b. "New Programs for Addicts: The Time Is Precious." *New York Times* (June 20), pp. A1, A11.

Treaster, Joseph. 1992c. "Television Ads Are Directed at Urban Youth and Drugs." *New York Times* (October 2), p. D13.

Twelve Steps and Twelve Traditions. 1953. New York: A.A. World Services, Inc.

Van Wormer, Katherine. 1994. "Hi, I'm Jane; I'm a Compulsive Overeater." Pp. 288–98 in *Feminist Perspectives on Eating Disorders.* Edited by P. Fallon, M. Katzman, and S. Woolley. New York: Guilford Press.

Van Wormer, Katherine. 1989. "Co-dependency: Implications for Women and Therapy." *Women and Therapy* 8, pp. 51–63.

Weisner, C. W. 1983. "The Alcohol Treatment System and Social Control: A Study in Institutional Change." *Journal of Drug Issues* 13, pp. 117–33.

Werblin, Jan Marie. 1992a. "Faulty Information Doesn't Compute." *Changes* (August), pp. 27–29.

Werblin, Jan Marie. 1992b. "Why Can't I Stop Eating?" *Changes* (October), pp. 52–53.

Wetzel, Janice Wood. 1991. "Universal Mental Health Classification Systems: Reclaiming Women's Experience." *Affilia* 6, pp. 8–43.

White, Mimi. 1992. *Tele-Advising: Therapeutic Discourse in American Television.* Chapel Hill: University of North Carolina Press.

Williams, Raymond. 1975. *Television: Technology and Cultural Form.* New York: Schocken Books.

Woititz, Janet Geringer. 1984. *Co-dependency: An Emerging Issue.* Deerfield Beach, Fla.: Health Communications, Inc.

Wolf, Naomi. 1991. *The Beauty Myth.* New York: William Morrow.

Zimring, Franklin, and Gordon Hawkins. 1991. "What Kind of Drug War?" *Social Justice* 18, pp. 104–21.

Index